"If this book contained only David Bradshaw's marvelous introduction, it would still be well worth the cover price. But the stellar essays that follow are a goldmine for anyone who cares about the things of God. Drawing upon oft-neglected sources as well as the Church Fathers and St. Gregory Palamas, the authors showcase the extraordinary richness of Orthodox reflection upon the existence of God—while also addressing the standard charges against natural theology. Refreshing, stimulating, and utterly timely, this book marks a brilliant start for the IOTA series."

— **Matthew Levering**
James N. and Mary D. Perry Jr. Chair of Theology,
Mundelein Seminary, Mundelein, Illinois

"This is an exciting, superb collection of insightful essays on natural theology in the Orthodox tradition. Its publication should radically alter the current canon of natural theology as limited to the West from Aquinas to Paley to the current revival of natural theology in Anglo-American philosophy. This volume is fascinating both in terms of the history of ideas and religious practice, and in its challenge to both religious and secular skeptics of the power and promise of natural theology."

— **Charles Taliaferro**
Overby Distinguished Chair and Professor of Philosophy,
St. Olaf College, Northfield, Minnesota

"Anyone acquainted with the Fathers of the Church is well aware of the fact that natural theology is an intrinsic, albeit secondary and subordinate, component of their theology. In the twentieth century, however, many Orthodox theologians, including Vladimir Lossky and Christos Yannaras, rejected natural theology for the sake of a one-sided emphasis on experience and apophaticism. This book is an admirable effort to reopen the discussion in a nuanced and balanced way that will hopefully make a distinct contribution to the wider debates of our times."

— **Fr. Demetrios Bathrellos**
Visiting Professor, Institute for
Orthodox Christian Studies, Cambridge, UK

"Natural theology has been rather neglected and indeed often dismissed within modern Orthodox theology. This splendid volume stands to change that. Assembling an impressive range of contributors, this book amply demonstrates natural theology's long patristic pedigree and ongoing vital importance while also bringing in perspectives from the medieval and early modern West. This *tour de force* will generate considerable theological discussion and, one hopes, further work on the topic. It should also serve to underline further the indispensability of the Orthodox witness within contemporary academic theology and philosophy."

— **Marcus Plested**
Professor of Greek Patristic and Byzantine Theology and
Henri de Lubac Chair, Marquette University, Milwaukee, Wisconsin

"A must-read for philosophers of religion and very beneficial for other scholars of religion, this volume makes a distinctively Orthodox contribution to contemporary natural theology. It brings into the discussion both well-known patristic authors and some who may be unknown to a broader audience—Fiodor Golubinskii, Viktor Kudriavtsev-Platonov, Panayiotis Nellas, and Fr. Dumitru Staniloae. It is without question a very insightful book."

— **Kirill Karpov**
Senior Research Fellow, Institute of Philosophy,
Russian Academy of Sciences, Moscow, Russia

"The idea that Orthodoxy has nothing to do with natural theology and the use of discursive reason is widespread. The present collected volume offers a careful survey of the patristic tradition and contemporary Orthodox theology, suggesting that a certain role is preserved for reason in discussing the existence of God. As the essays of the volume demonstrate, reason is part of the Incarnation, and as such is capable of knowing and participating in God. Hence, natural theology is still a valuable means of doing Orthodox theology."

— **Pantelis Kalaitzidis**
Director, Volos Academy for Theological Studies, Volos, Greece

Natural Theology *in the* Eastern Orthodox Tradition

David Bradshaw & Richard Swinburne

editors

Published in the United States of America by IOTA Publications, St. Paul, Minnesota. IOTA Publications is a part of the International Orthodox Theological Association (IOTA). IOTA is a community of scholars, clergy, and professionals dedicated to the dissemination of knowledge within the context of the Orthodox tradition. IOTA is a 501(c)(3) nonprofit organization, registered in the State of Illinois.

Text and cover design: Klaas Wolterstorff /kwbookdesign.com
Cover image: "Let there be lights in the dome of the sky" (Gen. 1:14).
Mosaic of Monreale Cathedral, Palermo, Sicily. MARKA / Alamy Stock Photo.

Natural Theology in the Eastern Orthodox Tradition /
edited by David Bradshaw and Richard Swinburne.
ISBN 978-1-7352951-3-8 (paperback)
ISBN 978-1-7352951-4-5 (e-book)

Library of Congress Cataloguing in Publication Data

1. Natural theology.
2. Eastern Orthodox Church.
I. Bradshaw, David. II. Swinburne, Richard.

Contents

Contributors

David Bradshaw is Professor of Philosophy at the University of Kentucky. He is the author of *Aristotle East and West: Metaphysics and the Division of Christendom* (2004) and the editor of *Philosophical Theology and the Christian Tradition: Russian and Western Perspectives* (2012) and *Ethics and the Challenge of Secularism: Russian and Western Perspectives* (2013). He is also the editor of "The Greek Christian Tradition" in *Medieval Philosophy: A Multicultural Reader*, ed. Bruce Foltz (2019).

Richard Cross is the John A. O'Brien Professor of Philosophy at the University of Notre Dame. He is the author of *The Physics of Duns Scotus* (1998), *Duns Scotus* (1999), *The Metaphysics of the Incarnation* (2002), *Duns Scotus on God* (2005), *The Medieval Christian Philosophers* (2014), *Duns Scotus's Theory of Cognition* (2014), and *Communicatio Idiomatum: Reformation Christological Debates* (2019). He is currently working on monographs on Christology in the thirteenth–fourteenth and seventeenth centuries, and on an edition of book three of Peter Auriol's commentaries on the *Sentences*.

Travis Dumsday is Associate Professor of Philosophy at Concordia University of Edmonton. He is the author of *Dispositionalism and the Metaphysics of Science* (2019) and *Assisted Suicide in Canada: Moral, Legal, and Policy Considerations* (2021). A third completed book manuscript, dealing with an important series of Marian apparitions within the Coptic Orthodox Church, is currently undergoing peer review.

Alexey R. Fokin is a senior researcher at the Department of Philosophy of Religion, Institute of Philosophy of Russian Academy of Sciences, Moscow;

and Professor of Theology and Patristics at SS. Cyril and Methodius Theological Institute for Postgraduate Studies, Moscow. He is the author of the following monographs (all in Russian): *Latin Patrology: Pre-Nicene Period* (2005); *The Christian Platonism of Marius Victorinus* (2007); *St. Jerome of Stridon: Biblical Scholar, Exegete, Theologian* (2010); *The Formation of the Trinitarian Doctrine in Latin Patristics* (2014).

Paul L. Gavrilyuk is the Aquinas Chair in Theology and Philosophy at the University of St. Thomas and the Founding President of the International Orthodox Theological Association. He is the author of *A History of the Catechumenate in the Early Church* (in Russian, 2001), *The Suffering of the Impassible God: The Dialectics of Patristic Thought* (2004), *Georges Florovsky and the Russian Religious Renaissance* (2013), the co-editor of *The Spiritual Senses: Perceiving God in Western Christianity* (with Sarah Coakley, 2012), and the editor of *On Christian Leadership: The Letters of Alexander Schmemann and Georges Florovsky (1947–1955)* (2020) and *Pilgrims toward the Kingdom: The Beginnings of the International Orthodox Theological Association* (2020).

Dionysios Skliris is a Teaching Fellow in Patristics at the Theological Department of the University of Athens. He is the author of *On the Road to Being: Saint Maximus the Confessor's Syn-odical Ontology* (2018) and *Logos – Mode – Telos: A Study in the Thought of Saint Maximus the Confessor* (2018, in Greek), and the editor of *Slavoj Žižek and Christianity* (2018).

Richard Swinburne is Emeritus Professor of the Philosophy of Religion at the University of Oxford, and a Fellow of the British Academy. He is best known for a trilogy on the meaning and justification of theism, *The Coherence of Theism*, *The Existence of God*, and *Faith and Reason* (all summarized in the short *Is There a God?*). He has written many books on the meaning and justification of central Christian doctrines, including *Revelation* and *The Resurrection of God Incarnate* (summarized in the short *Was Jesus God?*). He has also written in defense of the view that human beings consist of two parts, a body and a soul, especially in his books *Mind, Brain, and Free Will* and *Are We Bodies or Souls?* His book *Epistemic Justification* discusses the criteria which determine how probable some evidence makes some hypothesis. He has given many lectures around the world.

Preface

Founded in 2017, the International Orthodox Theological Association (IOTA) is a global network of over one thousand scholars, church leaders, and professionals dedicated to the worldwide exchange of knowledge within the context of the Orthodox Christian tradition. An important aspect of IOTA's mission is the engagement of contemporary culture in light of the Orthodox tradition with a view to contributing to the growth and renewal of the Church. To advance its mission, IOTA established a publishing house in 2020. IOTA Publications seeks to bring out Orthodox Christian scholarship of the highest caliber, which speaks to the contemporary situation out of the depth of the Church's historical and theological heritage. The Advisory Board of IOTA Publications consists of fifty prominent Orthodox scholars who also serve as group chairs. This collection of essays is co-edited by two internationally renowned Orthodox philosophers, David Bradshaw and Richard Swinburne, who co-chair IOTA's Philosophy of Religion Group. For many years they have dedicated much effort to bringing the worlds of Eastern European and Anglo-American Christian philosophy together. Reflecting IOTA's pan-Orthodox orientation, the volume includes contributions from an international group of philosophers from six countries: Canada, Greece, Russia, Ukraine, the United Kingdom, and the United States. We hope that this publication will inspire other worthwhile research and book projects within IOTA. Following this pattern of international cooperation, IOTA Publications aspires to become the gold standard of Orthodox scholarship worldwide.

The present volume makes a case for the rich history and contemporary relevance of natural theology in Eastern Orthodoxy. Natural theology has had a checkered history in modernity and, despite some groundbreaking work in the last decades, its epistemological credentials continue to be contested. In the ongoing debate about natural theology, with some notable exceptions, Orthodox theologians have most often joined on the side of its detractors rather than the supporters. The primary motivations for this attitude are twofold. The first one is historical: patristic authorities are typically represented as sanctioning an experiential rather than speculative paradigm of religious knowledge. Patristic theology is then contrasted with Western scholasticism, which allegedly privileged the operation of unaided reason, detached the supernatural from the natural, and created other dichotomies that were detrimental to Christian theology in the second millennium. By contrast, Eastern Orthodox theology is represented as successfully eschewing the pitfalls of Western scholasticism, especially its overreliance on the powers of reason unaided by revelation.

The second motivation is related to the first and comes from the fields of theological anthropology and religious epistemology: there is a tendency in twentieth-century Orthodox theology to insist on the unknowability of God and then to assert (following Vladimir Lossky or Christos Yannaras) that only the deified human *nous* is capable of apprehending that which is knowable in God. Among Orthodox believers, it is not uncommon to hear negative remarks about the role of discursive reasoning in theology, especially when it attempts to prove the existence of God or to provide an account of divine action and attributes. Such attempts are dismissed as obsolete, presumptuous, futile, and misguided, or worse still, clear signs of Orthodoxy's continuing Western captivity. Since God's existence is a matter of direct experience rather than rational investigation, to involve discursive reasoning in the attempt to establish the existence of God is a category mistake.

The essays in this volume mount a serious challenge to both motivations and invite us to think of natural theology less superficially and more constructively. Historically, the appeals to general features of the world as evidence for the existence of God and as a justification of various divine attributes are an integral part of the patristic tradition. Thus, contrary to a common misconception, the Church Fathers did not disparage discursive reasoning, even if some held the contemplative agency of the deified *nous* in higher regard. Furthermore, the appeals to revelation, religious experience, and the testimony of the Church Fathers, should not be understood as displacing reason or rendering it superfluous, but as presupposing reason's auxiliary role. Discursive reasoning has a modest, yet indispensable role to play in the human quest for the knowledge of God.

In sum, the contributors show that from the Fathers to present-day

Orthodox philosophers, there is an abiding tradition of natural theology in Eastern Orthodoxy. Contrary to a widespread misrepresentation, this tradition has not been entirely eclipsed in modernity, but in fact has had some outstanding if largely overlooked and underappreciated proponents. Moreover, as the present volume demonstrates, this tradition has been creatively revived by a number of contemporary Orthodox theologians and philosophers. When this legacy is fully acknowledged, recovered, and appropriated, it will bear much fruit in the Church's mission of bringing the message of Christ to the spiritually confused and religiously doubting contemporary world.

Paul L. Gavrilyuk
Founding President of IOTA
Feast of the Annunciation, March 2021

Abbreviations

ANF	*Ante-Nicene Fathers*, ed. Alexander Roberts, James Donaldson, and A. Cleveland Coxe (Buffalo, NY: Christian Literature Publishing Co., 1885)
GCS	*Die griechischen christlichen Schriftsteller* (Leipzig)
GNO	Gregory of Nyssa, *Gregorii Nysseni Opera*, ed. Werner Jaeger (Leiden: Brill, 1952–98)
NPNF	*A Select Library of Nicene and Post-Nicene Fathers of the Christian Church*, ed. Philip Schaff and Henry Wace (Buffalo, NY: Christian Literature Publishing Co., 1894)
PG	*Patrologia graeca*, ed. Jacques-Paul Migne (Paris: J.-P. Migne, 1857-66)
PL	*Patrologia latina*, ed. Jacques-Paul Migne (Paris: J.-P. Migne, 1857-66)
SC	*Sources chrétiennes* (Paris: Éditions du Cerf, 1941-)
ST	Thomas Aquinas, *Summa theologiae*

Introduction

DAVID BRADSHAW

Natural theology is the attempt to support the existence of God, and to investigate the divine attributes, through philosophical reasoning. More specifically, it seeks to do so starting (as Richard Swinburne observes later in this volume) "from propositions which theist and atheist alike can recognize as obviously true." In this it differs from philosophical theology, which allows theological teachings and other beliefs based on revelation to figure among its premises. Natural theology does engage with historical evidence, such as that for miracles and for various forms of religious experience, but it does so based on the publicly accessible historical record. It bears a close relation to apologetics, and indeed natural theological arguments are often used within apologetic strategies. However, apologetics is not limited to philosophical reasoning (embracing, for example, historical arguments for the veracity of Scripture) and it explicitly seeks to convert, whereas natural theology merely seeks to elucidate a line of philosophical reasoning.[1]

The term "natural theology" (*theologia naturalis*) is first attested in St. Augustine's report of the views of the first-century B.C. Roman scholar, Varro.[2] For Varro, natural theology was the kind of theology taught by the philosophers, as opposed to the mythical theology of the poets and the civil theology of the state. Varro himself refers to it as *physicon*, indicating that the

1. There is also a hybrid form of reasoning known as "ramified natural theology" which seeks to argue, not just for a general form of theism, but for the specific doctrines of a particular religion or denomination. Anselm's philosophical arguments for the necessity of the Incarnation and substitutionary atonement are a prominent example. Although our main focus here is on simple natural theology, the boundaries between the simple and ramified forms are fluid, and many arguments used in the former lend themselves to the latter as well.

2. See Augustine, *City of God* 6.5–7.

term (and probably the three-fold distinction) had a Greek origin, although it is no longer found in surviving sources. However that may be, the practice of natural theology goes back to Xenophanes and Anaximander and was developed in elaborate detail by Plato and Aristotle. It has a long and complex history stretching from antiquity through the Middle Ages and modern philosophy, one that was by no means brought to an end (as is sometimes supposed) by Hume and Kant. Although it went into eclipse in the first half of the twentieth century, owing to the dominance of phenomenology on the Continent and of positivism and ordinary language philosophy in the Anglophone world, it came roaring back with the revival of metaphysics that began in the 1960s.[3] Today natural theology is a flourishing enterprise that includes a wide range of argument types and strategies, some of them drawn from classical sources and many others of more recent vintage.

Despite its prominence in the ancient world, natural theology has from the beginning evoked varied responses within Christianity. St. Paul's sweeping dismissal in 1 Corinthians of the "wisdom of this world" (1:20), and his warning in Colossians against "philosophy and vain deceit" (2:8), certainly offer grounds for caution. As regards belief in the existence of God, the author of the book of Hebrews states in his encomium of faith that "by faith we understand that the world was created by the word of God, so that what is seen was made out of things which do not appear" (Heb 11:3).[4] A few verses later he brings divine goodness within the scope of the act of faith: "Without faith it is impossible to please him; for whoever would draw near to God must believe that he exists and that he rewards those who diligently seek him" (11:6). There is no reason to assume that the author wishes thereby to exclude an important role for reason—and indeed, the book of Hebrews offers careful and elaborate reasoning on many points. Nonetheless, these passages make plain that effectual and salvific belief in God only comes through faith, and whatever role reason plays must in some way be complementary to that.

Another important passage was St. Paul's discussion of the natural knowledge of God in Romans 1. There we read that "ever since the creation of the world the invisible things of God, namely his eternal power and deity, are clearly perceived, being understood from the things that are made" (v. 20). This is a classic proof text on behalf of the possibility of some form of

3. See on these developments *The Blackwell Companion to Natural Theology*, ed. William Lane Craig and J. P. Moreland (Malden, MA: Wiley-Blackwell, 2012), particularly the Introduction by the editors. See also the chapter by Travis Dumsday in this volume.

4. Biblical quotations are from the Revised Standard Version, slightly modified in some cases.

natural theology.[5] It must be admitted that St. Paul probably did not have philosophical arguments in mind, however, for he goes on to add, "so that they [that is, pagan idolators] are without excuse." Evidently he is thinking of a kind of knowledge that is available even to the unlearned and those who lived prior to the rise of philosophy. Nonetheless, his statement does imply that it is possible to reason from the facts of creation to the existence of an eternal and mighty Creator. We also know from his speech at the Areopagus that he was quite willing to draw upon pagan philosophy when he saw it as convergent with the truth.[6] Hence it seems likely that, despite his dismissal of the "wisdom of this world," Paul would have welcomed the use of arguments drawn from natural theology in a limited and subordinate role.

At any rate, early Christian authors—beginning with the Greek Apologists and continuing with St. Athanasius, the Cappadocians, and others—readily drew from existing philosophical arguments in their efforts to articulate and defend Christian belief. They did so not only in apologetic works like Athanasius's *Contra Gentes* and philosophical works like St. Gregory of Nyssa's *On the Soul and Resurrection*, but in works aimed at systematically presenting Christian belief to a Christian audience, such as Gregory's *Great Catechism* and St. John of Damascus's *On the Orthodox Faith*. The use of natural theological arguments was thus a firmly entrenched element of patristic thought, and such arguments continued to be repeated and elaborated throughout the Byzantine era.

Despite this patristic consensus, however, modern Orthodox thought has been markedly cool in its attitude toward natural theology. A number of leading Orthodox thinkers, such as Sergius Bulgakov, Vladimir Lossky, Christos Yannaras, and Metropolitan John Zizioulas, have criticized it sharply. Their arguments are varied, but in general they view natural theology as at best religiously useless, in that it does not lead to a true knowledge of or encounter with God; and at worst positively harmful, in that it can be a kind of substitute for faith (Lossky) and has contributed through its overreach to the rise of modern atheism (Yannaras). These are important concerns that deserve to be taken seriously. Our hope is that the present

5. See also the critique of idolatry in Wisdom of Solomon 13:1–9, especially the statement, "from the greatness and beauty of created things comes a corresponding perception of their Creator" (v. 5).

6. Paul's allusion, "as even some of your poets have said, 'For we are indeed his offspring'" (Acts 17:28), is probably a reference to the Stoic Cleanthes of Assos and the Stoic-influenced Aratus of Soli, who both make this statement. (I presume, in common with the patristic and Orthodox tradition, that Acts correctly represents the teaching of the Apostle.)

volume will give them a fair hearing while at the same time doing justice to the varied and important roles that natural theology has played within the Orthodox tradition.

Faith and reason in patristic thought

Before proceeding to a description of the contents of this volume, I would like to offer some context to help situate the role that natural theology played during the patristic era. I choose this period in part because of its intrinsic interest and in part because of its importance for the Orthodox tradition as a whole. My aim is not to offer a survey of the uses of natural theology among the Church Fathers (ably provided in Chapter 1 by Alexey Fokin), but to attempt to situate natural theology in relation to the broad contours of the patristic understanding of faith and reason. This is an important preamble to any attempt to assess its role today.

The first sustained discussion of faith in Christian literature is in the *Stromata* of Clement of Alexandria. One is surprised to find there not an analysis of the pertinent biblical passages (which would be complex enough), but instead a philosophical discussion drawing eclectically from Aristotle, Epicurus, and the Stoics. Clement begins by offering the sweeping statement, "Now the ways of wisdom are various that lead right to the way of truth. Faith is the way."[7] Faith (πίστις) is here a comprehensive term for all the ways that lead to knowledge, whatever they may be. After briefly discussing the ways to wisdom as they are taught in Proverbs, Clement adds: "Such is the way of wisdom ('for whom the Lord loves he chastens' [Prov. 3:12]), causing pain in order to produce understanding, and restoring to peace and immortality."[8] The reference here to pain and chastening indicates that Clement means his initial definition seriously: faith is not solely a matter of confidence or belief, but a way of growing into knowledge that necessarily requires pain and struggle. Indeed, to come to see in one's suffering the tutelage of God is itself an act of faith. Clement's reference to the verse from Proverbs is a reminder to the reader of this important biblical theme.

After this initial orientation, Clement goes on to offer a number of definitions of faith drawn from various sources. In light of his initial sweeping definition, these are best seen not as rivals but as descriptions of the var-

7. Clement of Alexandria, *Stromata* 2.2.4 (GCS 2:114–15; trans. ANF 2:348).

8. Clement of Alexandria, *Stromata* 2.2.4 (GCS 2:115; ANF 2:348).

ious forms faith may take in the growth to wisdom. The first is that it is a "voluntary preconception (πρόληψις ἑκούσιος), the assent of piety—'the substance of things hoped for, the evidence of things not seen' [Heb. 11:1]."[9] He continues in a terse and complex passage:

> Others have defined faith as a thoughtful assent (ἐννοητικὴν συγκατάθεσιν) to an unseen object, as indeed demonstration is the manifest assent to an object that was previously unknown. If then it is choice, being desirous of something, the desire is in this instance intellectual (ἡ ὄρεξις νῦν διανοητική). And since choice is the beginning of action, faith is discovered to be the beginning of action, being the foundation of rational choice for anyone who exhibits the demonstration to himself in a preliminary way through faith.[10]

Faith is here the ability to grasp beforehand that which may later be demonstrated. Clement highlights that as a *voluntary* preconception, faith is a choice. Yet it is hardly an arbitrary choice, for it is "thoughtful," "intellectual," the "beginning of action," and the "foundation of rational choice." In some way, then, faith both exhibits and enables rationality. We gain further insight into this a bit later when Clement cites Epicurus on what it means that faith is a preconception:

> Epicurus, too, who very greatly preferred pleasure to truth, supposes faith to be a preconception of the mind (πρόληψιν διανοίας); and defines preconception to be a grasping at something evident (ἐπιβολὴν ἐπί τι ἐναργὲς) and at the clear understanding of the thing; and asserts that, without preconception, no one can either inquire, or doubt, or judge, or even argue.[11]

Although Clement is our only surviving source for Epicurus's identification of faith as a preconception, the general Epicurean doctrine of preconception is attested by Diogenes Laertius. There a preconception is defined as a "universal idea stored in the mind; that is, a recollection of an external object

9. Clement of Alexandria, *Stromata* 2.2.8 (GCS 2:117; ANF 2:349).

10. Clement of Alexandria, *Stromata* 2.2.9 (GCS 2:117; ANF 2:349, modified). Clement's use of the term συγκατάθεσις here suggests a Stoic source, to which he welds an Aristotelian element in the understanding of choice as ὄρεξις διανοητική (drawn from *Nicomachean Ethics* 6.2 1139b4).

11. Clement of Alexandria, *Stromata* 2.4.16–17 (GCS 2:121; ANF 2:350).

often presented," and the point is made that without such preconceptions (for example, of man, or horse, or cow) we would not be able to inquire what something is.[12] One can see here the inspiration for Clement's point that preconceptions are, in general, necessary for action and rational choice. But to define faith as a *voluntary* preconception, and thereby itself a kind of choice, seems to be Clement's own innovation.

Although Clement's terminology is new, one need not look far to find a philosophical antecedent for the idea that some sort of voluntary preconception is necessary if there is to be rational thought and action. This is a prominent theme in two of Plato's best-known dialogues, the *Apology* and *Phaedo*. Socrates is presented there as a model of one who has faith in the sense of a persistent voluntary determination to live, think, and act as one who trusts in reason. We can distinguish two aspects of this Socratic faith, one subjective and one objective.[13] From a subjective standpoint, it is Socrates's response to the repeated call issued to him by "the god" (*Apology* 33c). As the Delphic oracle mentioned in the *Apology* illustrates, that call did not come with its meaning written on its face. Socrates's faith consisted precisely in seeking to ferret out its meaning by heeding the call daily, in an ongoing practice of seeking truth and virtue and urging others to do the same, regardless of the consequences. That is what his faith consisted in for him from the standpoint of his own experience. Considered objectively, in terms of its propositional content, it was above all a faith in the value of reason. Nothing that Socrates did makes sense unless there was at his core the conviction that reason is a precious gift that is to be honored at all costs. As he explains at length in the *Phaedo*, it is a gift from the gods for which we are responsible, and the gods will welcome us if we use it well. Seen in that light, Socrates's faith was not only in the gods, but in the goodness of the cosmos and the justice of the cosmic order. He saw reason as precious because it enables us to apprehend and, to the extent possible, conform ourselves to that order.

Far from being opposed to reason, faith is here its essential complement and presupposition. This point has sometimes been lost on commentators because Plato does not explicitly identify the attitude adopted by Socrates

12. Diogenes Laertius, *Lives of the Eminent Philosophers* 10.33; ed. and trans. R. D. Hicks, *Diogenes Laertius: Lives of Eminent Philosophers*, 2 vols. (Cambridge, MA: Harvard University Press, 1970), 2:563. See further Valerie Tsouna, "Epicurean Preconceptions," *Phronesis* 61 (2016): 160–221.

13. See my "God as the Good: A Critique of H. Tristram Engelhardt, Jr.'s *After God*," *Journal of Medicine and Philosophy* 43 (2018): 650–66, from which I draw in the remainder of this paragraph.

as one of faith (πίστις). This is hardly surprising, for *pistis* did not bear the meaning of "voluntary preconception" in Plato's time; indeed, it acquired such a meaning only in these very passages from Clement.[14] Nonetheless, the idea is there already in Plato's portrayal of Socrates. It may well have been partly for this reason that many early Christians ardently admired Socrates and readily associated his cause with their own. In the Gospels as well, faith is very much a voluntary preconception or (less technically) orientation of the soul, one that is open to the divine call and responds with alacrity to what God requires. Clement found in the general concept of a voluntary preconception that is necessary for rational thought and action a way of translating this biblical notion into a recognizable philosophical idiom.

Clement proceeds to offer two further definitions—again, not as rivals to the preceding, but as ways of explicating the forms faith may take in various aspects of life. One is that faith is "the judgment which follows knowledge," and accordingly "something superior to knowledge, and its criterion."[15] Faith is here certainty or conviction, which is a "criterion" of knowledge in that we do not think we know something until we have confidence in it.[16] The other definition is that faith is a sort of "natural art" that contributes to learning, one that involves docility and receptivity to sound teaching.[17] Faith in this sense leads to repentance, for it is open to acknowledging an act to be sin. And beyond repentance it leads to hope, for Scripture promises good things to one who is faithful.[18]

With these fruits we enter into recognizably Christian territory. Unfortunately, Clement does not explain explicitly how faith in the sense he has defined leads to Christian belief, nor how it relates to the use of reason. For insight on these points we must turn to another great Alexandrian, St. Athanasius. Athanasius in his *Contra Gentes* offers a sweeping account of the nature of human cognition of God. He begins by positing that God, in

14. Clement does near the end of 2.4 offer a few passages where Plato takes a positive view of *pistis*, but they seem to be about faith only in the sense of confidence or conviction. A closer precedent would be *Phaedo* 70a–b, where Cebes asserts (and Socrates accepts) that belief in the immortality of the soul requires *pistis*.

15. Clement of Alexandria, *Stromata* 2.4.15 (GCS 2:120; ANF 2:350).

16. Clement attributes this definition to Aristotle. The nearest source among Aristotle's surviving works would seem to be the teaching that one must believe more firmly (πιστεύειν μᾶλλον) the premises of a syllogism than the conclusion in order for the conclusion to count as knowledge (*Post. Anal.* 1.2 72a25–33).

17. Clement of Alexandria, *Stromata* 2.6.25–26 (GCS 2:126; ANF 2:353).

18. Clement of Alexandria, *Stromata* 2.6.26–27 (GCS 2:127; ANF 2:353).

creating man in his image and likeness, "made man perceptive and understanding of reality through his similarity to him, giving him also a conception and knowledge of his own eternity, so that as long as he kept this likeness he might never abandon his concept of God or leave the company of the saints."[19] In this original and fully natural state, man "is filled with admiration when he grasps God's providence towards the universe. He is superior to sensual things and all bodily impressions, and by the power of his mind clings to the divine and intelligible realities in heaven."[20] Yet although Adam perceived God within the natural world, he had no need for any intermediary, for he also knew God directly within his own soul: "The purity of the soul makes it able to behold God as in a mirror (τὸν θεὸν κατοπτρίζεσθαι), as the Lord himself said, 'Blessed are the pure in heart, for they shall see God.'"[21]

Returning to this subject later, Athanasius explains that the original paradisaical state is still available even now:

> The road to God is not as far from us or as extraneous to us as God himself is high above all, but it is within us and we ourselves can find its beginning, as Moses taught: "The word of faith is within your heart" [Deut. 30:14]. This the Savior also indicated and confirmed, saying: "The kingdom of God is within you" [Luke 17:21]. So since we have faith and the kingdom of God within us, we can quickly come to contemplate and apprehend the King of all, the saving Word of the Father.[22]

Faith is here the essential means by which we can recover the knowledge of God. It is both something innate, a kind of residuum from our state of primeval bliss, and something that must be cultivated in order to come to full realization. This is much like the view of Clement that faith begins as an essential (but voluntary) preconception and grows through time into a living relationship with God.

19. Athanasius, *Contra Gentes* 2; ed. and trans. Robert W. Thompson, *Athanasius: Contra Gentes and De Incarnatione* (Oxford: Clarendon Press, 1971), 6–7. Athanasius may have in mind here Wisdom 2:23, "For God created man for incorruption, and made him the image of his own eternity."

20. Athanasius, *Contra Gentes* 2; ed. and trans. Thompson, *Athanasius*, 6–7.

21. Athanasius, *Contra Gentes* 2; ed. and trans. Thompson, *Athanasius*, 6–9 (modified).

22. Athanasius, *Contra Gentes* 30; ed. and trans. Thompson, *Athanasius*, 82–82. Athanasius adds the words "of faith" to the quotation of Deuteronomy.

The place of natural theology

What role does rational argument play in this process? Athanasius goes on to explain that, although it is possible to behold the divine image directly within the soul when it is cleansed, many remain tied to earthly and sensual attachments. In that case God can still be known indirectly through creation:

> If this instruction on the part of the soul itself is not adequate because of external influences which disturb its mind and prevent it from seeing the better course, it is still possible to grasp knowledge about God from visible phenomena, since creation through its order and harmony, as it were in writing, indicates and proclaims its master and maker.[23]

This is the preface to a long presentation of what today would be considered a version of the argument from design. Much of the argument is framed, not as an inference, but as a description of what can be immediately perceived by one who is attentive. Just as someone hearing a lyre without seeing the player can perceive that there is a musician playing, so we can perceive from the harmony of the world that it has a single Ruler and King.[24] This perceptually-framed form of the argument is interestingly different from one that frames it as an inference.[25] Nonetheless, the argument is sufficiently rich that it can readily be translated into inferential form, as Richard Swinburne suggests later in this volume.

Although it takes center stage in *Contra Gentes*, the argument from design is only one among several ways that God can be known indirectly even in our current fallen state. In *On the Incarnation* Athanasius lists it as one of three ways God has provided for those who fail to come to know him through the divine image within. This passage is worth quoting at length, for it provides a classic description of the place of natural theology within the broader divine economy.

> The grace of God was sufficient for one to know God the Word and through him the Father. But because God knew the weakness of men

23. Athanasius, *Contra Gentes* 34; ed. and trans. Thompson, *Athanasius*, 94–95.

24. Athanasius, *Contra Gentes* 38; ed. and trans. Thompson, *Athanasius*, 104–07.

25. For discussion of the difference between perceiving and inferring design see Del Ratzsch, "Perceiving Design," in *God and Design*, ed. Neil Manson (New York: Routledge, 2003), 124–44; C. Stephen Evans, *Natural Signs and the Knowledge of God: A New Look at Theistic Arguments* (Oxford: Oxford University Press, 2010).

> he anticipated their negligence, so that if they failed to recognize God by themselves, through the works of creation they might be able to know the Creator. Because the negligence of men sank gradually to the worse, God again provided for such weakness of theirs and sent the law and the prophets, who were known to them, so that if they were reluctant to raise their eyes to heaven and know the Creator, they would have schooling from those close by. For men can learn more directly from other men about more advanced things. So they could lift their eyes to the immensity of heaven, and discerning the harmony of creation know its ruler, the Word of the Father, who by his providence in the universe makes the Father known to all men, and for that reason moves the universe, in order that by him all men should know God. Or if they were reluctant to do this, they could meet the saints and through them learn of God the Creator of the universe, the Father of Christ, and that the worship of idols was godless and full of all impiety. They could also, by knowing the law, desist from all wickedness and lead lives of virtue. For the law was not for the Jews only, nor on their account only were the prophets sent—though they were sent to the Jews and persecuted by the Jews—but they provided holy instruction to the whole world about the knowledge of God and the conduct of one's soul.[26]

Natural theology—represented here by coming to know God through the "works of creation"—is only the first of the ways God has provided to know him within the sensible world. There are also the prophets and saints, whose holiness is such that in merely meeting them, one can come to know God.[27] And there is the law which they teach; this too can be a way of knowing God, in that it leads away from godlessness and impiety toward a life of virtue.

For the full completion of this line of thought we must turn to a third of Athanasius's works, the *Life of Antony*. The *Life* is the literary portrayal of a saint in a way that enables the reader to experience, to the extent possible through the written word, what it is like to encounter someone holy. Its immense influence through the centuries is a testament to its success.[28] Much as in the *Contra Gentes*, Athanasius emphasizes that the direct knowledge

26. Athanasius, *On the Incarnation* 12; ed. and trans. Thompson, *Athanasius*, 162–63.

27. Thompson states in a footnote that "the saints" (οἱ ἅγιοι) here are solely the Old Testament prophets, but that seems unlikely inasmuch as meeting them is supposed to be widely available to all of humanity.

28. See in particular the story of its effect on the two friends of Ponticianus, and thereby on Augustine, in Augustine's *Confessions* 8.6–7.

of God Antony has achieved is not something alien to his humanity, but is simply the restoration of his natural state. When Antony emerges from the desert fortress where he has spent twenty years in battling demons, Athanasius describes him as "altogether guided by reason and abiding in a natural state (ἐν τῷ κατὰ φύσιν ἑστώς)."[29] Shortly thereafter, in his discourse to his disciples, Antony explains that virtue itself is something natural and innate.

> Fear not to hear of virtue, nor be astonished at the name. For it is not far from us, nor is it outside of us, but its work is within us and the performance is easy if only we are willing. . . . For when the soul has its spiritual faculty (τὸ νοερὸν) in a natural state, virtue is formed. And it is in a natural state when it remains as it was made—and it was made beautiful and perfectly straight.[30]

We can see in these passages the connection between Athanasius's second way of coming to the knowledge of God, the encounter with holiness, and the third, the moral law. Both are ways of recalling the soul to its natural state—the one by external example and inspiration, and the other by internal transformation. To the extent that the soul returns to its natural state, it has a direct knowledge of and communion with God, much as does Antony himself.

Can something similar be said for the first of the three ways of knowing God, natural theology? Although Athanasius does not address this question explicitly, an answer emerges near the end of the *Life* in the famous conversation between Antony and some visiting philosophers. The philosophers begin by mocking the Gospel, to which Antony replies by pointing out its superiority to pagan myths.[31] He then continues:

> But as you prefer to lean upon demonstrative arguments, and as you, having this art, wish us not to worship God until after such proof, tell me first how things in general and especially the recognition of God are accurately known. Is it through demonstrative knowledge or the working of faith (δι' ἐνεργείας πίστεως)? And which is better, faith which comes through such inworking (ἡ δι' ἐνεργείας πίστις) or demonstration by arguments?[32]

29. Athanasius, *Life of Antony* 14 (PG 26, 865A; trans. H. Ellershaw, NPNF 2/4:200).
30. Athanasius, *Life of Antony* 20 (PG 26, 872C–873A; NPNF 2/4:201, modified).
31. Athanasius, *Life of Antony* 74–76 (PG 26, 945B–949B; NPNF 2/4:215–16).
32. Athanasius, *Life of Antony* 77 (PG 26, 949B–952A; NPNF 2/4:216).

Perhaps surprisingly, the philosophers answer that faith (or perhaps merely "confidence," πίστις) that comes through inworking is superior to demonstrative knowledge. Antony replies:

> You have answered well, for faith arises from disposition of soul, but dialectic from the skill of its inventors. Wherefore to those in whom the inworking through faith (ἡ διὰ πίστεως ἐνέργεια) is present, demonstrative argument is needless, or even superfluous. For what we know through faith this you attempt to prove through words, and often you are not even able to express what we understand. So the inworking through faith is better and stronger than your sophistical arguments.[33]

It might seem that Antony here decisively rejects any important role for rational argument. Such a conclusion would be premature, however, for he immediately continues:

> We Christians therefore hold the mystery not in the wisdom of Greek arguments, but in the power of faith richly supplied to us by God through Jesus Christ. And to show that this statement is true, behold now, without having learned letters, we believe in God, knowing through his works his providence over all things. And for evidence that our faith is effective, see now that we are supported by faith in Christ, but you by sophistical logomachies.[34]

The reference to knowing God's providence through his works shows that we are here not far from the design argument.[35] Antony goes on to list a whole series of evidences that Christian faith is effective: the decline of paganism and the rise of Christianity, the power of the Cross over demons, the virtue and self-control exhibited by Christians, the courage of the martyrs. This appeal to evidence makes it clear that he is not rejecting rational argument in general, but only the specific role given to demonstrative reasoning by the philosophers.

Much depends, in reading this episode, on what is meant by the faith that comes by divine inworking (ἡ δι' ἐνεργείας πίστις) and the inworking

33. Athanasius, *Life of Antony* 77 (PG 26, 952A; NPNF 2/4:216, modified).

34. Athanasius, *Life of Antony* 78 (PG 26, 952B; NPNF 2/4:216, modified).

35. More specifically, this is true of the form the argument takes in the *Contra Gentes*, where God's providence can be immediately perceived in his works; there is no hint of an attempt to recast the argument in deductive form.

that is through faith (ἡ διὰ πίστεως ἐνέργεια). It is tempting to see in these a mere passive receptivity to divine enlightenment. Read in that way, Antony would be saying that God gives faith to some and not to others, and for those to whom He does give it, it is a sufficient warrant for belief. But that cannot be right, for Antony's whole purpose is to persuade the philosophers to embrace faith, and indeed to do so on rational grounds.

It is crucial to recognize that for the Greek Fathers, faith is never simply a divine gift; rather, it is an active and freely chosen response to God's continual presentation of the good. This is a view based largely on the Pauline usage of *energeia, energein*, and related terms.[36] Antony invokes it earlier in the *Life*, alluding to Romans 8:28 (in a minority reading): "Wherefore, children, let us hold fast our discipline, and let us not be careless. For in it the Lord is our fellow-worker (συνεργόν), as it is written, 'to all that choose the good, God works with them for the good (συνεργεῖ ὁ θεὸς εἰς τὸ ἀγαθόν).'"[37] The faith that comes by divine inworking is thus not something imparted by God to a passive recipient, but requires active cooperation. This is significant for our purposes because it shows that the choice Antony puts before the philosophers is not one between reason and blind faith. Both alternatives require reason, although exercised in different ways. Indeed it is the choice of faith that enables reason properly understood—that is, as the correct apprehension of reality—to come to full fruition.

Yet it remains true that Athanasius nowhere attributes to philosophical reasoning a capacity to restore and vivify the soul like that of the encounter with holiness or obedience to the divine law. Its role remains that which it has in the *Contra Gentes*: that of clearing away error and establishing an initial basis for belief in God. And even in that work, as noted earlier, Athanasius is less concerned to present a demonstrative argument (although his argument can be construed in that way) than to awaken the perception of the reader to what should already be obvious.

This Athanasian understanding of the respective roles of faith and reason became prevalent in the Christian East. We recognize it in the frequent assertions that virtue in general, and faith in particular, are innate to the human

36. See David Bradshaw, "The Divine Energies in the New Testament," *St. Vladimir's Theological Quarterly* 50 (2006): 189–223, and "St. John Chrysostom on Grace and Free Will," *Common Ground Journal* 12, no. 2 (Fall 2015): 30–36, http://www.commongroundjournal.org/volnum/v12no2.pdf.

37. Athanasius, *Life of Antony* 19 (PG 26, 872A; NPNF 2/4:201). Athanasius substitutes "all that choose the good" for "those that love God" found in all surviving witnesses, and also inserts ὁ θεὸς after συνεργεῖ in accordance with a relatively well attested minority reading.

soul.[38] We recognize it also in the way that Eastern authors tend to approach arguments for the existence of God as a matter of spiritual instruction, the first step to be taken by one who is presumed to be fundamentally open and receptive to learning. St. Maximus the Confessor, introducing what today would be considered a version of the design argument, explains his task as that of describing how "the saints learned of the Creator's existence from the things created by Him."[39] Equally telling is the way St. John of Damascus carefully introduces his arguments for the existence of God in *On the Orthodox Faith*. This passage illustrates well the fundamental orientation toward natural theology found among the Greek Fathers:

> The knowledge of the existence of God is implanted in us by nature. But since the wickedness of the Evil One has prevailed so mightily against man's nature as even to drive some into denying the existence of God, that most foolish and woeful pit of destruction (whose folly David, revealer of the divine meaning, exposed when he said, "The fool has said in his heart, there is no God" [Ps. 13:1, LXX]), so the disciples of the Lord and his apostles, made wise by the Holy Spirit and working wonders in his power and grace, took them captive in the net of miracles and drew them up out of the depths of ignorance to the light of the knowledge of God. In the same way their successors in grace and worth, both pastors and teachers, having received the enlightening grace of the Spirit, by the power of miracles and the word of grace enlightened those walking in darkness and brought back the wanderers into the way. But as for us who are not recipients either of the gift of miracles or the gift of teaching (for indeed we have rendered ourselves unworthy of these by our passion for pleasure), come, let us discuss a few of those things that have been delivered to us on this subject by the expounders of grace, calling on the Father, the Son, and the Holy Spirit.[40]

38. See Basil, *Hexaemeron* 9.4; Evagrius, *Praktikos* 81, *On Thoughts* 31; Pseudo-Macarius, *Homilies* 8.2; Maximus the Confessor, *Dispute with Pyrrhus* (PG 91, 309B–312A); John of Damascus, *On the Orthodox Faith* 58 (= 3.14).

39. Maximus the Confessor, *Ambigua* 10.35; ed. and trans. Nicholas Constas, *Maximos the Confessor: On Difficulties in the Church Fathers*, 2 vols. (Cambridge, MA: Harvard University Press, 2014), 1:285.

40. John of Damascus, *On the Orthodox Faith* 3 (= 1.3); ed. P. Bonifatius Kotter, *Die Schriften des Johannes von Damaskos*, 8 vols. (Berlin: De Gruyter, 1969–1988), 2:10–11; trans. S. D. F. Salmond, NPNF 2/9:2 (modified).

John then proceeds to give a form of the cosmological argument (based on identifying the mutable with the created) and a form of the design argument. Although he shows no sign of doubting the soundness of these arguments, they are plainly for him a kind of second-best, necessary only because the personal witness of the apostles and saints has not been available to all.

In sum, although the Greek Fathers certainly recognized a distinction between faith and reason, they tended to think of them as mutually supportive and interpenetrating. Faith begins as an innate orientation toward the good, and reason, which depends on faith, is the attempt to bring this innate orientation to its full realization. No point in this process is autonomous and self-directed, for God *is* the Good and he is constantly active presenting the good to us in various forms, so that every choice we make is always in some way a response to him.[41] It is this doubly synergistic view—involving the synergy of human faith and reason and of both with God—which determines the definite but subordinate role that the Greek Fathers gave to natural theology.

We may note in passing that natural theology is not to be confused with another way of coming to know God through nature that was richly developed in the Greek patristic tradition. This is natural contemplation (θεωρία φυσική), the second of the three stages of the spiritual life distinguished by Evagrius and the tradition that followed him.[42] Natural contemplation is the direct perception of the divine *logoi*—essences, meanings, intentions—within nature. It constitutes a much richer form of the knowledge of God than is sought by natural theology, one that comes about only through ascetic discipline (πρακτική) and is in turn oriented toward the yet higher state of pure prayer (θεολογία). Although natural contemplation is an important topic in its own right, it lies beyond our scope here.

41. See in particular John Chrysostom, *Homilies on Philippians* 8.1 (commenting on Phil 2:12–13), with discussion in Bradshaw, "St. John Chrysostom on Grace and Free Will." For God as the Good to whom we are innately drawn see Basil the Great, *Long Rules*, Q. 2; Gregory of Nyssa, *On Virginity* 11; Dionysius the Areopagite, *Divine Names* 4; Maximus the Confessor, *Ambigua* 7.11–13.

42. See Andrew Louth, *The Origins of the Christian Mystical Tradition: From Plato to Denys*, 2nd ed. (Oxford: Oxford University Press, 2007), 102–13; Julia Konstantinovsky, *Evagrius Ponticus: The Making of a Gnostic* (Farnham: Ashgate Publishing, 2009), 47–66.

Contents of the present volume

As mentioned earlier, natural theology has undergone a remarkable renaissance in recent years. Some of the best minds of contemporary philosophy have given it their attention, producing arguments and counter-arguments at a dizzying pace. Many of these discussions pertain to the traditional arguments for the existence of God (ontological, cosmological, teleological, and moral) or against it (the problem of evil as well as various concerns about the coherence of theism). Many others address new topics, ranging from the so-called problem of "divine hiddenness," to the evidentiary value of religious experience, to new approaches to understanding divine attributes such as omnipotence, eternity, and foreknowledge.

The present volume is presented in the hope that it will initiate a vigorous discussion about whether and how Orthodoxy should draw upon these contemporary developments; as well as, conversely, what distinctive insights Orthodoxy can contribute to this rich and growing discipline. Although the coverage of Orthodox perspectives on natural theology offered here is far from complete—whether from a historical, geographical, or systematic standpoint—we believe that it offers enough to provide a helpful starting point for further investigation.

The first essay, by Alexey Fokin, offers an overview of patristic arguments for the existence of God. As Fokin observes, the Fathers commonly hold that we can know "that" the divine nature or essence exists, but not what it is. This element of negative theology establishes the context for their appropriation of the classical arguments for the existence of God. Fokin divides these arguments under six headings: (1) the argument from the innate conception of God, (2) the design (or teleological) argument, (3) the cosmological argument, (4) the argument from an ideal or formal cause, (5) the argument from degrees of perfection, and (6) moral arguments. Of these, (4)–(6) are found only in Augustine and Boethius and so had little influence within the Orthodox tradition. The most popular among the Greek Fathers were (1) and (2), although (1) was scarcely developed beyond a simple appeal to the *consensus omnium*. The design argument, by contrast, was developed in some detail and typically bore the weight of establishing belief in God, whether for apologetic or systematic purposes. The cosmological argument appears in a few of the more philosophical authors (Augustine, Maximus, John of Damascus) although it too was not developed in much detail. Notably, arguments for the existence of God never became a subject of controversy among the Church Fathers of either East or West, and so were not subjected to detailed critique and analysis as occurred later among the scholastics.

The next article is my own short contribution on natural theology in the work of St. Gregory Palamas. Palamas is of course best known for his teaching about the vision of the uncreated light and the essence–energies distinction. Nonetheless, there are at least three passages in his work that show a favorable attitude toward natural theology. One of these, a statement of the design argument in the *Triads*, is very much in keeping with earlier patristic tradition. The others are somewhat more innovative. One of them, found in his early correspondence with Akindynos, speaks of how it is possible to take in together in a single glance (συνορᾶν) God with creatures when the latter are seen rightly, as evincing divine forethought, goodness, and wisdom. The other, from the *Chapters*, identifies God as the ongoing, sustaining cause of all things in their mere existence out of nothing. I argue that these latter two passages are best read in light of that on the design argument, and that the three together offer a way of educating one's perception so as to "see together" creatures with their divine cause.

The next article, by Richard Cross (the sole non-Orthodox contributor), shifts attention to the West. It offers a concise and richly informative survey of the course of natural theology from Anselm to Kant. Cross describes some of the sharp disagreements over arguments for the existence of God within medieval scholasticism, including over questions such as the validity of the ontological argument, the possibility of an *a priori* argument for the Trinity, and even (with Ockham) whether God can be shown to be single rather than many. Luther and Calvin introduced a new form of skepticism, questioning whether the God of natural theology can be known as the true God apart from revelation; and, if not, whether natural theology itself constitutes a kind of idolatry. Calvin also introduced (or revived) the idea that to recognize God in creation is less an act of inference than an act of immediate perception, one that he famously dubbed the *sensus divinitatis*.[43] The Reformation and the Scientific Revolution, with their accompanying intellectual and cultural turmoil, led to new motivations for natural theology, both epistemological (Descartes) and metaphysical (Leibniz). In these efforts natural theology was invoked as a way of resolving systematic philosophical problems. Kant sought to cut the ground out from under all such attempts by denying the possibility of a necessarily existing being. As

43. Calvin was a major influence on Thomas Reid, who is a primary inspiration for those who adopt this view today (see above, n. 25).

Cross notes in conclusion, the contemporary revival of natural theology has been predicated upon a widespread rejection of Kant's view on this point.

Paul Gavrilyuk offers a groundbreaking study of the place of natural theology in modern Russian Orthodoxy, including both the Russian theological academies of the nineteenth century and the religious philosophers of the early twentieth century. His story begins with Fiodor Golubinskii, a professor at the Moscow Theological Academy who drew upon the natural theology of Anselm, Leibniz, Wolff, and others as a counter to the materialism of the *philosophes*. He gave an emphasis to religious experience that is not found in these authors, however, and indeed regarded it as the strongest of the "empirical proofs" of the existence of God. This theme was developed more fully by his successor, Viktor Kudriavtsev-Platonov. For Kudriavtsev, the belief in God formed through immediate experience is "basic" in the sense that it "undergirds our beliefs about the general features of the world." Viktor Nesmelov of the Kazan Theological Academy offered an interesting twist on this idea, denying that the innate awareness of God is a distinct conscious event and seeing it rather as "given in the nature of personality." A similar emphasis on the all-pervasive awareness of God is found in his contemporary, the religious philosopher Vladimir Solovyov. Solovyov built upon the work of the German philosopher Friedrich Jacobi to argue that the unity of subject and object within experience is itself an act of faith. (Students of early modern philosophy will recognize much in common here with Hume, save that Jacobi and Solovyov substitute faith for Hume's "habit and custom.") For Solovyov, God can be directly experienced both as the condition of the possibility of this unity and, more specifically, in feelings of religious awe. Solovyov's follower Sergius Bulgakov similarly gave priority to spiritual perception, but insisted that true faith must involve trust and a receptivity to divine revelation. For him, the awareness of God is not a concomitant to all experience, but the operation of a distinct faculty which he associates with the heart. The last philosopher Gavrilyuk discusses is Semen Frank, who offers a sophisticated reprise of the ontological argument as not an inference but simply a "recognition of the self-evidence of the Absolute." This bare summary scarcely does justice to Gavrilyuk's complex essay; anyone interested in the rational foundations of belief in God, or the reception of modern philosophy within Orthodoxy, will want to give it a close reading.

The next two papers turn to modern Orthodox criticisms of natural theology. Dionysios Skliris examines attitudes toward natural theology among modern Greek Orthodox theologians, particularly those of the so-called "generation of the Sixties." These attitudes have been mixed. Panagiotis Nellas and Fr. Dumitru Staniloae (a Romanian who was influential in Greece) were generally positive, although without developing natural theological arguments in detail. Better known are the criticisms offered by Christos Yannaras and Metropolitan John Zizioulas. Yannaras does not deny the possibility of knowing God through "natural contemplation" of the divine *logoi* in beings, but objects strongly to natural theology as it has been practiced in the mainstream of Western philosophy. He finds in the quest for rational necessity an implicit denial of personal freedom, as well as a tendency to "conquer and objectify God" so as to diminish the threat he poses (or seems to pose) to rational autonomy. Zizioulas similarly sees in natural theology a mistaken focus on establishing "that" God exists, while ignoring the far more important question of "how" God exists—namely, as a Trinity of divine persons who can be experienced in the life of the Church. Zizioulas sees natural theology as having contributed to the rise of atheism precisely by ignoring God's Trinitarian mode of being, thus reducing God to a mere substance. Skliris concludes his essay with a comparison between the thought of Zizioulas and that of Richard Swinburne. Despite their opposing stances toward natural theology, both defend a form of Social Trinitarianism on rational (and not only scriptural) grounds. Skliris also observes that Swinburne's probabilism and his emphasis on the crucial importance of the appeal to religious experience go at least some distance, if not all the way, toward addressing the concerns of Yannaras.

Travis Dumsday considers objections to natural theology in a range of modern Orthodox thinkers, including Sergius Bulgakov, Olivier Clément, H. Tristram Engelhardt Jr., and Vladimir Lossky, as well as Yannaras. Dumsday identifies three major themes in their criticisms. The first is that arguments for the existence of God are, in general, objectively unsound. The second is that such arguments are counterproductive from a religious standpoint, either because they fail to provide an actual experiential encounter with God or because, by their overreach, they indirectly contribute to atheism. The third is that such arguments are rhetorically ineffective in that they fail to persuade nonbelievers. Dumsday observes that the third claim is debatable, since many nonbelievers have in fact been persuaded by such arguments and even many believers have found them helpful in strengthening and clarifying their faith. The first claim, if true, would be more decisive, but it is also harder to establish and the authors in question do not make any serious effort to do so. Their central concern lies with the second point. To this Dumsday observes that, from the standpoint of a nonbeliever, there has to be some reason to seek to experience God within Christianity (and especially Orthodox Christianity), as opposed to doing so within some other religion or simply not at all. For this one needs at least some grounds for thinking that Christian beliefs about God are true. Such grounds need not be apodictic, and in fact are more likely to be convincing if they are advanced with some sense of epistemic humility; but that does not make them in any way less important.

The volume concludes with a paper by Richard Swinburne presenting in summary form a version of the design argument. This is an important element of the cumulative case for Christian theism that Swinburne has elaborated in a number of publications.[44] His view is that, given the preeminence of science in modern society, the most broadly persuasive argument will be one in which "the pattern of argument is just the same as that of science." Accordingly he first explains the criteria that are used to evaluate causal explanations in science (as well as elsewhere, for example, in criminal investigations). These include: (1) the simplicity of the hypothesis posited, (2) if the hypothesis is true, it is likely that the phenomena to be explained will occur, and (3) if the hypothesis is false, it is much less likely that they will occur. In the case of theism, the hypothesis posited is the existence of a God who has the traditional divine attributes such as perfect goodness, omnipotence, omniscience, and eternity. Swinburne first argues that (owing to the absence of any posited constraints or limitations on this being) such a hypothesis is highly simple. He then evaluates its explanatory success in relation to the existence of an orderly universe that includes creatures like us who are capable of choosing good and evil. He argues that the existence of such a God would make these phenomena at least fairly likely and the absence of such a God would make them highly unlikely. His conclusion is that the design argument, so construed, provides a "strong cogent" argument for the existence of God. It is important to note that this is not tantamount to claiming that the argument makes the existence of God likely, all things considered. To draw such a conclusion one must consider all the relevant evidence. That includes not only apparently countervailing evidence such as the existence of great human suffering, but also further confirmatory evidence such as religious experience and the historical evidence for the life and resurrection of Jesus. Swinburne's view is that, when this additional evidence is taken into account, the existence of God is "significantly more

44. See Richard Swinburne, *The Existence of God*, 2nd ed. (Oxford: Oxford University Press, 2004), *The Resurrection of God Incarnate* (Oxford: Oxford University Press, 2003), and *Was Jesus God?* (Oxford: Oxford University Press, 2008).

probable than not." However, he does not argue for that stronger conclusion here. Here his purpose is only to illustrate how the design argument can be stated in contemporary terms and the contribution it can make to a cumulative case for theism.

None of these essays is, or could be, the final word on its subject. The question of what role reason should play in the human quest for God is one that will not be finally settled as long as we "see through a glass darkly." Yet it is one that no reflective person can avoid. We offer these papers in the hope that they will help facilitate positive and constructive reflection on natural theology from within the Orthodox tradition.

1. Natural Theology in Patristic Thought: Arguments for the Existence of God

ALEXEY FOKIN

Introduction

This chapter offers a brief overview of arguments for the existence of God in patristic and Byzantine theological literature. I limit myself to the question of God's existence and not of his attributes, because the former constitutes the core of the natural theology of the Church Fathers, as well as the natural theology of our times.[1] The need to defend Christian faith in the one God, Creator and Governor of the universe, against polytheism, Epicureanism, and atheism gave rise to many arguments for the existence of God in the writings of both the Greek and Latin Fathers. In doing this they depended on some key biblical passages hinting at natural ways of the knowledge of God,[2] and, to a greater extent, on the classical philosophical tradition.[3] Thus, in various circumstances and for different purposes, the Fathers put forward many arguments for the existence of God which I will consider in a systematic way, following classifications widely used in contemporary philosophy of religion.[4]

1. See, for instance, William Lane Craig and J. P. Moreland, eds., *The Blackwell Companion to Natural Theology* (Chichester: Wiley-Blackwell, 2012), 1–2.

2. See especially Psalm 18:2; 96 (97):6; Job 12:7-9; 37-41; Wisdom 13:5; Romans 1:20; and Hebrews 3:4.

3. For various arguments for the existence of God in classical Greek and Roman philosophy, see Xenophon, *Memorabilia* 1.4.1–19, 4.3.3; Plato, *Laws* 10.886a–899d, *Philebus* 28d–30d; Aristotle, *Physics* 7.1, 8.5–10; *Metaphysics* 2.2; 12.6–10; Sextus Empiricus, *Adversus Mathematicos* 9.76–119; Cicero, *De natura deorum* 1.1.2, 2.2.4-14.39; *Tusculanae disputationes* 1.27-36.

4. See Richard Swinburne, *The Existence of God*, 2nd ed. (Oxford: Oxford University Press, 2004); Richard M. Gale and Alexander R. Pruss, *The Existence of God* (Aldershot: Ash-

Before I discuss these arguments, I would like to point out that the Church Fathers regarded the existence of God as a truth that can be grasped and understood by human reason. Gregory the Theologian in his Second Theological Oration, where he investigates the capability and limitations of human knowledge of God, clearly states that God's nature is incomprehensible and unknowable (φύσις ἄληπτός τε καὶ ἀπερίληπτος), not as to whether it *exists*, but in *what* it is (οὐχ ὅτι ἔστιν, ἀλλ' ἥτις ἐστίν).[5] He explains this point at length a little further:

> For it is one thing to be persuaded of the existence of a thing (τοῦ εἶναί τι πεπεῖσθαι), and quite another to know what it is (τὸ τί ποτέ ἐστι τοῦτο εἰδέναι). Now our very eyes and the law of nature (ὁ φυσικὸς νόμος) teach us that God exists and that He is the efficient and maintaining Cause of all things: our eyes, because they fall on visible objects, and see them in beautiful stability and progress, immovably moving and revolving if I may so say; the law of nature, because through these visible things and their order, it reasons back to their Author (τὸν ἀρχηγὸν τούτων συλλογιζόμενος). For how could this universe have come into being or been put together, unless God had called it into existence, and held it together? For every one who sees a beautifully made cithara, and considers the skill with which it has been fitted together and arranged, or who hears its melody, would think of none but the maker of this cithara, or the player of it, and would recur to him in mind, though he might not know him by sight. And thus to us also is manifested the One who made (τὸ ποιητικόν) and moves and preserves all created things, even though He is not comprehended by the mind. And very wanting in sense is he who will not willingly go thus far in following natural proofs (ταῖς φυσικαῖς ἑπόμενος ἀποδείξεσιν).[6]

---

gate, 2003); William Lane Craig and J. P. Moreland, eds., *The Blackwell Companion to Natural Theology* (Chichester: Wiley-Blackwell, 2012).

5. See Gregory of Nazianzus, *Orations* 28.5.9-10; Greek text SC 250:110. See also an interpretation of this passage proposed by Maximus the Confessor: "I did not say that the nature in question is incomprehensible in terms of whether or not it exists, but in terms of what it is" (ὅτιπερ ὑπάρχει, ἀλλὰ τί ὑπάρχει), Maximus the Confessor, *Ambigua* 17.10.17-19; Greek text and English translation in *Maximus the Confessor, On Difficulties in the Church Fathers: The Ambigua*, Vol. 1, ed. and trans. Nicholas Constas (Cambridge, MA: Harvard University Press, 2014), 392-95. See also Gregory Palamas, *Second Epistle to Barlaam* 23.

6. Gregory of Nazianzus, *Orations* 28.5.14–6.14 (SC 250:110-12; trans. Charles Gordon Browne and James Edward Swallow, NPNF 2/7:290, slightly modified).

It is noteworthy that Gregory considers the existence of God as a truth that *can be* and even *must be* understood by human reason, since our reason is naturally predisposed to the knowledge of God. It seems to me that our reason itself, or rather its predisposition to derive the knowledge of God from nature, is called here "the natural law" (ὁ φυσικὸς νόμος). A little further Gregory, like Justin before him (whom I will discuss later), calls this natural law "our most ancient law" (πρῶτος ἐν ἡμῖν νόμος), which leads us from visible things to their invisible Cause, "the reason derived from God and implanted in all" (ὁ ἐκ θεοῦ λόγος καὶ πᾶσι σύμφυτος).[7] In addition, Gregory refers here to the most popular patristic argument for the existence of God—in his words "the natural proof" (φυσικὴ ἀποδείξεσις)—that is, the argument from design, which I will discuss later.

The idea that we can know God's existence without fully comprehending the divine essence was shared by many Greek Fathers.[8] Gregory of Nyssa also considers the knowledge of God's existence as natural for every human person, in contrast with the knowledge of God's essence which surpasses all powers of the human mind. As he writes, "About the Creator of the world we know only that he exists (ὅτι μὲν ἔστιν οἴδαμεν), but we deny that we know the principle of his essence (τὸν τῆς οὐσίας λόγον)."[9] In a similar way John Chrysostom insists that we are in total ignorance of the essence (ἡ οὐσία) of God, not in respect to whether it exists, but in respect to what it is (οὐχ ὅτι ἔστιν, ἀλλὰ τί ἐστιν).[10] Commenting on the passage from the Second Theological Oration of Gregory the Theologian, quoted above, Maximus the Confessor notes that man "has come to know God, not in His essence and subsistence (οὐ κατὰ τό τί ποτε τὴν οὐσίαν εἶναι καὶ τὴν ὑπόστασιν)—for this is impossible and beyond our grasp—but only with respect to the simple

7. Gregory of Nazianzus, *Orations* 28.16.19–21. Cf. note 2 of the French translator in SC 250:134: "la «loi premièr» est identique à la «raison»." See also a notable comment of Maximus the Confessor on this passage from Gregory: "The law of nature (ὁ φυσικὸς νόμος) through the power of sight had already introduced the concept and belief that God exists" (τὴν περὶ τοῦ εἶναι Θεὸν ἔννοιάν τε καὶ πίστιν)." See Maximus Confessor, *Ambigua* 15.4.9-10, ed. and trans. Constas, 364.

8. It is likely that their common source was Philo of Alexandria. See especially Philo, *Quod Deus sit immutabilis* 62; *Quod deterius potiori insidiari soleat* 89; *De praemiis et poenis* 44. On the knowability and unknowability of God, see Vladimir Lossky, *The Vision of God* (Crestwood, NY: St. Vladimir's Seminary Press, 1963).

9. Gregory of Nyssa, *Contra Eunomium* 2.1.71.28–30; Greek text GNO 1:248 (my translation).

10. John Chrysostom, *Contra Anomoeos* 5.335–36.

fact that He exists" (κατ' αὐτὸ τὸ μόνον εἶναι)[11]. Finally, St. John of Damascus states as a rule of orthodoxy that "it is evident, that God exists (ὅτι ἔστι θεός), but what He is in His essence and nature (τί δέ ἐστι κατ' οὐσίαν καὶ φύσιν) is absolutely incomprehensible and unknowable."[12]

As we can see, the Church Fathers regarded the existence of God as a proposition that can be grasped by human reason, which has a natural inclination or disposition to the knowledge of God. As they saw it, even pagan philosophers could understand this truth and proposed various arguments in its favor.[13] Christian theologians likewise elaborated numerous similar arguments. Most of their arguments are *a posteriori*, such as the argument from the necessity of an efficient cause or of a prime mover, or arguments from design, including even a kind of "fine-tuning argument." There are also arguments from the ideal cause or from different degrees of perfection, as well as some moral arguments. Besides these there are also *a priori* arguments, including an argument from the "innate idea" of the one God and the historical argument. I will consider these arguments step by step, beginning with *a priori* arguments because of their overall importance in patristic thought.

A priori arguments: argument from *sensus divinitatis* and historical argument

Many Greek and Latin Fathers believed that all people in their very nature possess some kind of innate awareness of God, one that is very similar to John Calvin's later notion of the *sensus divinitatis,* developed by Alvin Plantinga.[14]

We meet this argument as early as the Christian apologists of the second and third centuries. Justin Martyr in his *Second Apology* notes that "the appellation 'God' (τὸ θεὸς προσαγόρευμα) is not a mere name, but a notion

11. Maximus Confessor, *Ambigua* 15.2.14–17; trans. Constas, 363-65.

12. John of Damascus, *Expositio fidei* 1.4.2–3; Greek text *Die Schriften des Johannes von Damaskos*, 6 vols, ed. Bonifatius Kotter (Berlin: De Gruyter, 1973), 2:12 (my translation).

13. See John of Damascus, *Expositio fidei* 2.3.

14. The idea of *sensus divinitatis* (literally "sense of the Divinity") we find in Thomas Aquinas, who was well informed about patristic arguments for the existence of God; see, for instance, *Summa Theologiae* I, q. 2, a. 1, ad 1; *Summa Contra Gentes* 1.11.4; 3.38.1–3; *De veritate* 22.7. But it was Calvin who made it a *terminus technicus*; see Calvin, *Institutes* 1.3.1-3. More recently, Alvin Plantinga has used this concept in his Reformed epistemology to build up his conception of "the basic true beliefs." See James F. Sennett, ed., *The Analytic Theist: An Alvin Plantinga Reader* (Grand Rapids, MI: Eerdmans, 1998), 97-186.

implanted in the nature of men of a thing that can hardly be explained" (πράγματος δυσεξηγήτου ἔμφυτος τῇ φύσει τῶν ἀνθρώπων δόξα).[15] Justin explains further that not only Christians, but all the human race possess "an innate seed of the Logos" (τὸ ἔμφυτον παντὶ γένει ἀνθρώπων σπέρμα τοῦ λόγου), or "a portion of the seminal Logos" (σπερματικοῦ λόγου μέρος), which enables them to grasp the divine Logos, who made the universe.[16] According to Irenaeus of Lyons, all men in the depth of their souls know that there is one true God and Lord of the universe because this knowledge has been revealed to them through "the rational principle implanted in their minds" (*ratio mentibus infixus*).[17]

Clement of Alexandria believes that the idea of God as the Father and Creator of the world is implanted in all human minds and does not require any special instruction to understand it (ἐμφύτως καὶ ἀδιδάκτως ἀντιλαμβάνεται).[18] All people originally possessed a certain "vague knowledge" of God (εἴδησις ἀμαυρά), but very soon they lost this knowledge and forgot it.[19] However, all nations in every part of the world could not live without belief in an Almighty (τῇ τοῦ κρείττονος πίστει); they all possess "one and the same anticipation" (μίαν καὶ τὴν αὐτὴν πρόληψιν) of the Lord of the universe; and such anticipatory awareness precedes their faith and the fuller knowledge of what God is and how he is our Lord, Father and Creator.[20] According to another great Alexandrian, Origen, many Greeks recognize the existence of the one God, Creator and Father of the universe; for "although no one is able to speak worthily of God the Father, it is nevertheless possible to gain some notion of Him from the fact of the visible creation and from those things which the human mind naturally perceives" (*humana mens naturaliter sentit*).[21] Moreover, elsewhere Origen argues that every human soul is aware of its "familiarity" with God (τὸ συγγενές ἐπιγνοῦσα) and feels "a

15. Justin Martyr, *Apologia* 1.6.3; trans. Marcus Dods and George Reith, ANF 1:190 (slightly modified).

16. See Justin Martyr, *Apologia* 2.8.1–2; 2.13.3. Cf. Clement of Alexandria, *Stromata* 1.7.37.2–3.

17. Irenaeus, *Contra Haereses* 2.6.1–2 (my translation).

18. Clement of Alexandria, *Stromata* 5.14.133.7; cf. 5.13.87.2–4. See also Eusebius, *Praeparatio Euangelica* 13.13.64.

19. Clement of Alexandria, *Stromata* 6.8.64.

20. Clement of Alexandria, *Stromata* 5.14.133.8–9; see also: *Stromata* 5.13.87–88; 5.14.134–135; 6.17.149; *Protrepticus* 6–9; Eusebius, *Praeparatio Euangelica* 13.13.64.

21. Origen, *De principiis* 1.3.1; trans. John Behr, *Origen: On First Principles*, Vol. 1 (Oxford: Oxford University Press, 2017), 67.

natural love" (φίλτρον φυσικόν) for its Creator; hence all people possess "the common notion" (ἡ κοινὴ ἔννοια) of God and his nature.[22]

Arguments from the innate notion of God were extremely popular among the early Latin apologists. For example, Minucius Felix notes that there is "a universal agreement of all men" (*consensus omnium*) concerning the existence of God. In Minucius's dialogue *Octavius*, the Christian Octavius addresses the pagan Cecilius, trying to convince him to acknowledge the existence of the one God by means of the following argument:

> What! Is it not true that I have in this matter [i.e. the existence of the one God] the consent of all men (*omnium de isto consensum*)? I hear the common people, when they lift their hands to heaven, say nothing else but *Oh God*, and *God is great*, and *God is true*, and *if God shall permit.* Is this the natural expression of the common people, or is it the prayer of a confessing Christian?[23]

Minucius combines here the argument from the *sensus divinitatis* (an *a priori* argument) with the historical argument, which is one of the *a posteriori* arguments. This combination was very typical of the Church Fathers.

Another Latin apologist, Tertullian, was convinced that every human soul possesses some kind of innate knowledge of the one God, and is "a Christian by nature" (*anima naturaliter christiana*).[24] He regards "the knowledge of God" (*conscientia Dei*) as a kind of "dowry" (*dos*) with which every human soul is born.[25] In his treatise *On the Testimony of the Soul* he demonstrates how every human soul naturally arrives at primary notions of the one God, good and evil, the soul's immortality, the Last Judgment, the soul's beatitude and punishment, and so on.[26] Like Minucius Felix, Tertullian regarded such exclamations of common people as "God is great," "God is good," "God sees everything," "if God wishes," and "God will judge between us" as evidence of this innate knowledge of the one true God. According to Tertullian, these expressions testify that there exists (*esse*) the One whose

22. Origen, *Contra Celsum* 3.40.

23. Minucius Felix, *Octavius* 18.11, PL 3, 291B; trans. Robert Ernest Wallis, ANF 4:183 (slightly modified). Cf. Cicero, *De natura deorum* 2.3.

24. Tertullian, *Apologeticum* 17.

25. Tertullian, *Adversus Marcionem* 1.10.

26. Tertullian, *De testimonio animae* 2–6; cf. *De resurrectione carnis* 3, 5.

power and will our soul acknowledges.[27] This innate awareness Tertullian calls "the testimony of soul" (*testimonium animae*),[28] "the teaching of nature" (*doctrina naturae*), and "a silent errand of congenital and innate knowledge" (*congenitae et ingenitae conscientiae tacita commissa*).[29] Along with this argument from innate awareness, Tertullian, like Minucius Felix, puts forward the argument from the common agreement of all nations concerning the existence of the supreme God, or "the God of gods" (*conscientia populi contestantis Deum deorum*).[30]

We find similar arguments in later Latin Fathers, like Cyprian of Carthage[31] and Lactantius.[32] Hilary of Poitiers also indicates that not only Christians, but also many pagans "followed the public belief (*opinione publica*) in asserting the existence of a God."[33] According to Jerome, the words of the Gospel of John, "That was the true Light, which enlightens every man that comes into the world" (John 1:9), clearly demonstrate that the notion of God is implanted in all men by nature (*natura omnibus Dei inesse notitiam*), so that without God as the true Light, no one can either be born or possess the seeds of wisdom, justice, and other virtues.[34]

Augustine also notes that the notion of the one true God was somehow available to every man even before the advent of Jesus Christ:

> For that he is called God, this name could not have been totally unknown to every creature, even to all nations before they believed in Christ. For this is the elemental power of true Divinity (*vis verae divinitatis*), that it cannot altogether and utterly be hidden from a rational creature from the time it makes use of its reason. For with the exception of a few in whom nature has been exceedingly perverted, the whole human race declares that God is the author of this world (*universum genus humanum Deum mundi huius fatetur auctorem*). Therefore, in respect of this fact, that he made this world, clearly visible in its sky and land,

27. Tertullian, *De testimonio animae* 2; cf. *Apologeticum* 17; *Adversus Marcionem* 1.10; *De anima* 41; *De resurrectione carnis* 3.

28. Tertullian, *De testimonio animae* 5; *Apologeticum* 17.

29. Tertullian, *De testimonio animae* 5.

30. Tertullian, *De resurrectione carnis* 3.

31. Cyprian, *De idolorum vanitate* 9.

32. Lactantius, *Divinae Institutiones* 1.2.4.

33. Hilary of Poitiers, *De trinitate* 1.4, PL 10, 28A (my translation).

34. Jerome, *Commentarius in Epistolam ad Galates* 1.1.15, PL 26, 326B; cf. *Commentarius in Epistolam ad Titum* 1.10.

> even before they were imbued in the faith of Christ, God was known to all nations (*notus omnibus gentibus Deus*).[35]

Later Greek Fathers also proposed similar arguments from the innate notion of God. Nemesius, bishop of Emesa, puts forward such an argument in favor of divine providence:

> No mean indication of there being also a providence (πρόνοια) over particulars is the naturally ingrained knowledge of it in men (φυσικῶς ἐγκατεσπάρθαι τοῖς ἀνθρώποις τὴν γνῶσιν αὐτῆς). For in the grip of necessity we immediately take refuge with the divine (ἐπὶ τὸ θεῖον) and with prayers, as if nature led us untaught to its aid (τῆς φύσεως ἀγούσης ἡμᾶς ἀδιδάκτως ἐπὶ τὴν ἀπὸ τούτου βοήθειαν). But nature would not have led us untaught to what was not of a nature to happen; for also in sudden disturbances and fears we involuntarily call upon God without even thinking. But everything that follows something naturally (φυσικῶς ἑπόμενον) provides a strong proof (ἰσχυρὰν τὴν ἀπόδειξιν) which admits of no denial.[36]

Maximus the Confessor similarly notes that our spontaneous appeal to God in difficult circumstances is a sufficient proof that there is "a Providence of God, which encompasses everything" (περὶ τοῦ εἶναι τὴν ἐπὶ πάντα τοῦ Θεοῦ πρόνοιαν), for "our nature itself teaches us about it" (αὐτὴν καθ' ἑαυτὴν τὴν φύσιν . . . σαφῶς οὖσαν διδάσκαλον) and "it does this without any prior instruction (ἀδιδάκτως), as if it were pushing us toward God, whenever it leads us to seek salvation through prayer when we are beset by sudden, unforeseen emergencies and crises."[37] It is remarkable how close Maximus's and Nemesius's arguments from the consensus of humankind are to those of Tertullian and other Latin apologists. This illustrates the unanimity of Christian theologians in different times and circumstances on the questions before us. John of Damascus included the argument from the innate knowledge or

35. Augustine, *Tractatus in Joannis Evangelium* 106.4.2, PL 35, 1910A; trans. John W. Rettig, *St. Augustine: Tractates on the Gospel of John: A New Translation*, 5 vols. (Washington, DC: Catholic University of America Press, 1994), 4:268.

36. Nemesius of Emesa, *De natura hominis* 43.132.13–21; trans. R. W. Sharples and Philip J. van der Eijk, *Nemesius of Emesa: On the Nature of Man* (Liverpool: Liverpool University Press, 2008), 217.

37. Maximus the Confessor, *Ambigua* 10.103.1–7; trans. Constas, 317.

common notion of God's existence in his compendium of rational proofs of the existence of God, placing it before all others in his *De fide orthodoxa*:

> That God exists, then, is no matter of doubt to those who receive the Holy Scriptures, the Old Testament, I mean, and the New; nor indeed to most of the Greeks. For, as I said before,[38] the knowledge of the existence of God is implanted in us by nature (ἡ γνῶσις τοῦ εἶναι θεὸν φυσικῶς ἡμῖν ἐγκατέσπαρται).[39]

Elsewhere John viewed this innate knowledge of God as a commonly accepted opinion or common notion: "A common notion (κοινὴ ἔννοια) is what is recognized by all (ἡ παρὰ πάντων ὁμολογουμένη), such as that God exists (ὅτι ἔστι θεός)."[40] John Chrysostom also regards the existence of God as "the common opinion of all men (τὴν κοινὴν ἁπάντων ψῆφον) and the experience of their affairs (τὴν ἀπὸ τῶν πραγμάτων πεῖραν)."[41] Thus, as compared with the pagan Greek philosophers, the Church Fathers put much more stress on the argument from the innate knowledge of God, which together with the historical argument occupied an important place in patristic natural theology.[42]

Arguments from design

No less important and popular among Christian theologians were arguments from design, a form of *a posteriori* argument based on sense perception and rational inference. In fact, various arguments from design, or (in Kant's classification) teleological arguments, were the oldest and most widespread in the writings of both the Greek and Latin Fathers.[43] The core of these arguments is defined by Athanasius of Alexandria in this way:

38. Cf. John of Damascus, *Expositio fidei* 1.1.14–15; Greek text *Die Schriften des Johannes von Damaskos*, 2:7.

39. John of Damascus, *Expositio fidei* 1.3.4–5; Greek text *Die Schriften des Johannes von Damaskos*, 2:10; trans. S. D. F. Salmond, NPNF 2/9:3b (slightly modified).

40. John of Damascus, *Fragmenta philosophica* (e cod. Oxon. Bodl. Auct. T. 1.6) 18.72–73; Greek text *Die Schriften des Johannes von Damaskos,* 1:172 (my translation).

41. John Chrysostom, *De diabolo tentatore* 1.8, PG 49, 257E.

42. See Basil Studer, "God," in Angelo Di Berardino, ed., *Encyclopedia of Ancient Christianity,* 3 vols. (Downers Grove, IL: IVP Academic, 2014), 2:151-152.

43. On the history of this argument in antiquity and the Church Fathers see M. Chossat,

> It is further possible to attain to the knowledge of God from the things which are seen (ἀπὸ τῶν φαινομένων τὴν περὶ τοῦ Θεοῦ γνῶσιν καταλαβεῖν), since creation, as though in letters (ὥσπερ γράμμασι), declares in a loud voice, by its order and harmony (διὰ τῆς τάξεως καὶ ἁρμονίας), its own Lord and Creator.[44]

Because arguments from design, while having many common features, differ greatly from one another in their variety of forms and richness of details, it is impossible to discuss them all here in full. Instead I will consider select examples from different periods of patristic thought.

Arguments from design are very old: we find them as early as the second- and third-century Christian apologists. For example, Aristides of Athens in his *Apology* argues against those Greeks who believe that the heaven is God:

"Dieu. Son existence," in *Dictionnaire de théologie catholique*, vol. 4 (Paris: Librairie Letouzey et Ané, 1924), 874–948; Arthur Stanley Pease, "Caeli Enarrant," *Harvard Theological Review* 34 (1941): 163-200 (esp. 191-98 for patristic sources). It seems that for many Greek Fathers the common source was Philo of Alexandria. See Philo, *De praemiis et poenis*, 41-42; *De specialibus legibus* 1, 33-35; *De Abraham* 70, 84; *De opificio mundi* 17-21.

44. Athanasius, *Contra Gentes* 34.4; Greek text SC 18B:166; trans. Archibald Robertson, NPNF 2/4:22. See also: "By the order of the world (ἐκ τῆς τοῦ κόσμου τάξεως) one ought to perceive God its Maker and Artificer, even though He is not seen with the bodily eyes . . . He so arranged creation that although He is by nature invisible He may yet be known by His works" (ἐκ τῶν ἔργων, *Contra Gentes* 35.2; NPNF 2/4:22). Very similar concise definitions of the substance of the teleological argument can be found in many Church Fathers. Basil of Caesarea notes: "In our belief about God, first comes the notion that God exists (ἡ ἔννοια ἡ περὶ τοῦ ὅτι ἐστὶ Θεός), and this notion we gather from His works (ἐκ τῶν δημιουργημάτων). For, as we perceive His wisdom, His goodness, and all His invisible perfections (πάντα αὐτοῦ τὰ ἀόρατα) from the creation of the world (ἀπὸ τῆς τοῦ κόσμου κτίσεως), so we know Him," Basil the Great, *Epistola* 235.1.10; trans. Blomfield Jackson, NPNF 2/8:275 (slightly modified). See also *Homiliae super Psalmos* 33, PG 29, 357A. Gregory of Nazianzus also states that "we comprehend the Maker from his works" (ἐκ τῶν δημιουργημάτων τὸν δημιουργὸν καταλαμβάνοντες), *Homilia* 43.11.6-7; Greek text in Grégoire de Nazianze, *Discours funèbres en l'honneur de son frère Césaire et de Basile de Césarée*, ed. F. Boulenger (Paris: Picard, 1908) (my translation). Maximus the Confessor, referring to Wisdom 13:5, asks: "Who, in contemplating the beauty and the magnificence of creatures (τὸ κάλλος καὶ τὸ μέγεθος τῶν τοῦ Θεοῦ κτισμάτων) does not immediately understand that God is the One who has brought all them into existence, since he is the Origin and Cause and Creator of all beings? And would not such a person's thoughts subsequently ascend to God alone, leaving all these things below . . . in his desire to grasp immediately the One whom he has come to know through the medium of His works (διὰ μέσων τῶν ἔργων)?" *Ambigua* 10.88.1–7; trans. Constans, p. 285-87.

> For we see that the heaven revolves, moves by necessity and consists of many parts, that is why it is called "the world" (κόσμος), that is "arrangement." But the arrangement needs a certain artificer (τινος τεχνίτου), and everything that is arranged has a beginning and an end. But the heaven with all its luminaries moves out of necessity; and the stars move in a strict order (τάξει) and distance from one edge to another: some of them decline, while others rise, and they pass their way at proper time, determining summer and winter in accordance with how they have been arranged by God (καθὰ ἐπιτέτακται αὐτοῖς παρὰ τοῦ θεοῦ). And they together with the whole heavenly order (τῷ οὐρανίῳ κόσμῳ) do not transgress their limits determined by the inevitable necessity of nature, whence it is clear that the heaven is not a god, but the work of God (ἔργον θεοῦ).[45]

Another Greek apologist, Athenagoras, not only emphasizes the order and beauty of the world, but also uses an analogy with an artificial object, a cithara,[46] to explain how we can infer that the whole world is an excellent work of the Creator:

> Beautiful without doubt is the world, excelling, as well in its magnitude as in the arrangement of its parts, both those in the oblique circle and those about the north, and also in its spherical form. Yet it is not this, but its Artificer (τὸν τεχνίτην αὐτοῦ), that we must worship. . . . If, therefore, the world is an instrument in tune, and moving in well-measured time (ὄργανον κινούμενον ἐν ῥυθμῷ), I adore the One who gave its harmony (τὸν ἁρμοσάμενον), and strikes its notes, and sings the accordant strain, and not the instrument. For at the musical contests the adjudicators do not pass by the players of the citharas and crown the citharas themselves.[47]

Similar arguments and even more complex analogies can be found in

45. Aristides, *Apologia*, fr. 4.2; Greek text C. Vona, ed., *L'apologia di Aristide* (Rome: Facultas Theologica Pontificii Athenaei Lateranensis, 1950), 117–26 (my translation).

46. As we have seen, this analogy was also used by Gregory of Nazianzus in his Second Theological Oration.

47. Athenagoras, *Legatio pro Christianis* 16.1–3; trans. B. P. Pratten, ANF 2:136 (slightly modified).

other Greek apologists, such as Theophilus of Antioch,[48] Clement of Alexandria,[49] and Origen.[50]

Moreover, various arguments from design were also extremely popular among the Latin Fathers. Minucius Felix, depending mostly on the Stoics,[51] proposed several teleological arguments against Epicureans who denied that the world was perfectly arranged by divine reason (*divina ratione*) and an excellent intelligence (*praestantissimae mentis*), asserting that it was heaped together by certain fragments casually adhering to each other. He starts from observation of the heaven and the regular motions of the stars and planets, inferring that there must be "the marvelous and divine balance of the Supreme Governor (*summi moderatoris*) engaged therein." Then he proceeds to the regular circuit of the sun and the moon and the recurring changes of darkness and light, and of the seasons with their own weather and fruits, all of them presupposing "the Supreme Artist and perfect Reason" (*summi opificis et perfectae rationis*) to arrange them. Then Minucius observes the greatness of the sea and the ocean, and of the fountains and rivers, which always roll on in regular courses, and of the mountains, hills, and plains. Finally he turns to animals and to various functions of their limbs, and especially to human beings, noting that "the very beauty of our own figure especially confesses God to be its Artificer: our upright stature, our upward-looking countenance, our eyes placed at the top, as it were, for outlook; and all the rest of our senses as if arranged in a citadel."[52] Thus Minucius demonstrates that not only the world as a whole, but even every part of it and every creature, gives sufficient evidence about its Creator and Ruler.[53]

A similar cluster of arguments occurs in another Latin apologist, Lactantius, who wrote a special treatise *On the Workmanship of God*, also dedicated to refuting the Epicureans, where he describes how skillfully and intelligently different parts and limbs of animals or of the human body have been arranged,[54] testifying that they all are "a wonderful work of God" (*mirificum*

48. See Theophilus, *Ad Autolycum* 1.5–7.

49. See Clement of Alexandria, *Protrepticus* 4.63.1; *Stromata* 4.23.148.1-2.

50. See Origen, *Contra Celsum* 1.23.

51. See especially Cicero, *De natura deorum* 2.4; 2.15; 2.120–40; *Tusculane disputationes* 1.68–70; Seneca, *De beneficiis* 7.1.7; *Epistola* 90.42.

52. Minucius Felix, *Octavius* 17.3-11, PL 3, 285B-287A; trans. Robert Ernest Wallis, ANF 4:182.

53. Minucius Felix, *Octavius* 18.1-7, PL 3, 287A-290A.

54. See Lactantius, *De opificio Dei* 5-14.

Dei opus).[55] He also uses an analogy of an architect to explain the miracles of life, whose artificer is God and his providence:

> Since, therefore, all things which we see are produced with reference to a rational plan (*cum ratione nata sunt*)—for nothing but a rational plan (*ratio*) can effect this very condition of being born—it is manifest that nothing could have been born without a rational plan. For it was previously foreseen in the formation of everything, how it should use the service of the limbs for the necessities of life; and how the offspring, being produced from the union of bodies, might preserve all living creatures by their several species. For if a skillful architect (*peritus architectus*), when he designs to construct some great building, first of all considers what will be the effect of the complete building, and previously ascertains by measurement what situation is suitable for a light weight, in what place a massive part of the structure will stand, what will be the intervals between the columns, what or where will be the descents and outlets of the falling waters and the reservoirs—he first, I say, foresees these things, that he may begin together with the very foundations whatever things are necessary for the work when now completed—why should any one suppose that, in the contrivance of animals, God did not foresee (*Deum . . . non ante providisse*) what things were necessary for living, before giving life itself? For it is manifest that life could not exist, unless those things by which it exists were previously arranged.[56]

Lactantius concludes that "the divine mind of God (*divina mens Dei*), being extended through all parts of the universe, runs to and fro, and rules all things, governs all things, being everywhere present, everywhere diffused," just as the human mind by its intellectual power transgresses the barriers and limits of its body and wanders everywhere without restraint.[57] This same apologist gives us an excellent example of an argument similar to the modern argument of "fine-tuning," or at least an argument that the world in which rational creatures came to existence must be a product of a no less rational Creator.[58] Indeed, according to Lactantius,

55. Lactantius, *De opificio Dei* 11, PL 7, 52A.

56. Lactantius, *De opificio Dei* 6, PL 7, 28AB; trans. William Fletcher, ANF 7:287.

57. Lactantius, *De opificio Dei* 16, PL 7, 66A.

58. In this argument Lactantius depends on the Stoics. See Sextus Empiricus, *Adversus Mathematicos* 9.101–3, 118–19; Cicero, *De natura deorum* 2.6–8; *Tusculanae disputationes* 1.27.66.

> There is therefore a divine providence . . . by the energy and power of which all things which we see were both made and are governed. For so vast a system of things with such arrangement and such regularity in preserving the settled orders and times, could neither at first have arisen without a provident Artificer (*provido artifice*), nor have existed so many ages without a powerful inhabitant, nor have been perpetually governed without a skillful and intelligent Ruler (*perito ac sentiente rectore*); and reason itself (*ratio ipsa*) declares this. For whatever exists which has reason (*rationem*), must have arisen from Reason (*ratione sit ortum*). Now reason is the part of an intelligent and wise nature; but a wise and intelligent nature (*sapiens sentiensque natura*) can be nothing else than God. Now the world, since it has reason (*mundus . . . rationem habet*), by which it is both governed and kept together, was therefore made by God, who is the Maker and Ruler of the world.[59]

In a similar way Augustine in his *City of God* puts forth an argument from design in its classical form: for him "the world itself, by its well-ordered changes and movements, and by the most beautiful appearance of all visible things, bears a testimony of its own, both that it has been created, and also that it could not have been created save by God, whose greatness and beauty are unutterable and invisible.[60]

We can also find various arguments from design in the later Greek Fathers. Athanasius in his *Against the Heathen* proposes several reasons and analogies to prove that the world, consisting of different and contrary elements and parts combined into a perfect order and harmony, must be a wonderful work of the one true God.[61] He concludes his reasoning as follows:

> Since then, there is everywhere not disorder but order (τάξις), not disproportion but proportion (συμμετρία), not disarray but arrangement (κόσμος), and the perfectly harmonious order of the world (κόσμου παναρμόνιος σύνταξις), we must infer and perceive the notion of the Master that put together and compacted all things, and produced har-

59. Lactantius, *De ira Dei* 10.50–53; Greek text SC 289:142; trans. William Fletcher, ANF 7:268 (slightly modified). See also *De ira Dei* 10.42–44; *Divinae Institutiones* 2.8.35–36; and Tertullian, *De anima* 16.

60. Augustine, *De civitate Dei* 11.4.2, PL 41, 319; trans. Marcus Dods, NPNF 1/2:207 (slightly modified). Concerning the beauty of creatures testifying to their Creator, see also *Confessions* 10.6.9-10.

61. See Athanasius, *Contra Gentes* 35-37.

> mony in them. For though He is not seen with the eyes, yet from the order and harmony of contrary elements it is possible to perceive their Ruler, Arranger, and King (ἄρχοντα καὶ κοσμήτορα καὶ βασιλέα). For in like manner as if we saw a city, consisting of many and diverse people, great and small, rich and poor, old and young, male and female, in an orderly condition, and its inhabitants, while different from one another, yet at unity among themselves, and not the rich set against the poor, the great against the small, nor the young against the old, but all at peace in the enjoyment of equal rights—if we saw this, the inference surely follows that the presence of a ruler enforces concord, even if we do not see him; (for disorder is a sign of absence of rule, while order shows the governing authority: for when we see the mutual harmony of the members in the body, that the eye does not strive with the hearing, nor is the hand at variance with the foot, but that each accomplishes its service without variance, we perceive from this that certainly there is a soul in the body that governs these members, though we see it not); so in the order and harmony of the universe (ἐν τῇ τοῦ παντὸς τάξει καὶ ἁρμονίᾳ), we must perceive God the Governor of the universe (τὸν τοῦ παντὸς ἡγεμόνα Θεόν), and that He is one and not many. So then this order of its arrangement, and the concordant harmony of all things, shows that its Ruler and Governor is not many, but one—that is the Logos.[62]

John Chrysostom also proves the existence of God by making an analogy to a ship and a shipmaster:

> For if a ship having few sailors, and passengers, would not be conducted safely for one mile even, without the hand which guides it, much more, such a world as this, having so many things in it, composed of different elements, would not have continued so long a time, were there not a certain providence presiding over it, both governing, and continually maintaining this universe (πρόνοια ἥν τις ἐφεστῶσα, καὶ τόδε τὸ πᾶν συγκρατοῦσα καὶ συνέχουσα διηνεκῶς).[63]

As we have seen, many Church Fathers note both the perfect harmony and order in the world as a whole and also the skillful and wise arrange-

62. Athanasius, *Contra Gentes* 38.1-3; SC 18B:176-78; NPNF 2/4:24 (slightly modified).

63. John Chrysostom, *De diabolo tentatore* 1.8, PG 49, 257E; trans. T. P. Brandram, NPNF 1/9:186.

ment of the human body, the different functions of its parts, and the various faculties of the human soul that governs it. Thus, Cyril of Jerusalem, like Lactantius before him, notes that human nature most eloquently testifies about its Creator:

> Enter now into yourself, and from your own nature consider its Artificer (ἐκ τῆς σῆς ὑποστάσεως νόησον τὸν τεχνίτην). What is there to find fault with in the framing of your body? . . . Who prepared the recesses of the womb for child-bearing? Who gave life to the lifeless thing within it? Who knitted us with sinews and bones, and clothed us with skin and flesh (cf. Job 10:11), and, as soon as the child was born, brought streams of milk out of the breasts? How grows the baby into a boy, and the boy into a youth, and then into a man; and, still the same, passes again into an old man, while no one notices the exact change from day to day? Of the food, how is one part changed into blood, and another separated for excretion, and another part changed into flesh? Who gives to the heart its unceasing motion? Who wisely guarded the tenderness of the eyes with the fence of the eyelids? For as to the complicated and wonderful contrivance of the eyes, the voluminous books of the physicians hardly give us explanation. Who distributes the one breath to the whole body? You see, O man, the Artificer (τὸν τεχνίτην), you see the wise Creator (τὸν σοφὸν δημιουργόν).[64]

A similar appeal to twofold human nature testifying to the existence and nature of its Creator appears in Basil the Great:

> An exact comprehension of yourself (ἡ ἀκριβὴς σεαυτοῦ κατανόησις) will be sufficient to show you the way leading to the notion of God (τὴν ἔννοιαν τοῦ θεοῦ). Indeed, if you pay attention to yourself (προσέχῃς σεαυτῷ, cf. Deut. 19:5), you will not need to investigate the Maker from the arrangement of all things (ἐκ τῆς τῶν ὅλων κατασκευῆς), but in your own self as in a particular small arrangement (μικρῷ τινι διακόσμῳ), you will see the great wisdom of the One who made you.[65]

64. Cyril of Jerusalem, *Catecheses* 9.15; Greek text *Cyrilli Hierosolymorum archiepiscopi opera quae supersunt omnia*, vol. 1, *Catecheses ad illuminandos 1-18*, eds. W. C. Reischl and J. Rupp (München: Lentner, 1848); trans. Edwin Hamilton Gifford, NPNF 2/7:15.

65. Basil of Caesarea, *Homilia 3 in illud: Attende tibi ipsi*; Greek text *L'homélie de Basile de Césarée sur le mot "Observe-toi toi-même,"* ed. S. Y. Rudberg (Stockholm: Almqvist and Wiksell, 1962), 35.12-15 (my translation). See the whole argument in pp. 35.12-37.16.

Moreover, Basil also provides us with many arguments from design based on the observation of the harmony in the universe, as he does in his *Hexaemeron*:

> Thus, then, to show that the world is a work of art (τεχνικόν κατασκεύασμα) displayed for the observation of all people; to make them know Him who created it, Moses does not use another word. *In the beginning*, he says, *God created*. He does not say God worked, God formed, but *God created*. . . . He did not make the thing itself the cause of its existence. Being good, He made it a useful work. Being wise, He made it everything that was most beautiful. Being powerful He made it very great. Moses almost shows us the finger of the supreme Artisan (τεχνίτην) taking possession of the substance of the universe, forming the different parts in one perfect accord, and making a harmonious symphony result from the whole.[66]

Basil's younger brother, Gregory of Nyssa, begins his famous *Great Catechism* with the argument from design, pointing out that anyone who does not believe in God could from consideration of "the skillful and wise governing of all things, which are in the world, be brought to acknowledge that there exists a certain Power surpassing the whole universe (τινα δύναμιν τὴν . . . τοῦ παντὸς ὑπερκειμένην) and manifested through these things."[67] In his *On the Soul and Resurrection* Gregory belabors this argument at length. He agrees with the psalmist (Ps. 18:2) that not only the heavens, but "the whole creation of all things (ἡ κτίσις τῶν ὄντων) enunciates its Creator through its wonders (διὰ τῶν ἐν αὐτῇ θαυμάτων) to the audience of the eye, with a skillful and artistic utterance (τοῦ σοφοῦ τε καὶ τεχνικοῦ λόγου) that reaches the heart."[68] He further explains these "wonders of the creation" by pointing out the improbability of different and even opposite natures coming together and binding themselves in a harmonious unity:

> We see the universal harmony (τὴν τοῦ παντὸς ἁρμονίαν) in the won-

66. Basil of Caesarea, *Homiliae in Hexaemeron* 1.7.12-32; Greek text SC 26B:114–16; trans. Blomfield Jackson, NPNF 2/8:55–56. See also *Homiliae in Hexaemeron* 1.6.11-16; 3.10.27-36; *Homiliae super Psalmos* 32-33, PG 29, 329, 357.

67. Gregory of Nyssa, *Oratio Catechetica,* prologue, 32–37; Greek text SC 453:140 (my translation). This argument was borrowed from Gregory of Nyssa by later Byzantine theologian Euthymius Zigabenus; see his *Panoplia dogmatica: Titulus A*, PG 130, 33.

68. Gregory of Nyssa, *De anima et resurrectione*; Greek text GNO III.3, pp. 11.14-17; trans. William Moore and Henry Austin Wilson, NPNF 2/5:431 (slightly modified).

> drous sky and on the wondrous earth; how elements essentially opposed to each other are all woven together in an ineffable union (διά τινος ἀῤῥήτου κοινωνίας) to serve one common end, each contributing its particular force to maintain the whole; how the unmingling and mutually repellent do not fly apart from each other by virtue of their peculiarities, any more than they are destroyed, when compounded, by such contrariety; how those elements which are naturally buoyant move downwards, the heat of the sun, for instance, descending in the rays, while the bodies which possess weight are lifted by becoming rarefied in vapor, so that water contrary to its nature ascends, being conveyed through the air to the upper regions; how too that fire of the firmament so penetrates the earth that even its abysses feel the heat; how the moisture of the rain infused into the soil generates, one though it be by nature, myriads of differing germs, and animates in due proportion each subject of its influence; how very swiftly the polar sphere revolves, how the orbits within it move the contrary way, with all the eclipses, and conjunctions, and measured intervals of the planets. We see all this with the piercing eyes of mind, nor can we fail to be taught by means of such a spectacle that a skillful and wise Divine Power (θεία δύναμις ἔντεχνός τε καὶ σοφή) is manifesting itself in all these things, and, penetrating each portion, combines those portions with the whole and completes the whole by the portions, and encompasses the universe with a single all-controlling force, self-centered and self-contained, never ceasing from its motion, yet never altering the position which it holds.[69]

Gregory of Nazianzus in his Second Theological Oration also carefully investigates the way that leads us from the visible things to their invisible Creator and Artificer, who bound together different elements and parts of the universe:

> For what gave order (τὸ τάξαν) to things heavenly and earthly and to all that pass through air and live under water, and more than that to what came before them—I mean heaven, earth, air, and the element

69. Gregory of Nyssa, *De anima et resurrectione*; GNO III.3, pp. 12.1–13.5; NPNF 2/5:432. See also GNO III.3, pp. 14.7–10. The same insistence upon the improbability of the different opposite elements forming a unity, which would be "supernatural" (ὑπὲρ φύσιν) for them, is found in John of Damascus (*Expositio fidei* 1.3.38–43, see below) and Pseudo-Athanasius (*Quaestiones ad Antiochum ducem*, *Quaestio* 136, PG 28, 681–84).

> of water themselves? Who combined these elements and divided them out? What a wonderful communion they have with each other, and also harmony (συμφυΐα) and agreement (σύμπνοια)! I praise the man, non-Christian though he was, who asked: "What set these elements in motion and leads their ceaseless, unimpeded flow?" It was surely their designer (ὁ τεχνίτης), who implants in all things reason (λόγον) whereby the universe is conducted and carried along. And who is their designer? Surely he who made them and brought them into existence. Great power like this cannot be ascribed to chance (τῷ αὐτομάτῳ). Supposing chance brought them into existence, what gave them order (τὸ τάξαι)? Granting this possibility too, if you like, to chance, what preserves and guards (τὸ τηρῆσαι καὶ φυλάξαι) them in the conditions of their first constitution? Chance again, or something else? Clearly something beyond chance. What can this "something" be if not God? Thus God-derived reason (ὁ ἐκ Θεοῦ λόγος), bound up, connected, with the whole of nature, man's most ancient law, has led us up from things of sight (ἐκ τῶν ὁρωμένων) to God.[70]

It is noteworthy that Gregory uses here what is now known as the argument or inference "from the best explanation": he demonstrates that to explain the perfect harmony of the universe and its regular motions by an intelligent Creator is far more reasonable than to explain it by chance or spontaneous accident. Moreover he distinguishes here three aspects of the world: its existence, its order, and the preservation of this order. From there we can deduce three different types of arguments for the existence of God: from the need for an efficient cause (cosmological argument), from intelligent design (teleological argument), and from the need for a preservative cause (argument from providence).

Although Gregory himself fails to develop these three arguments separately, we find them in later Byzantine Fathers, such as John of Damascus, who develops all three types of Gregory's arguments in his *De fide orthodoxa*.[71] He carefully distinguishes the argument from the efficient cause

70. Gregory of Nazianzus, *Orations* 28.16.7–25; SC 250:132-34; trans. Lionel Wickham, *St Gregory of Nazianzus: On God and Christ* (Crestwood, NY: St. Vladimir's Seminary Press, 2002), 49 (modified). See also Georgius Acropolites, *In Gregorii Nazianzeni sententias* 5.20-27.

71. See John of Damascus, *Expositio fidei* 1.3.22-53. I will consider them separately later. These three arguments were repeated later in the twelfth century by Euthymius Zigabenus (*Panoplia dogmatica*, prologue, PG 130, 28) and in the thirteenth century by Josephus Racendytes (see Pseudo-Cyril of Alexandria, *De sancta trinitate* 2, PG 77, 1121-24).

(which I will discuss later) and the argument from the preservative cause of the universe:

> Even the very continuity of creation (ἡ τῆς κτίσεως συνοχή), and its preservation and government (συντήρησις καὶ κυβέρνησις), teach us that there does exist a God who supports and maintains and preserves and ever provides for this universe. For how could opposite natures, such as fire and water, air and earth, have combined with each other so as to form one complete world, and continue to abide in indissoluble union, were there not some omnipotent Power (τις παντοδύναμος δύναμις) which bound them together and always is preserving them from dissolution?[72]

As we can see, various arguments from design have a very important place in the natural theology of the Church Fathers. Nevertheless, the Fathers did not confine themselves to these arguments and from time to time proposed *a posteriori* arguments of a different kind, such as cosmological arguments, which I will briefly consider next.

Cosmological arguments

There are different types of the cosmological argument. First I will consider the one that is based on Aristotle's notion of the prime mover.[73] We can find it as early as the *Apology* of Aristides, who presents it in the following way:

> When I have observed the world and all things which are in it, that they move by necessity, I understood that the One who moves it and holds it (τὸν κινοῦντα καὶ διακρατοῦντα) is God. For everything that moves is stronger than the thing that it moves, and everything that holds is stronger than the thing that it holds.[74]

72. John of Damascus, *Expositio fidei* 1.3.38-43; cf. 1.1.15-17. See also Nicephorus Blemmydes, *De theologia* 16.19-21.

73. See Aristoteles, *Physics* 7.1, 241b 34–243a 30; 8.5, 256a 4–8.10, 267b 27; *Metaphysics* 12.6, 1071b 2–12.10, 1076a 6.

74. Aristides, *Apologia*, fr. 1.2; Greek text *L'apologia di Aristide* (my translation).

Another apologist, Athenagoras, explicitly refers to the Peripatetics while using their notion of the prime mover for his apologetic purpose:

> If, as the Peripatetics say, the world is a substance and a body, we do not bow down to "the wretched and weak elements," neglecting to worship God who is the cause of the body's motion (τὸν αἴτιον τῆς κινήσεως τοῦ σώματος θεόν), and adoring passible matter instead of "impassible spirit" (as they call it).[75]

Nemesius of Emesa also mentions Aristotle's notion of the prime mover when he describes the contemplative activity of man, which acts without spatial movement or change, noting that "not every activity is a movement, but there is also an activity which is without movement, through which the first God acts" (ὁ πρῶτος ἐνεργεῖ Θεός), for the first mover is unmoved (τὸ γὰρ πρῶτον κινοῦν ἀκίνητον).[76] However, Nemesius does not propose here any argument for the existence of God. The first among the later Greek Fathers who worked out the argument for such a prime mover was Maximus the Confessor. In order to demonstrate that the world has an origin and a beginning, Maximus starts from the notion of movement, which presupposes two things: the one that is moved, and the one that moves it.

> Whatever is moved has a beginning of its motion. And no motion is without beginning, since it is not without a cause. For its beginning is the mover (τὸ κινοῦν), and its cause (αἰτίαν) is the end that calls it and attracts it, and toward which it is also moved. But if the mover is the beginning of every motion of everything that is moved, and if the cause toward which whatever is moved is carried along is the end (τέλος)— for nothing moves without a cause—then no being is unmoved, except the Prime Mover (τὸ πρώτως κινοῦν)—for the Prime Mover is absolutely unmoved, since it is without beginning—from which it follows, that no beings are without a beginning, since none of them is unmoved.[77]

75. Athenagoras, *Legatio pro Christianis* 16.3; trans. Cyril Richardson, *Early Christian Fathers* (New York, NY: Touchstone, 1996), 314.

76. Nemesius, *De natura hominis* 18.79.15–17; trans. Sharples and van der Eijk, 139. See also: John Philoponus, *In Aristotelis physicorum libros commentaria*, vol. 17, p. 885.28; 887.6; *In Aristotelis libros de anima commentaria*, vol. 15, p. 20.36–37; 96.24–25.

77. Maximus the Confessor, *Ambigua* 10.88.8–17; trans. Constas, 287.

It is noteworthy that Maximus uses here not only Aristotle's argument of the prime mover, which moves without being moved, but also Plato's notion of the idea of the Good,[78] toward which all beings are moved as to their ultimate end. This reminds us of another notion of Aristotle's, that of the *causa finalis*. According to him, it is the same prime mover or universal intellect that thinks of itself and moves everything as an object of desire (κινεῖ δὴ ὡς ἐρώμενον).[79] We may say that we have here an anticipation, not only of the cosmological argument, but also of an argument to the final cause.

John of Damascus was the Greek theologian who gave to the cosmological argument for the prime mover its classical form. He writes:

> Everything that is moved is moved by another thing. And who again is it that moves that? And so on to infinity till we at length arrive at something motionless. For the Prime Mover is motionless (τὸ πρῶτον κινοῦν ἀκίνητον), and that is God . . . who alone is motionless, moving the universe without being moved (δι' ἀκινησίας τὰ πάντα κινοῦν).[80]

This argument was occasionally repeated by later Byzantine theologians.[81] Nonetheless it was another version of the cosmological argument, also proposed by John of Damascus, that became much more widespread.

I will call this argument the argument from the efficient cause or from mutability of creatures.[82] This argument is based on the notion of the mutability of things, which presupposes a cause of their existence that itself is uncaused. According to the Damascene, all things in the world are either "created or uncreated" (κτιστά ἐστιν ἢ ἄκτιστα). If things are created, they are mutable, since everything that has a beginning of its existence must also be mutable, whether in its nature or in its will. On the other hand, if we admit that things are uncreated, they must also be immutable. However, our experience shows that everything is subject to change or alteration or

78. See Plato, *Republic* 508b–509a; 517bc.

79. See Aristoteles, *Metaphysics* 12.7, 1072b 3.

80. John of Damascus, *Expositio fidei* 1.4.7–21; Greek text *Die Schriften des Johannes von Damaskos*, 2:12 (my translation).

81. See, for instance, Josephus Racendytes (Pseudo-Cyril of Alexandria), *De sancta trinitate* 2, PG 77, 1125; Georgius Acropolites, *In Gregorii Nazianzeni sententias* 6.19–29.

82. See the recent discussion of the patristic arguments from corruptibility and mutability of creatures in connection with the Arian controversy in Nathan A. Jacobs, "On the Metaphysics of God and Creatures in the Eastern Pro-Nicenes," *Philosophy and Theology* 28 (2016): 3–42 (esp. 25–35).

movement. So we have to admit that mutable things are also created or have a cause of their existence. From this it follows that things that are created must be the work of some maker. But the Maker (τὸν δημιουργόν) himself cannot have been created. For if he had been created, he also must surely have been created by someone else, and so on until we arrive at something uncreated (τι ἄκτιστον) and wholly immutable (ἄτρεπτος), and that is no other than God.[83] In addition to the premise of Plato's *Timaeus*, "that which has come into existence must necessarily have come into existence by reason of some cause,"[84] John here depends on the Aristotelian premise that prohibits the regress to infinity, in this case not regarding causes of movement, but regarding causes of existence or efficient causes.

A similar argument from the mutability of creatures and their need for the Creator is in the *Confessions* of Augustine, where he writes:

> See, heaven and earth exist, they cry aloud that they are made (*facta sint*), for they suffer change and variation (*mutantur enim atque variantur*). But in anything which is not made (*factum non est*) and yet is, there is nothing which previously was not present. To be what once was not the case is to be subject to change and variation. They also cry aloud that they have not made themselves: "The manner of our existence shows that we are made. For before we came to be, we did not exist to be able to make ourselves." And the voice with which they speak is self-evidence (*ipsa evidentia*). You, Lord, who are beautiful, made them for they are beautiful. You are good, for they are good. You are, for they are.[85]

Argument from the ideal or formal cause

In Augustine we also can find another argument for the existence of God, which I will call the argument from the ideal or formal cause. It depends on Plato's doctrine of the Forms, in which many different things participate and thereby receive their forms and qualities. Platonic forms include the ideas of

83. John of Damascus, *Expositio fidei* 1.3.22–37. Cf. Gregory of Nyssa, *Oratio Catechetica* 8.161–68.

84. Plato, *Timaeus* 28c, trans. R. G. Bury, *Plato*, 12 vols. (Cambridge, MA: Harvard University Press, 1989), 11:51.

85. Augustine, *Confessiones* 11.4.6, trans. Henry Chadwick, *Saint Augustine: Confessions* (Oxford: Oxford University Press, 1998), 224.

being, beauty, the good, the just, and so on. According to Augustine, all of these ideas are impressed *a priori* on human minds. One of the most popular arguments of this kind is based on the idea of the good (*bonum*). Augustine notes that all things in the world are good in some way:

> This thing is good and that good, but take away this and that, and regard good itself if you can. Thus will you see God, not good by a good that is other than Himself, but the Good of all good (*bonum omnis boni*). For in all these good things . . . we could not say that one was better than another, when we judge truly, unless a notion of the Good itself had been impressed upon us (*impressa notio ipsius boni*), such that according to it we might both approve some things as good, and prefer one good to another. . . . Whenever then you are told of this good thing and that good thing, which things can also in other respects be called not good, if you can put aside those things which are good by the participation of the good (*participatione boni bona sunt*) and discern that Good itself (*ipsum bonum*) by participation in which they are good (for when this or that good thing is spoken of, you understand together with them the Good itself also): if, then, I say you can remove these things, and can discern the Good by itself (*per se ipsum bonum*), then you will have discerned God.[86]

As we see from this passage, Augustine's argument is concerned not only with the one idea in many different things, but also with the different degrees of good or perfection which we observe in many things. This argument is very close to another of Augustine's arguments, to which I now turn.

Argument from degrees of perfection

This argument begins with the premise that all things in the world possess different degrees or levels of perfection, so that from the less perfect things we can come to more perfect things, and so on until we come to the best or the most perfect thing (*summum ac praestantissimum bonum*),[87] which is God. In his *On Christian Doctrine* Augustine argues that there exists an

86. Augustine, *De trinitate* 8.3.4–5; trans. A. W. Haddan, NPNF 1/3:117 (slightly modified). See also *De diversis quaestionibus* 24.

87. Cf. Augustine, *Contra Secundinum Manichaeum* 9.

unchangeable Life and Wisdom which transcends all other forms of life and intellect and which is God. Indeed, as he notes, we naturally prefer what is living to what is dead; we know that it is by life that everything lives or does not live, and that life is superior in dignity and worth to the bodily mass which is quickened and animated by it. Then, when we go on to look into the nature of the life itself (*ipsam vitam*), if we find it mere nutritive life (*vitam vegetantem*), such as that of plants, we should consider it inferior to sentient life (*sentientem*), such as that of animals; and above this, again, we place intelligent life (*intellegentem*), such as that of men. And, perceiving that even this intelligent life is obviously subject to change, we place above all these kinds of life the unchangeable Life (*incommutabilem illam vitam*) which cannot at one time be foolish, at another time wise, but on the contrary is Wisdom itself (*ipsa sapientia*). Augustine argues that the very "rule of truth" by which we affirm that the unchangeable Life must be more excellent, is itself unchangeable: and we cannot find such a rule, except by going beyond our own nature (*supra suam naturam*), since we find nothing in ourselves that is not subject to change. Thus, this unchangeable Life and excellent Wisdom cannot be other than God.[88]

Moreover, Augustine anticipates the Anselmian ontological argument, which is also based on the notion of perfection.[89] According to Augustine, we must understand and believe that "God is the supreme Good in all respects, better than which nothing can be or can be conceived" (*summum bonum omnino et quo esse aut cogitari melius nihil possit*).[90]

Another example of the argument from degrees of perfection to the perfect being occurs in Boethius's *Consolation of Philosophy*, book 3:

> It cannot be denied that there is something which is as it were the fountain of all goods (*omnium fons bonorum*). For all that is said to be imperfect is so termed for the want it has of perfection (*inminutione perfecti*). Whence it follows that if in any kind we find something imperfect, there must be something perfect also in the same kind. For if we take away perfection we cannot so much as devise how there

88. Augustine, *De doctrina christiana* 1.8.8 (paraphrase of translation by J. F. Shaw, NPNF 2/2:524–525). A similar, but much more complex argument from different degrees of perfection occurs in Augustine's treatise *On Free Will*; see Augustine, *De libero arbitrio* 2.3.7–15.39.

89. See Anselm, *Proslogion* 2.

90. Augustine, *De moribus Ecclesiae catholicae et de moribus Manichaeorum* 2.11.24 (my translation). See also *De libero arbitrio* 2.6.14; *De doctrina christiana* 1.7.7; Boethius, *De consolatione philosophiae* 3.10.25–26 (see below). See M. Chossat, "Dieu. Son existence," 879–880.

should be any imperfection. For the nature of things began not from that which is defective and not complete, but, proceeding from entire and absolute (*ab integris absolutisque*), falls into that which is extreme and enfeebled.[91]

Moral arguments

Although patristic literature lacks arguments from morality in their classical Kantian sense,[92] we do find in Augustine and Boethius a kind of moral argument based on human awareness of true happiness. Augustine observes that all men have a natural desire for happiness or beatitude (*beatitudo*). But before we become truly happy (*beati*) there is already a notion of happiness imprinted in our mind (*impressa notio beatitatis*), according to which we know that we possess a kind of happiness in ourselves. However, no one can be truly happy if he does not possess the highest Good (*summum bonum*), which is none other than God.[93]

A similar but more elaborate argument is presented by Boethius. He notes that all men seek to attain true happiness, which is "that good which, being once obtained, nothing can be further desired" (*id bonum quo quis adepto nihil ulterius desiderare queat*). This true happiness is "an estate replenished with all that is good" (*status bonorum omnium congregatione perfectus*), and this estate all men seek to obtain by different ways, for in men's minds there is "naturally inserted an earnest desire of that which is truly good" (*veri boni naturaliter inserta cupiditas*). Nevertheless, most people because of "deceitful error" (*devius error*) misunderstand that true good and true happiness and seek to obtain that which falsely seems to them to be such, thus falling into various delusions. They seek only transitory earthly goods, which can furnish only a vanishing and imperfect happiness; therefore, there must be an eternal, everlasting and perfect happiness, which is the supreme Good (*summum bonum*) and is none other than God. Indeed, as confirmed by "the common conceit of human minds" (*communis humanorum conceptio animorum*), "nothing can be imagined better than God" (*nihil Deo melius excogitari queat*), who is "that Good than which nothing is better"

91. Boethius, *De consolatione philosophiae* 3.10.7-18; trans. H. F. Stewart, *Boethius, The Theological Tractates, The Consolation of Philosophy*, LCL 74, eds. H. F. Stewart and E. K. Rand (Cambridge, MA: Harvard University Press, 1968), 266-67.

92. See Richard Swinburne, *The Existence of God*, 212-18.

93. Augustine, *De libero arbitrio* 2.9.26–27.

(*id quo melius nihil est bonum*). From this it follows that "the supreme God is most full of supreme and perfect good" (*summum Deum summi perfectique boni esse plenissimum*); but, as has been shown, "perfect good is true happiness, wherefore true happiness must necessarily be placed in the supreme God" (*veram igitur beatitudinem in summo Deo sitam esse*).[94]

Thus, from the natural desire for happiness implanted in all men, both Augustine and Boethius conclude to the existence of the one true God as the supreme Good and the true Beatitude, without whom men's desire for happiness cannot be explained properly.

Conclusion

This brief overview of the main arguments for the existence of God in patristic and Byzantine theological literature shows that many Church Fathers regarded the existence of God as a truth that can be grasped and proved by human reason, inasmuch as the latter has a natural inclination or predisposition to the knowledge of God. Christian theologians of the patristic era successfully worked out different types of arguments for the existence of God, including both *a priori* and *a posteriori*. In doing this they combined the biblical and philosophical traditions. In contrast to the Greek philosophers, however, they put considerable stress on the argument from the innate knowledge of God, which along with the historical argument was prominent in patristic natural theology. But the most widespread and popular form of argument was that from design, including arguments from the arrangement and order of the universe, from its composition out of opposing elements and parts, from the structure of living beings, and especially from the human body and mind. There were also arguments from the beauty and magnificence of the universe, from the perfect harmony within it, and from the preservation of this harmony and universal order by providence. Less popular and widespread were arguments from the efficient cause (including the arguments from motion and from the mutability of creatures), from the ideal or formal cause, and from different degrees of perfection and from morality (namely, from the natural desire for happiness). All of these arguments were not only borrowed from the Church Fathers by later Byzantine and Western medieval theologians, but also have made a considerable impact on modern and contemporary philosophy of religion.

94. Boethius, *De consolatione philosophiae* 3.2.2-79; trans. Stewart, 228-33; 3.10.23-38; trans. Stewart, 266-69 (slightly modified).

2. Natural Theology in St. Gregory Palamas

DAVID BRADSHAW

St. Gregory Palamas is one of the leading exponents in the Orthodox tradition of the experiential knowledge of God. His *Triads in Defense of the Holy Hesychasts* begins by addressing the view of his opponent, Barlaam of Calabria, that "God is knowable only through the mediation of His creatures."[1] Palamas roundly rejects such a view. He cites the pagan philosophers as a cautionary tale of what happens when one seeks to know God solely through creatures: "By examining the nature of sensible things, they arrived at a certain concept of God, but not at a conception truly worthy of Him and appropriate to His blessed nature . . . For if they had attained a worthy conception of God through rational thought, how could they have taken the demons for gods, and how could they have believed the demons when they taught man polytheism?"[2] Far superior to such partial and inadequate knowledge is the intellectual illumination (φωτισμὸς νοερός) that God brings about in those whose hearts have been purified through obedience to the divine commandments and consecration to prayer. Such illumination is "utterly different from knowledge, though productive of it."[3] Through it, "those who have obtained spiritual and supernatural grace do not gain knowledge only through created beings, but also know spiritually, in a manner beyond sense

1. Gregory Palamas, *Triads* 1.1.1; Greek text in *Défense des saints hésychastes*, ed. John Meyendorff, 2nd ed. (Louvain: Specilegium Sacrum Lovaniense, 1973), 5; trans. Nicholas Gendle, *Gregory Palamas: The Triads* (New York: Paulist Press, 1983), 25. See also the lengthy quotation from Barlaam on this point in 2.3.64.

2. Palamas, *Triads* 1.1.18; ed. Meyendorff, 51; trans. Gendle, 26 (modified).

3. Palamas, *Triads* 1.3.5; ed. Meyendorff, 119; trans. Gendle, 34.

and intelligence, that God is spirit, for they have become entirely God, and know God in God."[4]

In light of this strong emphasis on the experience of God, it is perhaps surprising that Palamas on several occasions speaks favorably of natural theological arguments. My purpose here is to examine several such passages in order to see what light they shed on his general attitude toward natural theology. I will focus on three passages that offer three separate arguments (or at least, sketches of arguments) for the existence of God. However, these arguments are not advanced explicitly *as* natural theology, that is, as part of a systematic attempt to establish the existence of God. It will therefore be necessary to examine them carefully to determine what Palamas thinks they can accomplish and what role they play within his larger thought.

The first occurs in the course of Palamas's correspondence with the monk Barlaam, who later became his primary opponent in the hesychast controversy.[5] This correspondence centered on the question of whether there can be a demonstrative refutation of the *filioque*. Barlaam had denied such a possibility in the course of his *Antilatin Treatises*, and Palamas took the opposite view. It is Palamas's defense of this point regarding the *filioque* that leads him to touch, albeit briefly, on the possibility of demonstrating God's existence.

Barlaam based his position on the teaching of Aristotle's *Posterior Analytics* that a demonstration (ἀπόδειξις) must proceed from premises that are both universal and causally prior to their conclusion.[6] Since nothing is causally prior to God, there can be no demonstration regarding him. Pala-

4. Palamas, *Triads* 2.3.68; ed. Meyendorff, 531–33; trans. Gendle, 69.

5. More specifically, it occurs in Palamas's first epistle to Akindynos, who at this stage served as an intermediary between Palamas and Barlaam. For discussion of the correspondence and the issues involved, see John Meyendorff, *A Study of Gregory Palamas*, 2nd ed. (Crestwood, NY: St. Vladimir's Seminary Press, 1974), 44–45, 116–20, 126–27; Robert Sinkewicz, "The Doctrine of the Knowledge of God in the Early Writings of Barlaam the Calabrian," *Mediaeval Studies* 44 (1982): 181–242; idem, "Gregory Palamas," in *La théologie byzantine et sa tradition*, vol. 2, ed. Carmelo Giuseppe Conticello and Vassa Conticello (Turnhout: Brepols, 2002), 131–88, at 132–33, 145–46; Katerina Ierodiakonou, "The Anti-Logical Movement in the Fourteenth Century," in *Byzantine Philosophy and Its Ancient Sources*, ed. Katerina Ierodiakonou (Oxford: Oxford University Press, 2002), 219–36; Stamatios Gerogiordakis, "The Controversy between Barlaam of Calabria and Gregory Palamas on Demonstrative and Dialectical Syllogisms Revisited," *Philotheos* 10 (2010): 157–69.

6. Aristotle, *Posterior Analytics* 1.2, 14–15. There are other requirements as well, such as that the premises must be necessary, indemonstrable, and better known than the conclusion, but they are not relevant to our purposes here.

mas defended instead a much more relaxed conception of demonstration that was more in line with the common patristic usage of the term.[7] His view allows that a demonstration can be based on premises that are singular or causally posterior to their conclusion, or both. In particular, despite the fact that nothing is causally prior to God, there can be demonstration about him based on the "things around God."[8] Palamas gives this term a broader scope than it normally has in patristic literature, embracing not only the common properties (κοινότητα) of the Trinity but also the unique properties (ἰδιότητα) of each Person.[9] We know the latter through divine revelation, which offers first principles that are self-certifying (αὐτοπίστους) and indemonstrable (ἀναποδείκτους).[10] Since such premises deal with individual members of the Trinity, they are not universal, and they are also not causally prior to their conclusion (although arguably they are not causally posterior, either). It is from premises pertaining to these unique properties of the Persons that Palamas believes there can be a demonstrative argument against the *filioque*. More specifically, one such argument runs as follows: "The superessential Spirit is by nature from God; that which is by nature from God has its source in God, i.e., possesses its being from the source of divinity; the Father alone is source of divinity; therefore, the Spirit is from the Father alone."[11]

Our concern, of course, is not with the *filioque* but with the demonstrability of the existence and nature of God. Palamas goes on to address this subject in the course of confirming the possibility of demonstration about God in general. He prefaces his remarks by observing that those who have been purified in heart have evidence in themselves, through the intelligible illumination they receive, that there is a God and that he is like light—or

7. See, for example, Basil, *On the Holy Spirit* 18.46, cited by Palamas, *First Letter to Akindynos* 8, ed. P. Chrestou, *Gregoriou tou Palama: Syngrammata*, 6 vols. (Thessalonica, 1962–2015), 1:211; Gregory Nazianzen, *Orations* 28.6. Basil and Gregory here merely follow the common usage of the term, which was far broader than the narrow technical meaning given it by Aristotle.

8. Palamas, *First Letter to Akindynos* 9–10; ed. Chrestou, 1:213–14; cf. Sinkewicz, "Doctrine," 199–200. Translations are my own except where noted.

9. Palamas, *First Letter to Akindynos* 9; ed. Chrestou, 1:214. For the meaning of the "things around God" in patristic literature see David Bradshaw, *Aristotle East and West: Metaphysics and the Division of Christendom* (Cambridge: Cambridge University Press, 2004), 166–67 (Cappadocians), 189–91 (Maximus), 207–8 (John of Damascus).

10. Palamas, *First Letter to Akindynos* 10; ed. Chrestou, 1:214.

11. I borrow here the paraphrase offered by Sinkewicz, "Doctrine," 201, based on Palamas, *First Letter to Akindynos* 11.

rather, that he is a fountain of immaterial and intelligible light.[12] Such knowledge possesses the highest certitude. Those who have not been so purified can still know that there is a God, however. While explaining how this can be, Palamas offers some thoughts that are relevant to our topic:

> Those who have not attained to this contemplation are able to apprehend (συνορᾶν) from the forethought (προμηθείας) about all things the common Forethought; from those who are made good, Goodness itself; from those who are made wise, Wisdom itself; and, in general, from all things the One who transcends all and is established above all, the many-named and unnameable Being beyond being. Are not all these immaterially contemplated around that One, whatever it may be? And is it not through them as evidence that there is a demonstration free from deceit (ἀψευδὴς ἀπόδειξις) that there is One who leads forth all, who before the ages has forethought for all, who is all-mighty, overseeing all, all-good, and the cause of all, transcending nature?[13]

Although this passage is not in itself an argument for the existence of God, it is a blueprint for such an argument. Palamas proposes that by considering the forethought evident in all things, we can infer to its divine source; from observing how things are made good, we can infer to Goodness itself; from observing how they are made wise, we can infer to Wisdom itself; and so on. One wonders precisely how these inferences are supposed to work. For instance, is it really true that there is forethought evident in all things, given the immense amount of evil and undeserved suffering in the world? Why should we understand what we see as a product of forethought rather than simply in terms of natural causes? Similarly, is it true that things are made good by some active agent, rather than becoming good on their own? And, if they are, why must this agent be a single thing, the Good itself? Indeed, what does it mean to be the Good, rather than simply one good among others? Similar questions can be asked about Wisdom and the other perfections toward which Palamas here gestures.

Perhaps, however, to speak of *inferring* from these effects to their cause is premature. What Palamas actually says is that one can take in together in a single glance (συνορᾶν) the effects and their cause. We often take in together effects and their cause in this way. I see the milk spilled and the flowers

12. Palamas, *First Letter to Akindynos* 12; ed. Chrestou, 1:216.
13. Palamas, *First Letter to Akindynos* 12; ed. Chrestou, 1:216.

knocked over, and I immediately see these effects as due to the cat, who has done such things in the past. I feel the car suddenly lose power and notice the gas gauge on zero, and I immediately perceive these effects as due to an empty gas tank. I hear voices through the window and perceive that there are people outside, even though I have not seen them or tried otherwise to confirm their presence.

One can certainly formulate the thought process involved in such cases as an inference to the best explanation, where "best" is assessed based on factors such as simplicity and prior likelihood. But this is an after-the-fact reconstruction of what is, in its actual occurrence, an immediate act of perception. It is true that to "perceive" a cause with its effects in this way requires a complex set of presuppositions and causal associations, many of which are acquired by learning. Someone with no prior knowledge of cats would not perceive the wreck on my kitchen counter as the work of a cat, nor would someone with no prior knowledge of cars perceive the car's sudden deceleration and the reading on the gauge as signs of an empty gas tank. Indeed, such a person might not group these phenomena into a single observation at all, regarding them instead as unrelated. Nonetheless, once such background knowledge has been acquired, it conditions perception so that the cause is perceived, as it were, within the effects, with no conscious intermediary act of inference.

Most normal acts of communication also involve perceiving the cause in the effects in this way. To understand the words you utter requires that I perceive them collectively as effects produced by a cause, namely, your mind and the meaning you intend to convey. I do not infer from the former to the latter; I perceive the meaning *in* the sounds. Notably, in this case not only is there no conscious act of inference, there is not even an implicit inferential chain that can be reconstructed after the fact. To understand speech is not normally a matter of correctly interpreting evidence, as in the case of the cat or the car; it is a skill that is acquired through countless acts of association and imitation. Of course, in learning a foreign language we may frequently rely on inference from evidence, and in fact it may be precisely through such inferential acts that we gradually acquire the skill. In such cases there is a spectrum ranging from inference to skill, rather than a sharp dichotomy. Nonetheless, the point remains that often (including when understanding our native tongue) we operate purely through an acquired skill whose operations cannot be reconstructed inferentially.[14]

14. Another even purer such case is that of reading the moods on someone's face. As Thomas Reid observed, we often could not say precisely what are the signs that indicate to us

In referring to "seeing together" the cause with the effects, then, Palamas is invoking an extremely widespread phenomenon. Yet such acts of seeing can be mistaken. I can wrongly blame the cat, when in fact the true cause was the dog; I can mistakenly think there are people outside when there are only voices from a neighbor's television set; and so on. Skill-based acts of perception can also be mistaken, as when I misunderstand what you have said and find in it a meaning you did not express. Of course, just as there are many ways to err, there are also many ways to prevent error, such as seeking out further evidence, checking one's perceptions against those of others, and reasoning through the implications of a given conclusion. Much depends on the correctness of the presuppositions with which one approaches a given act of "seeing in."

With what presuppositions does Palamas wish us to approach the perception of apparent acts of divine forethought, becoming good, and becoming wise? And how would he have us check our results for error? Regrettably, he does not tell us.[15] Let us turn, then, to the other places where Palamas offers arguments for the existence of God, in the hope of clarifying his overall strategy.

The next such passage occurs in the second of Palamas's *Triads in Defense of the Holy Hesychasts*. After arguing at some length for the superiority of faith over the knowledge allegedly gained through philosophy, Palamas seeks to strengthen his case by allowing, for the sake of argument, that philosophical knowledge is entirely true. Even so, he argues, it leads to the knowledge of God. I quote this passage in full since it is his most extended discussion of our topic:

> Let us suppose that the knowledge attained by philosophy is entirely true, and let us set before us those who have come to recognize (ἐπιγνόντας) God through this knowledge of creatures. The knowledge and contemplation that comes about through creatures is called

---

a given mood; yet even infants recognize moods, suggesting that this ability is to a large extent simply innate. See on this point Del Ratzsch, "Perceiving Design," in *God and Design*, ed. Neil Manson (New York: Routledge, 2003), 124–44.

15. A further question is whether, if he were to attempt to state the argument more fully, it would be a deductive inference like his argument for the *filioque* or (to use modern terminology) an inductive inference to the best explanation. His use of the term ἀπόδειξις does not necessarily require the former, since this term was used broadly (outside of the technical Aristotelian context) for any argument that was thought to be firm and conclusive. Fortunately not much hinges on this issue, for the argument could no doubt be formalized in various ways.

"natural law." Thus, even before the patriarchs and prophets and the written law, it summoned the human race and returned it to God, and showed indirectly (ὑπεδείκνυ) the Creator to those who did not abandon the natural knowledge of the wise among the Greeks. For who that possesses reason and beholds such manifest differences among beings—both the oppositions of hidden forces and the compensating kinetic impulses, and again stability that compensates in another way; the ceaseless resolutions arising out of contrary affections and the unconfused harmony arising out of irreconcilable strife; the cohesion of things that are distinct and the continuing distinction of those that are united, whether they be minds, souls, or bodies; the harmony among so many, their established positions and relations; the conformity of their states and ranks to their essence, the indissolubility of their connection—who that attends to all these points would not form a conception (ἐννοήσειεν) of the One who has so well established each thing in itself and wondrously harmonized each with the others, so as to come to know (γινώσκειν) God from his image and that which he has caused? And who that has known God in this way will consider him one of the things that are caused or set forth in his image? Thus he will also possess the knowledge of God that comes from denial (τὴν ἐξ ἀποφάσεως θεογνωσίαν). So the knowledge of creatures returned the human race to the knowledge of God before the Law and the prophets. And now again it returns to God virtually the whole of the inhabited world, as many as do not yield to the divine oracles of the Gospel; through it alone they now have no other God than the Creator of this universe.[16]

One recognizes here a form of the argument from design so beloved to patristic authors. In particular, Palamas reasons from the balance of opposing elements and natural forces to the necessity of some Designer and Sustainer who maintains them in harmony. This is a form of the design argument developed at length by St. Athanasius and deployed more briefly by St. Gregory of Nyssa and St. John of Damascus.[17] As Richard Swinburne has argued, it can be understood as a form of inference to the best explanation, where the item to be explained is the fact that the elements "fit together in such a way as

16. Palamas, *Triads* 2.3.44; ed. Meyendorff, 477–79 (my translation).

17. See Athanasius, *Contra Gentes* 36–38; Gregory of Nyssa, *On the Soul and Resurrection* (GNO III.3, p. 11); John of Damascus, *On the Orthodox Faith* 1.3. See also Alexey Fokin, "Natural Theology in Patristic Thought" in this volume, where these passages are quoted at length.

to produce an orderly world . . . fitted for humans."[18] So understood, the argument bears a marked resemblance to the so-called fine-tuning argument, although, of course, without the latter's mathematical precision.

Nonetheless, let us note some peculiarities in Palamas's own presentation of the argument. One is that Palamas refers to the created world as God's image. This is not an idea present in his sources or in the patristic tradition in general.[19] Palamas uses it primarily to point out how absurd it would be to consider God one of the things "set forth in his image." It thus contributes to a second peculiarity of this passage, Palamas's conclusion that the argument leads to *apophatic* knowledge of God. This is quite surprising. Palamas's purpose would seem to be to emphasize the relative completeness of the knowledge of God available through creatures, since it includes not only the certainty that God exists, but also the awareness of his radical difference from creation. Evidently for Palamas one does not truly know that it is *God* who exists if one does not grasp at the same time this radical difference.

It is likely that we find here at least part of the answer to our question about what presuppositions are necessary to perceive earthly events as pointing to divine forethought, goodness, and wisdom. The question of the source of harmony among the elements, and the attempt to answer this question through inference to the best explanation, has an objectivity about it that questions about forethought, goodness, and wisdom do not. Presumably it can be resolved by reference to criteria that govern other similar forms of inference. Having concluded that there is indeed no better explanation for cosmic harmony than an immensely powerful and intelligent Designer, it is far more plausible to see earthly events as governed by such an Intelligence. And if the Intelligence is indeed transcendent in the way Palamas suggests, it is plausible to see it as not only good, but the source of all good; as not only wise, but the source of all wisdom; and so on.

That, at least, would be one way to connect the dots between the two quite different argument-schemas presented in the correspondence and the *Triads*. It certainly fits well with the preeminence that the patristic tradition typically gave to the design argument.[20] However, there are problems facing such a design-first approach. Given the immense amount of undeserved

18. Richard Swinburne, "Gregory Palamas and Our Knowledge of God," in *Logic in Orthodox Christian Thinking*, ed. Andrew Schumann (Frankfurt: Ontos Verlag, 2013), 18–37, at 26.

19. There is no mention of it in the long entry on εἰκών (image) in G. W. H. Lampe, ed., *A Patristic Greek Lexicon* (Oxford: Clarendon Press, 1961).

20. See Fokin, "Natural Theology."

suffering and moral evil in the world, why should we conclude that the Designer is good? Would not moral indifference, or perhaps even a streak of evil, better fit the facts? Alternatively, we might suppose that the Designer is perfectly good but incompetent or limited in power; or perhaps even that the Designer is actually a committee of Designers who disagreed among themselves and settled on the current state of our world as a compromise.[21] The problem is not only that any number of hypotheses are consistent with the facts of natural order and harmony (although that is bad enough); it is that the facts actually seem to militate against the postulation of a Designer who is perfectly good, omniscient, and omnipotent.

We face here an intrinsic limitation of inductive reasoning. Any act of induction necessarily focuses on only a subset of the total available information. In many cases this produces no difficulty, for the boundaries of the relevant information are plain enough. When the goal is to infer from some subset of the total available information to the Cause of the universe, however, the question of where to set the boundaries becomes acute. In the case of the design argument, is the relevant information simply the existence of harmony among natural forces and elements; or is it this, plus the existence of undeserved suffering and moral evil; or is it these, plus particular facts about the design of living things—including (as evolutionists would urge) their apparent design flaws? Other things being equal, it seems that the more evidence one takes in, the more likely one's results are to be correct. But of course, other things are not equal, for the inclusion of new evidence tends also to produce new perplexities and to add complexity to possible explanations.

Theistic apologists are well aware of such difficulties and have long worked on strategies to overcome them. The most common is to deploy a number of arguments that complement one another so as to collectively produce something like the traditional conception of God.[22] Such a procedure is natural enough given the abundance of available theistic arguments, but it is also fraught with difficulty. Not only must each argument individually be sound; further arguments must be provided to show that the entities they postulate really are one and the same and that the different descriptions they offer complement one another so as to collectively amount to something like traditional theism. Furthermore, the attempt to do this well can end up defining what is meant by "God" in such a way as to impose an *a*

21. David Hume's *Dialogues Concerning Natural Religion* famously presents a number of such possibilities.

22. Aquinas's Five Ways are a classic example of such an approach.

priori constraint on biblical interpretation and one's general understanding of divine revelation. It was perhaps worries such as these that led Pascal to warn of the difference between the "God of the philosophers" and the God of Abraham, Isaac, and Jacob.[23]

It is not our task here to adjudicate such worries. Suffice to say that the attempt to deploy comprehensive and complementary arguments in this way is a far more ambitious project than what I have called the design-first approach to reorienting one's perception of the world. Although it seems likely that Palamas would have embraced the latter, there is no evidence that he embraced (or even had any interest in) the former. His deployment of the design argument is quite modest in intent. It seeks to show that God has not left those today who reject the Gospel (as he did not leave those who lived before the Gospel) bereft of any means to know him. It is less an act of apologetics than a vindication, from within the standpoint of faith, of divine goodness.[24]

It remains, however, to consider Palamas's third and perhaps most potent argument. It occurs at the outset of his most systematic work, the *One Hundred and Fifty Chapters*. This work begins with an argument from history that the world had a beginning:

> That the world had a beginning both nature teaches and history confirms; the truth of the arts, the introduction of laws and the government of states also clearly affirm this. For we know the founders of almost all the arts, those who established the laws, and those who first administered the states.[25]

23. This is not to deny that Pascal was also reporting an immediate experience. The opening lines of his famous "Memorial" (found at his death on a scrap of paper sewn into the lining of his coat) read: "The year of grace 1654, Monday, 23 November, feast of St. Clement, pope and martyr, and others in the martyrology. Vigil of St. Chrysogonus, martyr, and others. From about half past ten at night until about half past midnight, FIRE. 'GOD of Abraham, GOD of Isaac, GOD of Jacob' not of the philosophers and of the learned" (Vatican Observatory Foundation, "The 'Memorial' of Blaise Pascal," https://www.vofoundation.org/faith-and-science/memorial-blaise-pascal, accessed January 16, 2021). Here he reports the experience in such a way as to also constitute a warning, if only to himself.

24. The allusion at the end of the passage to how the knowledge of creatures "now again returns to God virtually the whole of the inhabited world" is particularly notable in this regard. As Meyendorff observes (*Study*, 119), it is evidently a reference to the rise of Islam. As such it shows that Palamas regarded the Muslims as, despite their erroneous theology, being led by the knowledge of creatures to worship the true God.

25. Gregory Palamas, *The One Hundred and Fifty Chapters* 1, ed. and trans. Robert E. Sinkewicz (Toronto: Pontifical Institute of Mediaeval Studies, 1988), 83.

After a few sentences on the superiority of the Mosaic account of the world's history over others, Palamas turns from history to nature:

> Since the nature of this world is such that it always requires a new cause in each instance and since without this cause it cannot exist at all, we have in these facts proof for an underived, self-existent primordial cause.[26]

Unfortunately this brief sentence is all that he says on this important matter. The next chapter continues in the same vein, taking the dependency of the world on a Cause as its starting point: "The nature of the contingent existence of realities (τῶν ἐνδεχομένων εἶναι) in the world proves not only that the world has had a beginning but also that it will have an end, as it is continually coming to an end in part."[27]

Brief though it is, this argument marks an important step beyond the patristic legacy. Already in the New Testament, the Logos is presented as the ongoing, sustaining cause of all things (Col 1:17, Heb 1:3). Patristic authors as early as St. Justin Martyr noticed the convergence between this teaching and that of Plato that the world remains in existence only through the will of the Creator.[28] In Plato, however, the reversion of the world to non-being would be merely a return to the initial chaotic state upon which the Demiurge imposed form. The patristic authors (with the exception of Justin) believed instead in creation *ex nihilo*. Yet they did not fully integrate this belief with their understanding of the ongoing sustenance of the world. Instead they speak rather vaguely of the danger of dissolution or decay of the elements or of the whole world "falling back into non-being" (τὸ μὴ εἶναι).[29] Palamas, in speaking of the world as "always requiring a new cause in each instance" (ἀεὶ προσφάτου τῆς καθ' ἕκαστον ἀρχῆς δεομένη), seems to have in mind specifically the maintenance of things in existence as opposed to sheer nothingness.

If this is correct, the argument points to a more radical kind of transcen-

26. Palamas, *One Hundred and Fifty Chapters* 1; trans. Sinkewicz, 83. The term translated "we have proof" is παρίστησι, more literally "it [the nature of the cosmos] presents or sets forth."

27. Palamas, *One Hundred and Fifty Chapters*, 85.

28. Justin Martyr, *Dialogue with Trypho* 5 (citing Plato, *Timaeus* 41a–b); see also Athanasius, *Contra Gentes* 41–42; Eusebius, *Demonstration of the Gospel* 4.13; Gregory Nazianzen, *Orations* 28.16; John Chrysostom, *Homilies on Colossians* 3.2, *Homilies on Hebrews* 2.3.

29. This is the phrase of Chrysostom, *Homilies on Hebrews* 2.3 (PG 63, 23).

dence than does the design argument. As Palamas observes in the *Triads*, the Designer cannot be one of the things that are made. This means, roughly, that he cannot be a spatio-temporal entity. But that does not preclude that he might be like the Demiurge in the *Timaeus*, who acts upon preexisting matter to create the world. By shifting the ground of argument to the mere continuance of things in existence, the *Chapters* provides the grounds for understanding God as the cause, not only of order and harmony, but of the entire spatio-temporal framework. The implications of this are twofold. First, it offers a philosophical foundation for the traditional belief in creation *ex nihilo*; and second, it clarifies that God's sustaining the being of the universe consists not only in maintaining harmony, but in sustaining things in any form of existence whatsoever.[30]

A much fuller version of an argument like that of the *Chapters* has been developed by David Braine in his *The Reality of Time and the Existence of God*.[31] Braine's version of the argument is too complex to summarize here. Still, he makes clear that it depends on a number of controversial assumptions, such as a broadly Aristotelian substance ontology and the rejection of Humean and Kantian accounts of causation.[32] The same would presumably be true of the *Chapters* argument if it were spelled out fully. Although this argument is in some ways more powerful than the design argument, then, it is not without its own presuppositions.

Unfortunately, just as in the other passages, Palamas makes no effort to examine or defend those presuppositions. So here again we find no evidence that he intended his various theistic arguments to be elements in a broader apologetic strategy. Writing as he did for a Christian audience in an age when a basic form of theism was widely taken for granted, apologetics was not his concern. Instead he has a number of other aims. In the correspondence with Barlaam he wishes to show the possibility of demonstrative knowledge of God, and in the *Triads* the real (although limited) value of pagan philosophy. In both works, too, there is an underlying concern to vindicate the good-

30. Although Palamas was (to my knowledge) the first author in the Greek tradition to give an argument for the latter view, the view itself is implicit in the teaching of Dionysius the Areopagite that God is "the being of things that are" (τὸ εἶναι τοῖς οὖσι, *Divine Names* 5.4 817D). I suspect it was through his long reflection on the Dionysian writings that Palamas arrived at this argument.

31. David Braine, *The Reality of Time and the Existence of God* (Oxford: Clarendon Press, 1988).

32. See analysis in David Bradshaw, "'All Existing is the Action of God': The Philosophical Theology of David Braine," *The Thomist* 60 (1996): 379–416.

ness of God by showing that he can be known even by those who have not received divine revelation. The *Chapters* has a different concern, aiming to show the utter dependence on God of all created nature.

Finally, I believe that we can see in these passages a spiritual aim as well. To "see together" creatures with their divine cause is not something that, for most of us, comes naturally. We are much like those beginning to learn a language who need to be taught how to recognize the meaning in what otherwise are bare sounds. Seen in that light, the arguments of the *Triads* and *Chapters* are part of the preparatory training that enables one to see God at work in all things. Not all need such training, for there are other ways of learning to perceive God's activity among creatures, as we see so vividly in the lives of many saints. But for those who lack such spiritual insight, or are for other reasons plagued with doubts, such arguments can be helpful.

Of course, to point out that Palamas's own aims were not apologetic does not mean that we cannot adapt his arguments for that purpose. An argument is sound, or not, independently of who may have stated it and what that person's aims may have been. It certainly seems that our cultural situation today calls for some form of apologetics. In that task Palamas provides some helpful pointers, but little more. The bulk of the work to be done, and the responsibility for doing it well, lie with us.

3. Medieval and Early Modern Natural Theology in the West

RICHARD CROSS

Arguments for God's existence come in two kinds, *a priori* and *a posteriori*—respectively arguments that do not as such require any kind of empirical experience of the world, and those that take such experience as their starting point. In what follows, I offer a brief summary of some of the more important discussions in the West during the medieval and early modern periods. Arguments for the existence of God frequently have more than one function. One, of course, is to prove the existence of God. But none of the authors I discuss in this essay holds the arguments to have any seriously apologetic purpose, although they doubtless held that the arguments could be used in such a way. Rather, the various thinkers I consider use the arguments to explore a range of second-order questions, issues that the arguments themselves either generate or solve. The identity of these topics shifts quite radically from the Middle Ages to the early modern period; and, in this latter period, sharply differs between the philosophers and the theologians. I shall be sensitive to all this in what follows.

Medieval thought

The most obvious use of the arguments for God's existence in the Middle Ages is to "demonstrate" God's existence in ways that, from the thirteenth century onwards, generally conform to the requirements of one of the strongest kinds of Aristotelian scientific argument. Another function of the arguments is meta-scientific, so to speak, as part of a way of distinguishing the subject matters of different intellectual disciplines ("sciences," in the medieval jargon): for example, physics and metaphysics; and, in the Christian context, theology and the purely natural sciences. To which of the former disciplines does an argument for God's existence belong? And what is the relationship between revealed theology and the philosophical enterprise of attempting to prove God's existence by natural reason? Another question relates to the requirements of human cognition: does all cognition in some sense presuppose cognition of God as the primary object of the intellect, or not? Yet a further function is strictly theological: the correct understanding of Romans 1:19–25. With the exception of the last, these questions are largely medieval or scholastic concerns; the question of Aristotelian science, for instance, becomes less pressing in the early modern period, at least outside scholastic circles.

Not only do we find arguments for God's existence in medieval theology; we find too what has become known as "ramified" natural theology: the extension of natural theology to include certain specific articles of the Christian faith. Arguments for the Trinity are the most popular extensions in the period. But we find too arguments for the truth of the Incarnation and the life of grace, as we shall see.

As far as I know the first, and certainly the most well-known, attempt to formulate an *a priori* argument for God's existence can be found in Anselm's *Proslogion*. The fundamental argument goes like this:

> [God is] something than which nothing greater can be thought. . . . That than which a greater cannot be thought cannot exist in the mind alone. For if it exists solely in the mind, it can be thought to exist in reality also, which is greater. If then that than which a greater cannot be thought exists in the mind alone, this same that than which a greater cannot be thought is that than which a greater can be thought. But this is obviously impossible. Therefore there is absolutely no doubt that something than which a greater cannot be thought exists both in the mind and in reality. . . . And . . . God . . . [is] this being.[1]

The argument relies on the presupposition, admittedly highly contentious, that one and the same thing can exist in two modes, so to speak: "in the mind" and "in reality." The idea is that a being characterized as Anselm defines "God" could not be such that it existed merely in the mind, since this

1. Anselm, *Proslogion* 2–3; trans. M. J. Charlesworth, *Anselm of Canterbury: The Major Works*, ed. Brian Davies and G. R. Evans (Oxford: Oxford University Press, 2008), 87–88 (modified).

would entail, absurdly, that the being both was and was not that than which nothing greater can be thought.

In another text from the *Proslogion*, Anselm apparently develops a different line of thinking:

> Something can be thought to exist that cannot be thought not to exist, and this is greater than that which can be thought not to exist. Hence, if that than which a greater cannot be thought can be thought not to exist, then that than which a greater cannot be thought is not the same as that than which a greater cannot be thought, which is absurd. Something than which a greater cannot be thought exists so truly then, that it cannot be even thought not to exist.[2]

Here, something that "cannot be thought not to exist" is a necessary being, and the idea is that necessary being entails being—an argument that does not depend on the strong version of the mind-world identity thesis that undergirds the first argument. Now, if this is the argument that Anselm intends, then he has overlooked a crucial additional required premise: to get from necessary being to actual being we need to show that the being of such an item is *possible* (I will return to this in a moment).[3] So the argument as stated does not establish its conclusion. In any case, it seems likely Anselm himself saw this additional argument as merely an attempt to spell out some of the implications or presuppositions of the first argument given: namely, that that than which a greater cannot be thought must, if it exists, be a necessary existent, since necessary existence is a great-making property.

Anselm famously places his argument in the context of a second-order discussion that focuses on the purpose of the argument. As he puts it in relation to the *Proslogion* itself,

> I began to wonder if it might perhaps be possible to find one single argument that for its proof required no other save itself, and that by itself would suffice to prove that God really exists, that he is the supreme good needing no other and is He whom all things have need of for their being and well-being, and also to prove whatever we believe about the Divine Being. . . . I have written the following short tract

2. Anselm, *Proslogion* 3; trans. Charlesworth, 88 (modified).

3. For the classic account of the two arguments in Anselm, see Norman Malcolm, "Anselm's Ontological Arguments," *Philosophical Review* 69 (1962): 41–62.

> dealing with this question as well as several others, from the point of view of one trying to raise his mind to contemplate God and seeking to understand what he believes. . . . [I have given it the title] "Faith Seeking Understanding."[4]

The idea is that understanding the faith ultimately involves being able to demonstrate the faith from first principles.

Anselm develops a very ambitious theological program around this basic idea. As he sees it, to understand the faith is to bracket the contents of the faith and attempt to explore what can be shown by reason alone. In the *Proslogion*, Anselm uses the notion of God's maximal greatness or perfection to show that God, as characterized in the arguments just given, must have all great-making properties: that is to say, the properties ascribed to God in classical theism.

Elsewhere, Anselm attempts to do the same thing for the Incarnation. Here is how he himself summarizes his objectives in relation to the two books of the relevant treatise, *Cur deus homo*:

> The first book . . . proves, by necessary reasons, that, supposing Christ were left out of the case (*remoto Christo*), as if there had never existed anything to do with him, it is impossible that, without him, any member of the human race could be saved. In the second book, similarly, the supposition is made that nothing were known about Christ, and it is demonstrated with no less clear reason and truth: that human nature was instituted with the specific aim that at some stage the whole human being should enjoy blessed immortality . . .; that it was inevitable that the outcome concerning mankind which was the reason behind man's creation should become a reality, but that this could only happen through the agency of a Man-God; and that it is from necessity that all the things which we believe about Christ have come to pass.[5]

The argument, in a nutshell, is this. Human beings are made for beatitude.[6] But sin places a bar to this,[7] and renders human beings liable to

4. Anselm, *Proslogion*, preface; trans. Charlesworth, 82–83.

5. Anselm, *Cur deus homo*, preface; trans. Janet Fairweather, *Anselm of Canterbury: The Major Works*, ed. Brian Davies and G. R. Evans (Oxford: Oxford University Press, 2008), 261–62.

6. Anselm, *Cur deus homo* 2.1, 4.

7. Anselm, *Cur deus homo* 1.4.

punishment.[8] God wills human salvation, but cannot simply forgive sin.[9] So some kind of recompense is necessary,[10] by way of paying the debt owed to God in virtue of the subjective harm ("dishonor") done to God.[11] God's honor is infinite, and a sin against God is infinite. So only the infinite God can pay the debt. But only humankind owes the debt. So only a God-man can pay what is owed.[12] Anselm assumes that this arrangement requires some kind of distinction in God, between the one who pays (the Son) and the one who is paid (the Father). So this gets us the Incarnation, the Trinity (at least inchoately), and redemption, all demonstrated from first principles.

Later theologians found this program too wildly ambitious to be workable. But the endeavor to see just how far unaided reason could take us into the Christian faith remained a feature of medieval theology in the West. Richard of St. Victor, for instance, in the twelfth century, accepts a version of Anselm's ontological argument, and thence derives an argument for the Trinity on the basis of perfect-being considerations. God's goodness entails God's lovingness.[13] But love requires a subject to love and a subject to be loved; and in the case of supreme love these subjects must be equal.[14] And supreme love requires that these two are united in their love for a third.[15] And this—mutual love and shared love—exhausts the varieties of love. But there is only one God since there can only be one omnipotent being;[16] and there can only be one omnipotent being because omnipotence includes the power "to render any other being powerless."[17] So the three subjects cannot be three Gods. They are three persons, in one God.

Since its formulation, Anselm's ontological argument has attracted a great deal of attention, and has provoked some strong reactions. Bonaventure's capacious approach to the arguments for God's existence allows him to affirm both *a priori* and *a posteriori* arguments for God's existence.[18] Indeed,

8. Anselm, *Cur deus homo* 1.9.

9. Anselm, *Cur deus homo* 1.12.

10. Anselm, *Cur deus homo* 1.19–20.

11. Anselm, *Cur deus homo* 1.11, 13.

12. Anselm, *Cur deus homo* 2.6–7.

13. Richard of St. Victor, *De trinitate* 2.16; in *Trinity and Creation: A Selection of Works of Hugh, Richard and Adam of St Victor*, ed. and trans. Boyd Taylor Coolman and Dale Coulter (Hyde Park, NY: New City Press, 2011).

14. Richard of St. Victor, *De trinitate* 3.2.

15. Richard of St. Victor, *De trinitate* 3.11.

16. Richard of St. Victor, *De trinitate* 3.8.

17. Richard of St. Victor, *De trinitate* 1.25; trans. Coolman and Coulter, 227.

18. See for instance the array of twenty-nine arguments set out at the beginning of the

Bonaventure holds, further, that God is understood "implicitly" in all human cognition.[19] We cannot understand the notion of substance without some understanding of a more general notion, that of being. And we cannot understand the notion of being without some understanding, in turn, of a less general notion, that of being as bracketed from all potency and defect. And this notion of being is the one realized in God. So reflection ("reduction," as Bonaventure calls it[20]) on our own cognitive acts leads us to realize that some kind of knowledge of God is presupposed in all human cognition.[21]

Aquinas takes a very different approach from this. To begin with, while he agrees with Bonaventure that knowledge of the notion of substance presupposes some notion of the more general notion of being, he denies that either of these requires knowledge of pure actuality, as Bonaventure posited. The intellect knows by abstraction from material objects, and we cannot simply abstract the notion of God from that of any material object.[22] In line with this, Aquinas prioritizes an *a posteriori* argument from Aristotle found in the science of physics, and couples it with similar arguments in the science of metaphysics, as we shall see in a moment. And he strongly rejects Anselm's *a priori* argument: "Given that someone understands this name 'God' to signify . . . that than which a greater cannot be thought, it does not follow from this that they understand that which is signified by the name to be in reality, but only in the apprehension of the intellect."[23] We can understand what a word means—the concept it signifies—but whether or not that concept is realized in reality cannot be established simply on the basis of the word's signification.

Aquinas's "five ways" of arguing for God's existence are almost too well-known to repeat: the argument from motion or change to an unchanged

---

Disputed Questions on the Trinity, q. 1, a. 1 (trans. Zachary Hayes [St. Bonaventure, NY: Franciscan Institute, 1979]).

19. For "implicitly," and Bonaventure's understanding of it, see *Commentaria in quatuor libros sententiarum* [= *In sent.*] 1, d. 28, dubium 1 (*Opera omnia*, 10 vols. [Quaracchi: Collegium S. Bonaventurae, 1882–1902]). I owe this reference to Daniel Matías Contreras Ríos, "*Primum Cognitum*: Bonaventure and Aquinas on the Foundations of Knowledge" (Ph.D. dissertation, University of Notre Dame, 2020), 35.

20. See the text referenced in the previous note.

21. For the whole discussion, see Bonaventure, *The Journey of the Mind to God* 3.3 (trans. Philotheus Boehner, ed. Stephen F. Brown [Indianapolis, IN: Hackett, 1993], 19).

22. See Aquinas, *ST* I, q. 12, a. 4; 1, q. 88, a. 3. For the texts, see *Corpus Thomisticum: S. Thomae de Aquino, Opera Omnia*, https://www.corpusthomisticum.org/iopera.html. All translations from Aquinas are my own.

23. Aquinas, *ST* I, q. 2, a. 1 ad 2.

changer, on the basis of the impossibility of an infinite regress and the impossibility of a self-mover; the argument from efficient causation to an uncaused cause, on the basis of the impossibility of an infinite regress and the impossibility of a self-cause; the argument to a necessary (i.e., eternal) being, on the basis that the existence of contingent beings requires something eternal else there would at some time have been nothing, and hence would be nothing now; the argument from degrees of perfection to a most perfect being, on the basis that degrees of perfection require a maximum against which their perfection can be graded; and the argument from the purposiveness of all things in the universe, on the basis that purposiveness requires rational intention.[24]

A contemporary argument that Aquinas rejects is one found in Bonaventure and originating in al-Ghazālī: the universe cannot be infinitely old, since if it were there would have been a day infinitely distant from the present one. And this is impossible, because any such day could be succeeded neither by a day finitely distant from the present one nor by one infinitely distant from the present one.[25] Aquinas rightly objects: even if the universe is infinitely old, "whatever past day is pinpointed, there are finitely many days from that one to this."[26]

After presenting the five ways, Aquinas goes on to show that any being or being satisfying these descriptions must be simple, perfect, good, infinite, omnipresent, immutable, eternal, and unique.[27] But he has no sympathy for the ramified natural theology fashionable in the twelfth century. He thinks that the project of demonstrating God's existence is simply a "preamble" to theology,[28] establishing the existence of theology's subject-matter: God.[29] Aquinas argues that our only way of knowing God by natural reason is derivatively, from creatures, as a cause is known derivatively from its effects. But "God's creative power is common to the whole Trinity, and thus pertains to the unity of essence, not the distinction of persons. Only those things, however, that pertain the unity of the essence, not those which pertain to the distinction of persons, can be known by natural reason."[30] And Anselm's argument for the necessity of a God-man fails on the

24. See Aquinas, *ST* I, q. 2, a. 3.
25. See Bonaventure, *In sent.* II, d. 1, p. 1, q. 2, arg. 3.
26. Aquinas, *ST* I, q. 46, a. 2 ad 6.
27. See Aquinas, *ST* I, qq. 3–11.
28. Aquinas, *ST* I, q. 2, a. 2 ad 1.
29. see Aquinas, *ST* I, q. 1, a. 7.
30. Aquinas, *ST* I, q. 32, a. 1 c.

straightforward grounds that God could in principle have chosen simply to forgive human beings.[31]

As Aquinas sees it, natural theology, despite not getting us knowledge of the Trinity, nevertheless gets us knowledge of the God of the Bible, the God of Abraham, Isaac, and Jacob. Thus we can correctly identify God simply by means of a sufficient agglomeration of divine attributes. At the end of each of the five ways, Aquinas says something like "and this all call God," or "all understand to be God." This is clearly provisional; it does not make it clear whether Aquinas thinks the end results of the five ways get us knowledge of *who* God is or merely of (in some sense) *what* God is, what kind of thing something that is a God is. But when discussing Romans 1:19–20, Aquinas claims that the merely natural theologians were at fault not necessarily for misidentifying God but only for not paying God the required service:

> That their first guilt was not from ignorance is showed by the fact that they had cognition of God but did not use it for good. For they knew God in two ways. In one way, as a being supereminent over all; and in this way they owed him the glory and honor that is due to supereminent beings. And for this reason they are said to be inexcusable, because "they know God but did not glorify him as God," either because they did not pay him the worship due [to him], or because they imposed a limit on his power and knowledge, taking away something from his power and knowledge. . . . Secondly, they knew him as the cause of all good things. Thus to him was owed thanks in all things, which however they did not pay him, but rather ascribed these good things to their own talent and power.[32]

Here it seems that we have knowledge of God even in the case that we limit God's power and knowledge. (It is not clear to me how many theological errors Aquinas thinks we might make before we simply fail to identify God at all.)

By far the most highly developed attempt at natural theology in the Middle Ages can be found in Duns Scotus. Scotus formulates a modal argument that has elements of both cosmological and ontological arguments. Scotus rejects the physical argument from change or motion, since he holds it to

31. See Aquinas, *ST* III, q. 1, a. 2.

32. Aquinas, *Super epistolam beati Pauli ad Romanos lectura*, c. 1, lect. 7.

be false that nothing is a self-mover,[33] and in any case the argument from motion would not allow one to arrive at the notion of a first *being*, rather than merely a first mover.[34] The subject of metaphysics is not God, as Averroes held, but being; one of the functions of this science is to demonstrate the existence of God.[35] Scotus lays out his arguments as a premise and sequence of conclusions. At each stage he shows how the conclusion follows from the previous one:

(P) "Something can be produced (*est effectibilis*)."[36]

(C1) "Some nature among beings can cause an effect (*est effectiva*)."[37]

(C2) "Something able to produce an effect is simply first."[38]

(C3) "What is able to cause effectively is simply first, because it is itself incapable of being caused."[39]

(C4) "A being able to exercise efficient causality which is simply first actually exists."[40]

Scotus argues from (C1) to (C2) by noting that some causal series are transitive—specifically, those in which a cause causes an effect to cause a further effect.[41] According to Scotus, such transitive causal series always have a causation-deficit: each member of such a series is "dependent,"[42] and thus "the whole series of dependents . . . is dependent . . . upon something which is not one of the group."[43] Scotus does not mention the impossibility of an infinite regress of causes in this totality: so presumably he holds that

33. See Scotus, *In libros metaphysicorum* 9, q. 14; in *Opera philosophica*, 5 vols., ed. G. Etzkorn et al. (St. Bonaventure, NY: Franciscan Institute, 1997–2006).

34. See Scotus, *In libros metaphysicorum* 6, q. 4, nn. 4–5.

35. See Scotus, *In libros metaphysicorum* 6, q. 4, nn. 1–3.

36. Scotus, *De primo principio* 3.5; ed. and trans. Allan B. Wolter, *A Treatise on God as First Principle* (Chicago, IL: Franciscan Herald Press, 1982), 42.

37. Scotus, *De primo principio* 3.4; trans. Wolter, 42.

38. Scotus, *De primo principio* 3.7; trans. Wolter, 44.

39. Scotus, *De primo principio* 3.16; trans. Wolter, 50.

40. Scotus, *De primo principio* 3.18; trans. Wolter, 50.

41. See Scotus, *De primo principio* 3.11; trans. Wolter, 47.

42. Scotus, *De primo principio* 3.11; trans. Wolter, 46.

43. Scotus, *De primo principio* 3.13; trans. Wolter, 46–48.

the overall dependence claim obtains whether the series has a beginning or is beginningless. (Scotus rejects the possibility of an infinite sequence given that such a sequence is *simultaneous*, on the grounds that "no philosopher assumes" a temporally simultaneous infinite set.[44])

The crucial step is the move to (C4):

> Proof of this [C4]: Anything to whose nature (*rationi*) it is repugnant to receive existence from something else, exists of itself if it is able to exist at all. To receive existence from something else is repugnant to the very notion of a being which is first in the order of efficiency [from C3]. . . . And it can exist [from C2].[45]

So the argument to (C2) is supposed to show that it is possible that there is a first cause. The argument to (C3) is supposed to show that any first cause is necessarily uncausable. And the argument to (C4) is supposed to show if it is possible that something is necessarily uncausable, then it is necessary that something is necessarily uncausable. So the argument turns into a complex variation of an Anselm-style argument; the cosmological component provides the attempt to demonstrate the possibility-condition required for such an argument to go through.

Scotus goes on to develop a complex argument in favor of the Trinity of persons. It requires taking rather literally the thought that the Son proceeds as a mental word and the Holy Spirit as an act of love. The idea is that the mind is necessarily productive of two (and only two) kinds of act: cognitive acts and appetitive acts. So God is thus productive. But God is simple, so what is produced cannot be in any accidental category such as quality, as would obtain in the human case. There is only one God, so what is produced cannot be a further god or gods. And there cannot be more than two productions, since there cannot be an actual infinity of divine persons, and there is no way of assigning a maximum to such productions other than if they are individuated by type.[46]

This is quite different from Richard of St. Victor's argument, and Scotus, indeed, vehemently opposes Richard's view. Richard's argument presupposes that it is mutual love of person for person that constitutes inner

44. See Scotus, *De primo principio* 3.13; trans. Wolter, 48.

45. Scotus, *De primo principio* 3.18–19; trans. Wolter, 52.

46. For discussion, see my *Duns Scotus on God*, Ashgate Studies in the History of Philosophical Theology (Aldershot: Ashgate, 2005), part 2.

divine love. Scotus holds that this is false, because the self-love of a divine person is quite as much a perfection as the love of that person for another. And all these forms of love are satisfied on the simpler condition that the divine *essence*, fully in each person, is the object of all divine love. So there is no argument from mutuality to a Trinity of persons.[47]

Having discussed some very optimistic approaches, cataphatic to greater or lesser degrees, I will briefly mention a dissenting voice. Ockham disagrees with the claim that an infinite regress of causes—even in cases that the causal relation is transitive—necessarily suffers from a causation-deficit. So he rejects any argument to a first efficient cause.[48] He is happy, however, with the thought that there must be a being "than which nothing is more noble and more perfect," else there would be infinitely many beings of ever increasing perfection, and an actual infinity, simultaneously actualized, is impossible. But Ockham does not believe that there is an argument to divine unicity: there could be many such perfect beings.[49]

It is perhaps curious that the Middle Ages should have been *par excellence* the age of natural theology. After all, in sharp contrast to their early modern philosophical successors, the medieval philosophers placed no great emphasis on the necessity for the grounds of a belief to be internally accessible to the believer in order for the belief to count as in some way rational—a condition that is, nevertheless, on the face of it satisfied by the deliverances of natural theology, with an emphasis on providing *reasons* for believing in the existence of God. Still, one way of interpreting the medieval theological and philosophical project would see it as an exploration of the limits of human reason; and given this understanding of scholasticism, God's existence, if not God's nature, lies well within such bounds.

Early modern theology

It is no surprise that in various ways the theologians of the Catholic reformation follow their medieval predecessors in all this.[50] But it is perhaps

47. See my *Duns Scotus on God*, 218–19.

48. See Ockham, *Quaestiones in libros Physicorum Aristotelis*, q. 135; in William of Ockham, *Philosophical Writings: A Selection*, ed. Philotheus Boehner and Stephen F. Brown (Indianapolis, IN: Hackett, 1990), 120.

49. Ockham, *Quodlibet* 1, q. 1 (*Philosophical Writings*, 126).

50. A good example is Suárez, who accepts an argument to the existence of God from the principle that "everything that is produced is produced by another" (*Disputationes meta-*

more surprising that their Protestant contemporaries do not reject all natural theology—although, as we shall see, they sharply circumscribe its scope. After all, in popular histories of the Reformation, Luther defined his whole theological program as a challenge to—and, indeed, rejection of—scholastic theology and its supposedly unwarranted trust in natural reason. In fact, however, Luther's innovative approach to natural theology adds a much more subtle nuance to the project of demonstrating God's existence. I will first of all set out his position, and then explain what is novel in it. In a useful essay on the subject, Ilmari Karimies highlights two pertinent texts: the *Lectures on Romans* (1515–16, before any sort of break with the Catholic Church), and the Heidelberg disputation (1518). The relevant parts of these works are both in effect commentaries on Romans 1:19–23.[51]

In the earlier work, Luther outlines two ways in which God is known antecedently to and independently of any kind of revelation. First of all, he holds (in line with Romans 1:19, "God has shown to [human beings what can be known about God]") that human beings have an innate "notion" of God's nature, and know that this notion is instantiated. Thus, human beings, independently of revelation, "hold that divinity is invisible . . . and that he who possesses it is invisible, immortal, powerful, wise, just, and gracious to those who call upon him," and "they hold fast to this idea so that they confess it also by works, by calling upon him, worshiping and adoring him of whom they think that divinity resides in him." This is *a priori*, the "insight of the conscience."[52]

Luther's evidence for this reading of Romans 1:19—as about natural knowledge of God—is that the subsequent verse (Rom 1:20: "Ever since the creation of the world his invisible nature, namely, his eternal power and deity, has been clearly perceived in the things that have been made") is

---

physicae, disp. 29, sect. 1, n. 20 [in *Opera omnia*, 28 vols. (Paris: Vivès, 1857–1878)]), coupled with the impossibility of an infinite regress (see *Disputationes metaphysica*, disp. 29, sect. 1, nn. 25–66). Suárez rejects the argument from motion since no reasoning in the science of physics could lead to the existence of something non-physical (see *Disputationes metaphysicae*, disp. 29, sect. 1, n. 17); and he rejects the ontological argument since we do not have knowledge of the divine essence such that we understand that God's existence "follows from the proper principles" of this essence (*Disputationes metaphysicae*, disp. 29, sect. 3, n. 1).

51. See Ilmari Karimies, "Lutheran Perspective on Natural Theology," *European Journal for Philosophy of Religion* 9 (2017): 119–38.

52. Luther, *Lecture on Romans*, scholium 1; trans Walter G. Tillmans in *Luther's Works*, vol. 25, *Lectures on Romans: Glosses and Scholia*, ed. Hilton C. Oswald (St. Louis, MO: Concordia, 1972), 157.

clearly about natural knowledge of God.[53] But Luther takes this verse itself to support a different kind of natural theology, an *a posteriori* one:

> One can see how one human being helps another, one animal another, yes, how one thing helps and assists another according as it has superior power and ability. At all times the higher and more privileged one helps or suppresses the lower and less privileged one. Therefore, there must be that in the universe which is above all and helps all.[54]

This knowledge of God is *inferential*, not in any sense immediate.

What is important about these two arguments is what Luther thinks they *fail* to achieve. They get us a notion of God's nature, and knowledge that this notion is instantiated. They get us, in other words, knowledge of the nature and existence of God: that there is a being with this nature. But they do not get us knowledge of the *identity* of God as the God of the Bible, the God of Abraham, Isaac, and Jacob. We can capture Luther's insight by attending to a distinction made by philosophers, medieval and modern, between two ways of knowing the content of a proposition. We can have *de dicto* knowledge of the proposition or *de re* knowledge of a proposition. The philosopher Robert B. Brandom offers a very clear account of the distinction:

> There are two ways to read: "Voltaire believes the man from whom Napoleon learned the most about the relations between war and diplomacy was a philosopher-prince." One reading makes this a false claim, the other true. It is false that Voltaire believed the dictum "The man from whom Napoleon learned the most about the relations between war and diplomacy was a philosopher-prince." If you had asked Voltaire, he would have denied that he endorsed this claim; after all, when Voltaire died in 1778, Bonaparte was only nine. In contrast, he would have endorsed the claim: "Frederick the Great was a philosopher-prince." This is a belief about the same *res*, since Frederick the Great was in fact the man from whom Napoleon learned the most about the relations between war and diplomacy. That is, Voltaire really did believe *of* or *about* the man from whom Napoleon learned the most about

53. See Luther, *Lectures on Romans*, scholium 1; *Luther's Works*, 25:156.
54. Luther, *Lectures on Romans*, scholium 1; *Luther's Works*, 25:158.

> the relations between war and diplomacy (namely Frederick the Great) that *he* was a philosopher-prince.[55]

De dicto knowledge is simply knowledge of the truth of a proposition, and in the example Voltaire wrongly believes that the proposition "the man from whom Napoleon learned the most about the relations between war and diplomacy was a philosopher-prince" is false. To have *de re* knowledge of the truth of the proposition, we need to know *who* the man from whom Napoleon learned the most about the relations between war and diplomacy actually was: namely, Frederick the Great.

I noted above that Aquinas believes that natural theology can get us knowledge of the God of the Bible: knowledge of God's *identity*. He believes, in other words, that it gets us both *de dicto* and *de re* knowledge of the proposition that God exists: a being with such-and-such attributes exists (the *de dicto* sense of the proposition), and this being is identified as the God of the Bible, the being with whom Abraham, Isaac, and Jacob interacted (the *de re* sense of the proposition). This distinction enables us to see what is innovative in Luther's approach. Luther thinks that in principle the arguments of natural theology could get us *de re* knowledge of the existence of God. Thus the merely natural theologian could have identified God descriptively, by spelling out the appropriate list of divine attributes, and had the natural theologians done this, "then without a doubt they would have been saved."[56] But they failed to do *merely* this; instead they "erred when they said and claimed: 'Now, this one,' that is, Jupiter or any other who is like this image, 'is of this type'"[57]—is the type of thing, that is to say, that has divine attributes. So that God exists is not known *de re* by the merely natural theologian. Luther's reason for this claim is Romans 1:23 (according to which the natural theologians "exchanged the glory of the immortal God for images resembling mortal man or birds or animals or reptiles"): "This was their error, that they did not worship this divinity untouched but changed and adjusted it to their desires and needs"[58]—with the result that they failed to identify the one God at all: "They worshiped not God but a figment of their own imagination."[59] In making this move, Luther might in addition

55. Robert B. Brandom, *Making It Explicit: Reasoning, Representing, and Discursive Commitment* (Cambridge, MA: Harvard University Press, 1994), 501.

56. Luther, *Lectures on Romans*, scholium 1; *Luther's Works*, 25:157.

57. Luther, *Lectures on Romans*, scholium 1; *Luther's Works*, 25:157.

58. Luther, *Lectures on Romans*, scholium 1; *Luther's Works*, 25:157.

59. Luther, *Lectures on Romans*, scholium 1; *Luther's Works*, 25:158.

be making the stronger claim that the merely natural theologian does not even have *de dicto* knowledge of the proposition that God exists, since they inevitably ascribe divine attributes to pagan deities.

The *Lectures on Romans* does not explain how God might indeed be known *de re*: how, in other words, to avoid the immediate move to idolatry. In the Heidelberg disputation, Luther attempts to plug this gap. Referring to Romans 1:22, he asserts of the merely natural theologian that "someone who discerns the invisible things of God understood through those things which have been made is not worthily called a theologian,"[60] and he contrasts this person with one who does deserve to be called a theologian, someone "who comprehends the visible and manifest things of God seen through suffering and the cross."[61] Knowledge of *Christ* gives *de re* knowledge of God: "He who does not know Christ does not know God hidden in suffering. . . . God can be found only in suffering and the cross."[62]

But just as in the *Lectures on Romans*, Luther does not mean to reject natural theology *tout court*.[63] The relation between the two—between a "theology of glory" and a "theology of the cross," in Luther's novel language post-1517—is, however, a rather delicate matter.[64] Luther's basic instinct in the Heidelberg disputation is to contrast them in a way that parallels exactly his Pauline contrast between the law and grace.[65] In both cases, the former without the latter is harmful. Thus "That wisdom which sees the invisible things of God in works as perceived by man is completely puffed up, blinded, and hardened";[66] and "The law brings the wrath of God, kills, reviles, accuses, judges, and condemns everything that is not in Christ."[67] But both natural theology and the law are fully acceptable in the context of

60. Luther, *Heidelberg Disputation*, th. 19: "Non ille digne Theologus dicitur qui invisibilia Dei per ea quae facta sunt intellecta conspicit," my translation (in Luther, *Werke: Kritische Gesamtausgabe*, 73 vols. [Weimar: Böhlau, 1883–2009], 1:354.17–18). The standard English translation—"The person does not deserve to be called a theologian who looks upon the invisible things of God as though they were clearly perceptible in those things which have actually happened" (in *Luther's Works*, vol. 31, *The Career of the Reformer: I*, ed. and trans. Harold J. Grimm [St. Louis, MO: Concordia, 1957], 52)—introduces a misleadingly negative appraisal absent in Luther's Latin.

61. Luther, *Heidelberg Disputation*, th. 20; *Luther's Works*, 31:52.

62. Luther, *Heidelberg Disputation*, th. 21; *Luther's Works*, 31:53.

63. See Kamires, "Lutheran Perspective," 121–22.

64. For the terminology, see Luther, *Heidelberg Disputation*, th. 21; *Luther's Works*, 31:53.

65. For the terminology, see Luther, *Heidelberg Disputation*, th. 26; *Luther's Works*, 31:56.

66. Luther, *Heidelberg Disputation*, th. 22; *Luther's Works*, 31:53.

67. Luther, *Heidelberg Disputation*, th. 23; *Luther's Works*, 31:54.

revealed theology and grace: "Yet that wisdom is not of itself evil, nor is the law to be evaded; but without the theology of the cross man misuses the best in the worst manner":[68] where "the best" is, respectively, the law and natural theology. Knowledge of God in Christ is what *de facto* allows us to secure *de re* knowledge of God, and thus to ascribe our *de dicto* knowledge of propositions about the divine nature and attributes, derived from natural theology, to the correct item.

We find something a little similar to all this in the final edition of Calvin's *Institutes* (1559)—I assume with Luther's Heidelberg disputation in the back of his mind.[69] Calvin holds that "there is within the human mind, and indeed by natural instinct, a perception of divinity (*sensus divinitatis*)."[70] He also maintains that God's existence and nature can be discerned in creation. But unlike Luther he does not think of this latter process as something inferential. Rather, Calvin repeatedly talks of it as a kind of perception: for example, "this skillful ordering of the universe is for us a sort of mirror in which we can contemplate God, who is otherwise invisible";[71] and

> the Lord manifests himself by his powers, the force of which we feel within ourselves and the benefits of which we enjoy. We must therefore be much more profoundly affected by this knowledge than if we were to imagine a God of whom no perception came through to us. . . . [We] contemplate him in his works whereby he renders himself near and familiar to us, and in some manner communicates himself.[72]

It is not clear to me whether or not Calvin wishes to exclude all inferential knowledge in this context. But it is certainly not his principal focus, and he does not expressly mention it.

Calvin seems to hold, like Luther, that in the absence of revelation this perception is not *de re* perception of an individual. It is in some sense a perception, if not of a *kind*, at any rate not of an individual that the perceiver is in a position to identify. Thus Calvin talks of it as a perception of *divinity*, or of

68. Luther, *Heidelberg Disputation*, th. 24; *Luther's Works*, 31:55.

69. Luther's *Lectures on Romans* was not published until the beginning of the twentieth century.

70. Calvin, *Institutes* 1, c. 3, §1; ed. and trans. Ford Lewis Battles, 2 vols. (Philadelphia, PA: Westminster Press, 1950), 1:43.

71. Calvin, *Institutes* 1, c. 5, §1; trans. Battles, 1:52–53.

72. Calvin, *Institutes* 1, c. 5, §9; trans. Battles, 1:62.

deity.[73] He claims too that what "is naturally inborn in all" is a "conviction . . . that there is some (*aliquem*) God,"[74] and thus, presumably, not that there is *this* God, the God of Abraham, Isaac, and Jacob. Calvin takes Scripture as a whole (and not just the theology of the cross, as in Luther), to fill the epistemic gap:

> Scripture, gathering up the otherwise confused knowledge of God in our minds, having dispersed our dullness, clearly shows us the true God. This, therefore, is a special gift, where God, to instruct the church, not merely uses mute teachers but also opens his own most hallowed lips. Not only does he teach the elect to look upon a god (*aliquem deum*), but also shows himself to be the one upon whom they are to look.[75]

Again, we have the contrast between *de dicto* and *de re* understandings of the claim that God exists (compare "a god" and the "true God [who] . . . shows himself to be the one"). But unlike Luther's approach, Calvin's seems to be highly experiential: to get *de re* knowledge of the claim that God exists we need direct contact with God.

In line with this, Calvin holds that, as a matter of inevitability given the Fall, natural knowledge of God in the absence of revelation leads either to idolatry[76] or (worse) hypocrisy[77], failure to acknowledge at all the existence of a deity who can nevertheless be perceived: a kind of self-deception. In relation to the former, Calvin appeals to Romans 1:21–2, and notes that idolaters "do not therefore apprehend God as he offers himself, but imagine him as they have fashioned him in their own presumption."[78] The similarities to Luther's treatment are striking, despite the various differences in details.

What is distinctive about these accounts in Luther and Calvin, relative to their medieval antecedents, is thus that they refuse to allow that merely natural theology achieves *de re* knowledge of God. This refusal naturally raises second-order questions about the function of natural theology, and both Luther and Calvin take it along Pauline lines as fundamentally laying humans open to just condemnation.[79]

73. Calvin, *Institutes* 1, c. 3, §1.

74. Calvin, *Institutes* 1, c. 3, §3; trans. Battles, 1:46.

75. Calvin, *Institutes* 1, c. 6, §1; trans. Battles, 1:70.

76. Calvin, *Institutes* 1, c. 4, §1–3.

77. See Calvin, *Institutes* 1, c. 4, §4.

78. Calvin, *Institutes* 1, c. 4, §1; trans. Battles, 1:48.

79. See Luther, *Lectures on Romans*, scholium 1 (*Luther's Works*, 25:157); Calvin, *Institutes* 1, c. 5, §14–15.

We find some highly contrasting accounts in the Protestant theologians of the seventeenth century. The foremost Lutheran theologian, Johann Gerhard, for example, repeats the standard *a posteriori* arguments found in the medieval theologians, more or less in the form they appear in Aquinas, whom he cites.[80] Unlike Aquinas, Gerhard holds that merely natural theology is not by itself sufficient for *de re* cognition of God. His reason, however, has nothing to do with the contingencies of the human condition, as in Luther and Calvin. Rather, his argument is that merely natural theology does not get us knowledge of the Trinity, and that such knowledge is necessary not just for salvation but even for *de re* knowledge of God: "The true God thus reveals himself in his Word, that he is one in essence, three in person: Father, Son, and Holy Spirit. Therefore whoever does not know him in this way does not know the true God"—and Gerhard appeals to John 5:23 and elsewhere in support of this.[81] I assume Gerhard ascribes to the central figures in the Hebrew Bible some kind of implicit or explicit knowledge of the Trinity.

Francis Turretin, the most important Genevan theologian of the seventeenth century, seems to reason along more standardly medieval lines. Turretin follows Calvin in supposing that there is both innate and acquired knowledge of God—the latter of which is "gathered from the book of creatures by argument."[82] Among the most significant such arguments are one from efficient causation; a series of versions of Bonaventure's arguments against the impossibility of an eternal world; one from the order of the world; and another from the purposiveness of creation.[83]

Turretin claims that these arguments get us knowledge "that God is" and knowledge of "what God is," including knowledge of the divine "nature and attributes." Knowledge of "who God is" comes about "by reason of the persons."[84] But Turretin does not seem to make knowledge of who God is necessary for *de re* knowledge of God. Thus, he argues that the fundamental purpose of postlapsarian natural theology is that human beings "might be persuaded that God exists and should be religiously worshiped,"[85]

80. Gerhard, *Exegesis* 2, c. 4, §61; in *Theological Commonplaces: On the Nature of God and on the Most Holy Mystery of the Trinity*, ed. Benjamin T. G. Mayes, trans. Richard J. Dinda (St. Louis, MO: Concordia, 2007).

81. Gerhard, *Exegesis* II, c. 4, §82; trans. Dinda, 85.

82. Turretin, *Institutio theologiae elencticae*, loc. 1, q. 3, §8; in *Institutio theologiae elencticae*, 3 vols. (Edinburgh: Lowe: 1847), 1:8 (my translation).

83. Turretin, *Institutio*, loc. 3, q. 1, §§6–12.

84. Turretin, *Institutio*, loc. 3, q. 1, §2 (1:153).

85. Turretin, *Institutio*, loc. 1, q. 3, §3 (1:7).

and claims that not all non-Christian religions are "impious and idolatrous" (which is to say that they lack *de re* knowledge of God); some are merely "false and erroneous" (which, given the contrast with impiety and idolatry, is presumably to say that they correctly identify God but nevertheless make false claims about God).[86] In line with this, Turretin apparently interprets Romans 1:19–20 as asserting that natural theology can get us genuine knowledge of the one God, but not *enough* of it to be salvific,[87] for the basic reason that knowledge of Christ is necessary for salvation.[88]

Early modern philosophy

We find none of these specifically theological considerations in the work of the philosophers. But neither do we find much apologetic content. A good starting point is to consider the well-known argument for God's existence found in Descartes's *Meditations on First Philosophy*:

> It is obvious to anyone who pays close attention that existence can no more be separated from God's essence than its having three angles equal to two right angles can be separated from the essence of a triangle, or than the idea of a valley can be separated from the idea of a mountain. Thus it is no less contradictory to think of God (that is, a supremely perfect being) lacking existence (that is, lacking some perfection), than it is to think of a mountain without a valley. . . . From the fact that I cannot think of God except as existing, it follows that existence is inseparable from God and that for this reason he really exists.[89]

Clearly, Descartes lacks the premise whose need was so clearly spotted by Scotus: that the argument requires that God's existence is possible. But more interesting than this is the difference from the theologians in terms of motivation and context. The aim of the *Meditations* is "to establish [something] firm and lasting in the sciences"—which is to say, to establish firm and lasting knowledge.[90] Descartes has a strikingly narrow criterion for knowledge, and,

86. Turretin, *Institutio*, loc. 1, q. 4, §2 (1:10).

87. See Turretin, *Institutio*, loc. 1, q. 4, §8.

88. See Turretin, *Institutio*, loc. 1, q. 4, §4.

89. René Descartes, *Meditation Five*; in *Meditations, Objections, and Replies*, ed. and trans. Roger Ariew and Donald Cress (Indianapolis, IN: Hackett, 2006), 37.

90. Descartes, *Meditation One*; trans. Ariew and Cress, 9.

indeed, for rational belief: "Reason now persuades me that I should withhold my assent no less carefully from opinions that are not completely certain and indubitable than I would from those that are patently false."[91] According to Descartes, I am not permitted to believe what I am not certain of. As is well known, Descartes holds that I can on the face of it reasonably doubt everything apart from my own existence as a thinking substance. Descartes's ontological argument is offered as a means of grounding my knowledge (in this narrow sense) of the external world: "Once I perceived that there is a God, and also understood at the same time that everything else depends on him and that he is not a deceiver, I then concluded that everything that I clearly and distinctly perceive is necessarily true."[92] We can be certain that we are not being systematically deceived; and thus we can be certain that the external world exists, as it seems to us to do. Obviously, in this context an *a posteriori* argument is not possible, since Descartes's aim is to appeal to God to ground his knowledge of the external world, not vice versa.

Descartes offers a second argument too, again a kind of *a priori* argument. He notes that ideas, as "not nothing," require causes.[93] Ideas of finite objects could have as their cause the finite human mind. But the idea of an infinite object could not:

> I understand by the name "God" a certain substance that is infinite, independent, supremely intelligent and supremely powerful, and that created me along with everything else that exists—if anything else exists. Indeed all these are such that, the more carefully I focus my attention on them, the less possible it seems they could have arisen from myself alone. Thus, from what has been said, I must conclude that God necessarily exists. For although the idea of substance is in me by virtue of the fact that I am a substance, that fact is not sufficient to explain my having the idea of an infinite substance, since I am finite, unless this idea proceeded from some substance which really was infinite.[94]

Descartes's motivation in both of these arguments is purely philosophical: a meditation on epistemology. Leibniz's motivation is equally ambitious, but in relation to a different area of philosophy: metaphysics. What Leibniz

91. Descartes, *Meditation One*; trans. Ariew and Cress, 9.
92. Descartes, *Meditation Five*; trans. Ariew and Cress, 37.
93. Descartes, *Meditation Three*; trans. Ariew and Cress, 23.
94. Descartes, *Meditation Three*; trans. Ariew and Cress, 25.

aims at is the formulation of a universal system of concepts in which we could in principle deduce the nature of the universe from the concepts of God and the divine attributes, concepts that Leibniz takes to be maximally simple. Clearly, this analysis requires that God exists, and Leibniz offers both *a priori* and *a posteriori* arguments in favor of this latter claim. Both arguments bear more than a passing resemblance to Scotus's, and perhaps both Leibniz's and Scotus's have their ultimate origin in Avicenna.[95]

Leibniz reports Descartes's ontological argument, and notes of the reasoning as found in Descartes "that the most you can draw out of this argument is that if God is possible, it follows that he exists."[96] He characterizes Descartes's claim to demonstrate God as an argument "that has already been rejected by Thomas Aquinas."[97] As Leibniz sees it, what is missing is an argument to show that God is possible. So Leibniz devotes some attention to the project of proving this. He adopts three basic approaches. The simplest is merely to maintain what we might call the "priority" of the possible: "There is always a presumption on the side of possibility, that is, everything is held to be possible until its impossibility is proved."[98] The second starts from the thought that the divine attributes are simples: "All the simple forms are compatible with each other. . . . If [this] proposition is granted, it follows that God's nature, which contains all the simple forms taken absolutely, is possible."[99] The final argument starts from the assumption of divine limitlessness:

> God alone, or the necessary being, has the privilege of necessarily existing if he is possible. And since nothing can prevent the possibility of that which is without any limits, without any negation, and consequently without any contradiction, this fact alone suffices to know the existence of God *a priori*.[100]

95. For Avicenna's argument for a necessary existent, see e.g. Jon McGinnis, *Avicenna*, Great Medieval Thinkers (New York: Oxford University Press, 2009), 160–68.

96. Gottfried Wilhelm Leibniz, "Meditations on Knowledge, Truth, and Ideas," in Gottfried Wilhelm Leibniz, *Philosophical Papers and Letters*, ed. and trans. Leroy E. Loemker, 2nd ed., Synthese Historical Library 2 (Dordrecht: Reidel, 1976), 292–93.

97. Leibniz, "Meditations on Knowledge, Truth, and Ideas," in *Philosophical Papers and Letters*, 293.

98. Leibniz, "Letter to Princess Elisabeth," in *Proofs of God in Early Modern Europe: An Anthology*, ed. and trans. Lloyd Strickland (Waco, TX: Baylor University Press, 2018), 114.

99. Leibniz, "Letter to Princess Elisabeth," 116.

100. Leibniz, "Monadology," §45, in *Philosophical Papers and Letters*, 647.

Sadly, Leibniz never develops any of these ideas further.

Ontological arguments are, obviously, modal in character. The same is the case for Leibniz's *a posteriori* argument. In it, Leibniz appeals to the so-called "principle of sufficient reason" particularly associated with himself and, earlier, Spinoza: "That there can be found no fact that is true or existent, or any true proposition, without there being a sufficient reason for its being so and not otherwise":[101]

> Besides the world or aggregate of finite things, there is a certain One which is dominant. . . . For a sufficient reason for existence cannot be found merely in any one individual thing or even in the whole aggregate and series of things. . . . Every subsequent state is somehow copied from the preceding one (although according to certain laws of change). No matter how far we may have gone back to earlier states, therefore, we will never discover in them a full reason why there should be a world at all, and why it should be such as it is. . . . Therefore, since there must be an ultimate root in something which has metaphysical necessity, and since there is no reason for an existing thing except in another existing thing, there must necessarily exist some one being of metaphysical necessity, or a being to whose essence belongs existence.[102]

A necessary being is one whose non-existence "implies a contradiction," such that the sufficient reason for its existence is simply its "necessity or essence itself."[103] (Leibniz sometimes talks of such a being as something "for which no reason can be given."[104]) Things other than such a necessary being—that is to say, contingent things—do not include their own sufficient reasons. Neither does the aggregate of such things, considered synchronically or diachronically ("every subsequent state is somehow copied from the preceding one"). So, as Leibniz notes, eternity and contingency are compatible: "We cannot escape an ultimate extramundane reason for things, or

101. Leibniz, "Monadology," §32, in *Philosophical Papers and Letters*, 646.

102. Leibniz, "On the Ultimate Origination of Things," in *Philosophical Papers and Letters*, 486–87.

103. Leibniz, "On the Ultimate Origination of Things," in *Philosophical Papers and Letters*, 486.

104. Leibniz, "On the Ultimate Origination of Things," in *Philosophical Papers and Letters*, 487.

God, even by assuming the eternity of the world."[105] Even an aggregate of contingent things everlasting in the past is itself contingent.

Both of these arguments rely on the claim that God is a necessary existent. The final thinker I shall consider—Kant—attempts to undermine both of Leibniz's arguments by the simple expedient of denying the possibility of a necessary existent.[106]

Kant tries a number of interrelating strategies to show this.[107] One is that positing the non-existence of something can never amount to positing a contradiction, since contradiction arises only in those predications in which the predicate "cancels" or negates something included in the subject. Even if existence is included in the subject ("its existence was comprehended within the range of its meaning"[108]), no contradiction results from canceling both subject and predicate: "If you cancel its existence, then you cancel the thing along with its predicates; where then is the contradiction supposed to come from?"[109]

A second argument makes use of the semantic distinction between analytic and synthetic propositions. An analytic proposition is one which is true simply in virtue of the meaning of its terms; a synthetic proposition is one which is not analytic. Existential predications cannot be analytic, Kant reasons, since if they were "existence would add nothing to the thought of the thing," and in this case either "the thought in you is the thing itself, or else you have presupposed an existence as belonging to possibility, and then inferred that existence on this pretext from its inner possibility, which is nothing but a miserable tautology."[110] The latter option here is not wholly clear. The idea seems to be that if existence is built into a concept (perhaps resulting in the concept *existing-thing*, or something like that), then stating that this concept is realized will amount to nothing more than a tautology: "An existing thing exists." And this is supposed to show, in turn, the absurdity of supposing that there could be an analytic existential proposition. We cannot get from a *concept's* inclusion of existence to the *real* existence of something in the world.

105. Leibniz, "On the Ultimate Origination of Things," in *Philosophical Papers and Letters*, 486–87.

106. For the application to the *a posteriori* argument, see Immanuel Kant, *Critique of Pure Reason*, A615/B653 (ed. and trans. Paul Guyer and Allen W. Wood [Cambridge: Cambridge University Press, 1998]).

107. For a recent discussion of these arguments, see Uygar Abacı, *Kant's Revolutionary Theory of Modality* (Oxford: Oxford University Press, 2019), 231–45.

108. Kant, *Critique of Pure Reason*, A594/B622; trans. Guyer and Wood, 565.

109. Kant, *Critique of Pure Reason*, A595/B623; trans. Guyer and Wood, 565.

110. Kant, *Critique of Pure Reason*, A597/B625; trans. Guyer and Wood, 566.

Thirdly, real predicates "add to the concept of a thing." Being does not do this, but merely "posit[s] a thing or . . . certain determinations in themselves."[111] If it added something, then "what would exist would not be the same as what I had thought in my concept, but more than that, and I could not say that the very object of my concept exists."[112] If being, in other words, were a real predicate, it would be impossible for the concept of a thing accurately to represent that thing, since the concept would fail to include a feature possessed by the thing: namely, its existence.

Kant ends on a rather humorous note:

> Thus the famous ontological (Cartesian) proof of the existence of a highest being from concepts is only so much trouble and labor lost, and a human being can no more become richer in insight from mere ideas than a merchant could in resources if he wanted to improve his financial state by adding a few zeros to his cash balance.[113]

The zeros are, I assume, to be placed at the front of the balance. Still, Leibniz may feel that Kant has missed the point. Affirming that God's properties include necessity does not mean that existence itself is a predicate. God's essence includes not existence but necessity, and in any case it might be thought that Kant's arguments presuppose, rather than demonstrate, that existence is not a predicate.

Natural theology has recently flourished in the West, despite Kant's criticisms—from which we might reasonably infer that not all philosophers and theologians have regarded these objections as evidently successful. A standard position simply denies that Kant has shown that all real existence is contingent.[114] A more radical approach has been adopted by others—notably, Richard Swinburne, who maintains that all real existence, including God's, is contingent, in the Leibnizian sense that neither it nor its denial implies a contradiction. In line with this, Swinburne appeals to properties other than necessity to support an argument for God's existence: in Swinburne's case, the explanatory power of simplicity.[115]

111. Kant, *Critique of Pure Reason*, A598/B626; trans. Guyer and Wood, 567.

112. Kant, *Critique of Pure Reason*, A600/B628; trans. Guyer and Wood, 567–68.

113. Kant, *Critique of Pure Reason*, A602/B630, trans. Guyer and Wood, 569.

114. See for instance Robert M. Adams, "Has It Been Proved that All Real Existence Is Contingent?," *American Philosophical Quarterly* 8 (1971): 284–91.

115. See Richard Swinburne, *The Existence of God*, 2nd ed. (Oxford: Oxford University Press, 2004).

4. Natural Theology in Modern Russian Religious Thought

PAUL L. GAVRILYUK

Introduction

Mikhail Bulgakov (1891–1940) opens his novel *The Master and Margarita* with a dialogue between two Soviet literati, a journal editor and a poet. The editor has commissioned the poet to write an anti-religious poem about Jesus, but the poet has not delivered the expected product. According to the editor, his colleague has failed to impress upon his readers that the Gospels are fables and that Jesus never existed at all. Their conversation is soon joined by the Devil, who has just arrived in Moscow disguised as a foreign tourist and a specialist in black magic. Having ascertained that the editor and the poet deny the existence of a historical figure called Jesus, the Devil inquires: "Forgive my intrusiveness, but is it true that in addition to denying the existence of Jesus, you also do not believe in God, do you? . . . I swear, I will not tell anyone." The editor, who is more versed in religious matters than the poet, replies: "Yes, we do not believe in God, but one may speak of this with complete freedom." Having been assured, to his great delight, that he has arrived in a country of widespread atheism, the Devil probes further: "I have to ask you, what are we to do about the five commonly known proofs of the existence of God?" The erudite editor replies: "Alas, not one of these proofs is worth anything, and humankind archived them long ago. For you would agree that there can be no proof of the existence of God in the realm of reason." The Devil is ecstatic: "Bravo! You have repeated the thought of my restless old pal, Immanuel. But here is a surprise: having utterly demolished all five arguments, he then played a prank on himself and constructed his own sixth proof!" The editor retorts: "Kant's proof is likewise unpersuasive. Schiller used to say that Kant's considerations could satisfy only slaves and

Strauss simply derided this proof."[1] Undeterred, the Devil proceeds to offer a proof of his own.

Bulgakov's acquaintance with natural theology, particularly the arguments for the existence of God (and their rebuttals), has to do with his upbringing: he was born into the family of a history professor who taught at the Kiev Theological Academy, which was one of the four elite graduate schools of theology in the pre-revolutionary Russian Empire (the other three were the academies of St. Petersburg, Moscow, and Kazan).[2] At the turn of the twentieth century, Orthodox theological schools boasted a well-established tradition of natural theology, which spread beyond the seminary walls and found a growing circle of readers. Unfortunately, this tradition remains largely unknown not only among non-Orthodox philosophers of religion, but also among scholars steeped in the Orthodox tradition. In Russia and Ukraine, scholars are only beginning to recover the Orthodox academic tradition of natural theology, which was "archived" for nearly a century.

My historical case for natural theology in modern Russian religious thought will proceed in two main steps. First, I will show that there was a well-developed, but largely forgotten trend of classical natural theology in the pre-revolutionary Russian Orthodox theological academies. For the purpose of this essay, I have chosen the three most outstanding representatives of this trend: Fiodor Aleksandrovich Golubinskii (1797–1854), Viktor Dmitrievich Kudriavtsev-Platonov (1828–1891), and Viktor Ivanovich Nesmelov (1863–1937). Second, I will consider the religious philosophy of all-unity associated with Vladimir Sergeevich Solovyov (1853–1900) and his followers, Sergius Nikolaevich Bulgakov (1871–1944) and Semen Liudvigovich Frank (1877–1952). Setting aside the arguments of classical natural theology, the first two representatives of this trend, Solovyov and S. Bulgakov, developed a theologically-informed philosophy of nature grounded in religious expe-

1. Mikhail Bulgakov, *Master i Margarita* (Sankt-Petersburg: Izdatel'stvo Azbuka, 1999), 10–12 (my translation; unless otherwise noted, all translations from Russian are my own). English translation by Mirra Ginsburg, *The Master and Margarita* (New York, NY: Grove Press, 1995).

2. According to Patrick Lally Michelson, "In sheer numbers, ranging from faculty members and graduates to publications and outreach programmes, it was the Church's four clerical academies, more so than the salons and societies of capital-city Russia, that constituted the centre of Russian Orthodox thought in the century leading up to the revolutions of 1917." See "Russian Orthodox Thought in the Church's Clerical Academies," in Caryl Emerson et al., eds., *The Oxford Handbook of Russian Religious Thought* (Oxford, UK: Oxford University Press, 2020), 94–110, at 95.

rience. As for Frank, while sharing Bulgakov's reservations concerning the methods of classical natural theology, he nevertheless offered an original version of the ontological argument. I conclude by comparing the general features of these two trends. I also discuss the implications that the recovery of Russian philosophical theism, especially its tradition of natural theology, has for present-day Orthodox theology.

I limit my historical inquiry to the nineteenth century and the first half of the twentieth century. This tumultuous period begins with Orthodoxy as a majority religion and the Orthodox Church as a protected state institution in the Russian Empire. The period ends with atheism in its Marxist-Leninist form established as an official state ideology and the Church nearly destroyed in the Empire's successor, the Soviet Union. In such circumstances, the historical context in which a particular type of natural theology or a-theology was proffered could become a matter of life and death. This Soviet context was profoundly different from that of the Russian Empire prior to the Bolshevik Revolution of October 1917.

Setting the Context: Philosophy in Nineteenth-Century Russia

The process of secularization began in Russia with the reign of Peter the Great in the early eighteenth century. Secularization affected primarily the upper classes and the emerging intellectual elites, rather than the peasantry, which generally remained religious. The Russian aristocracy and literary elites experienced the influence of Voltaire and other Freethinkers, and through them became familiar with the Western forms of deism, pantheism, materialism, and atheism. Generally speaking, skepticism and agnosticism, especially of the Humean type, have not been particularly attractive to Russian intellectuals. This is important to keep in mind since so much of contemporary Anglo-American natural theology engages predominantly skeptical and agnostic concerns, and is less focused on militant atheism or dogmatic materialism motivated by moral and political concerns for the remaking of society.

Even more importantly, Russia did not experience the Reformation and the subsequent intra-Christian wars of religion, which in turn led to the development of legislation in the direction of increasing religious tolerance. During the Enlightenment, such legislation searched for its ground in "natural religion," generic theism, and deism, for which there was no comparable political and legal demand in Russia. For example, when in 1769 a philosophy professor at Moscow State University published a dissertation on natural religion, the government responded by burning his work on the charges of atheism.[3] While such extreme measures were sporadic, the Russian Orthodox Church regularly used the power of the state to persecute and suppress other religious groups and anti-religious ideas.

In the first half of the nineteenth century, the best philosophy in Russia was done in the Orthodox theological academies (graduate schools of theology), rather than in the universities. Philosophy professorships were introduced into the academies with the provision that the holders of such positions could not profess anything undermining the central teachings of the Orthodox Church.[4] In addition to logic and metaphysics, academic curricula began to include classical natural theology, often referred to as "philosophical theism." By classical natural theology, I mean sustained reflection on the generally observable features of the world, which leads to sustained reflection on the existence, nature, and agency of one God, whose properties include some of the following: transcendence, immateriality, necessary existence, primary cause, perfect goodness, omniscience, omnipotence, simplicity, impassibility, and so on.[5] This type of natural theology is *classical* for three reasons: it (a) proceeds by way of deductive or inductive arguments and (b) concludes to the existence of the God of classical theism (c) without recourse to special divine revelation. The philosopher who introduced a robust version of classical theism into the educational system of the Russian Orthodox Church was Archpriest Fiodor Golubinskii.[6]

3. The case of Anichkov, as discussed in Vasily V. Zenkovsky, *Istoriia russkoi filosofii* (Leningrad: Ego, 1991), 1.1:117–18. English translation by George L. Kline, *A History of Russian Philosophy*, 2 vols. (London, UK: Routledge & Kegan Paul, 1953).

4. Georges Florovsky, *Puti russkogo bogosloviia*, 3rd ed. (Paris: YMCA Press 1937/1983), 237–38. English translation by Robert L. Nichols, *The Ways of Russian Theology*, 2 vols. (Vaduz: Büchervertriebsanstalt, 1987).

5. My working definition of "classical natural theology" agrees with that of Richard Swinburne in this volume.

6. I highlight Golubinskii's contribution because of his impact on nineteenth-century Orthodox theological education in Russia. I do not thereby wish to ignore or underestimate the important contributions of his predecessors, including the Ukrainian religious philosopher Georgii Savvich Skovoroda (1722–1794).

Fiodor Golubinskii: integrating natural theology into the seminary curriculum

Born into the family of an Orthodox clergyman, Golubinskii followed his father's path by attending an Orthodox seminary in his hometown of Kostroma. In 1814, he matriculated at the newly founded Moscow Theological Academy. While he majored in natural sciences, he also studied the history of philosophy under V. I. Kutnevich, who introduced him to contemporary German philosophy, especially Immanuel Kant. Recognizing his student's potential, Kutnevich retained Golubinskii as his teaching assistant. Golubinskii went on to become a professor of philosophy in his own right and remained at the Academy until his death in 1854. During his tenure, Golubinskii developed a two-year course in philosophy, which included epistemology, metaphysics, and natural theology, which he preferred to call "speculative theology."[7]

In his brief excursus into the history of natural theology, Golubinskii states that in patristic thought and in Western medieval scholasticism, natural and revealed theology were often mixed together, inasmuch as the scholastics appealed to the authority of Scripture and the Church Fathers in addition to purely rational arguments. According to Golubinskii, natural theology was first clearly differentiated from revealed theology during the time of Descartes.[8] Among the most outstanding proponents of classical natural theology, Golubinskii noted François Fénelon, Pierre Poiret, Gottfried Leibniz, and Christian Wolff. The Russian philosopher himself was particularly influenced by the ideas of Friedrich Jacobi.

Golubinskii's main contribution to Russian religious thought consists in synthesizing the eighteenth-century European natural theology and rearticulating it in response to materialist and idealist critique in the context of the Russian Orthodox theological academy. The materialist teachings that he criticized included those of Jean d'Alembert, Denis Diderot, Claude Helvé-

7. Golubinskii translated his preferred expression "speculative theology" into Latin as *theologia rationalis seu naturalis* ("rational or natural theology"). See F. A. Golubinskii, *Lektsii filosofii, umozritel'noe bogoslovie*, 4 vols. (Moscow: Tipografiia Snegireva, 1886), 4:4. The lectures were published posthumously in various editions. For the use of the adjectives "rational," "general," "fundamental," and "natural" as qualifying "theology" see N. P. Rozhdestvenskii, "Istoricheskii ocherk razvitiia khristianskoi apologetiki ili osnovnogo bogosloviia," *Khristianskoe chtenie* 7–8 (1883): 74–101, esp. 100.

8. Golubinskii, *Lektsii filosofii, umozritel'noe bogoslovie*, 4:10. On the origins of natural theology, see the introduction to this volume.

tius, and Voltaire. Golubinskii was also widely read in German philosophy and particularly grappled with the Kantian objections to natural theology. Golubinskii defined natural theology as "systematic knowledge of God, i.e. of his existence, properties, and actions, which can be obtained under the guidance of the ideas of the mind by means of observations from inner and outer experience."[9] In addition to properly functioning mental powers, the knowledge of God requires purification, attunement, and focus of the volitional and affective powers of the self. The inner experience has to do with the observation of the inner powers of the soul, such as the voice of conscience. Following the tradition leading back to Anselm and developed by Descartes and Leibnitz, Golubinskii held that prior to experience, humans find in their minds the idea of the Infinite. This idea cannot be derived from observing the physical world (outer experience) since everything in this world is finite. It is the idea of the Infinite that "leads us to seek an all-perfect being, which is the origin, prototype, and purpose of every perfection."[10] In other words, the idea of the Infinite guides the mind from the traces of the Infinite found in the external world to the existence, properties, and actions of God. According to Golubinskii, the purpose of natural theology is to find in the human spirit and in nature the confirmation of the truths of faith and revelation. Such a confirmation is especially important for communicating the revealed teaching to others.[11]

Most humans possess some awareness of the divine power, although such awareness is often vague, unstable, and uncertain. In order to render this awareness clearer, more permanent and certain, natural theology has recourse to the proofs of the existence of God. Such proofs are not a substitute for immediate awareness or for religious faith, but they may provide rational support for the doubtful and ammunition against atheists. Golubinskii is the first Russian philosopher to formally discuss the proofs, generally following the arguments that were common in the literature of his time: ontological, cosmological, physico-teleological (design), and Kant's ethico-teleological, adding to this list also the arguments from the general consensus of nations, from the highest needs of the human soul, and from the activity of God in the soul. The discussion of each argument is given a separate section, which includes the argument's different formulations, a survey of its intellectual history, major objections, and concludes with rebuttals of the objections.

9. Golubinskii, *Lektsii filosofii, umozritel'noe bogoslovie*, 4:14.
10. Golubinskii, *Lektsii filosofii, umozritel'noe bogoslovie*, 4:18.
11. Golubinskii, *Lektsii filosofii, umozritel'noe bogoslovie*, 4:21.

Golubinskii discusses the ontological argument in its classical Anselmian form (God is that than which nothing greater can be thought; if God exists only in the mind and not in reality, it is possible to conceive of something greater than God, which is a contradiction; therefore, God exists both in the mind and in reality) and its later versions. Golubinskii refutes the Kantian objection that existence is not a great-making property by observing that Anselm himself did not regard existence as a property, but considered it a substratum of all properties. If the infinitely perfect being exists only in the human mind, such an idea would be circumscribed by the human mind and, therefore, would be limited at least in one respect by not being an actual being, but only a possible being.

As in the case of the ontological argument, Golubinskii discusses various historical forms of the cosmological argument. The first premise of the cosmological argument is that there exists something rather than nothing. All existent things are contingent, rather than necessary: it is possible for anything to be thought of as non-existent and there was a time when a particular thing did not exist. Since the same consideration is applicable to the world as a whole, there was a time when there was nothing. Since out of nothing comes nothing, there has to be a non-contingent or necessary being. It may be objected that the chain of contingent causes may itself be infinite, even if each link in the chain is finite. However, in the absence of a first cause to start a causal chain, there will not be any intermediate causes to continue the chain. Golubinskii also overturns the materialist view that a material substance brought the world into existence. His general point is that a part cannot account for all features of the whole and that a divine being cannot be a part of the world, but has to transcend it. Similar to the ontological argument, the cosmological argument points to the existence of the Infinite being, the idea of which is innate to humans, as we saw earlier.

The physico-teleological argument proceeds from the order, connection, and harmony of various parts of the physical world. The attunement of the various parts of a complex organism and of the various parts of the physical world is a highly improbable event, if such attunement is to be attributed to pure chance. The principle of the world's order cannot be a part of the world, since such a partial principle would only be able to account for a particular part of the world rather than the world at large. Hence, there has to be a wise architect or designer, whose mind ordered all things. Golubinskii concedes that the argument leaves space for the conclusion that such a designer is not perfect or that the designer is not the creator of the world out of nothing. He rules out such alternatives by suggesting that the teleological argument needs to be taken in tandem with the cosmological argument (which establishes that God as the primary cause and the necessary being created the world out of nothing) and the innate idea of the Infinite Being, which is clarified by the ontological argument.

The argument from the general consensus of humankind is based on the observation that all nations have at least some form of religious practice. Even if some practices, such as Alaskan native shamanism, are questionable from the Christian point of view, no nation or state, taken as a whole, professed atheism in Golubinskii's time. The universal character of religious practice points to the existence in the human soul of a disposition to believe in a divine power, even if the associated beliefs may be confused or erroneous. For Golubinskii, the argument from the general consensus of humankind established that the seeds of faith are present in all human beings. Given favorable circumstances, such seeds could be cultivated and the associated beliefs purified.

A related matter is the presence in the human soul of such lofty aspirations as the desire for truth, holiness, and true happiness. These desires would be frustrated if they did not find their fulfillment in God, who is the sum of all perfections, including truth itself, holiness itself, and blessedness. These desires cannot be properly and fully satisfied by the physical world, but only by life with God, who is infinite perfection.[12] Specifically, as Kant pointed out, the fulfillment of one's moral duty often comes at the expense of self-sacrifice and suffering; the life of virtue is not always rewarded with happiness in this life. In order to assure the certainty of such a reward, it is necessary to postulate eternal life with God, in which there is a perfect harmony between virtue and happiness, to be enjoyed by the blessed. Golubinskii accepts this argument, but rejects Kant's contention that morality is the foundation of religion and that only the ethico-teleological argument is valid.

For Golubinskii, "among the empirical proofs of the existence of God, the strongest one is the awareness of God's action in oneself, when the person leads a life worthy of God."[13] When one feels God acting upon one's heart, no other proof is necessary. "As the sensual person cannot doubt the existence of air, because he constantly breathes it in and out, the spiritual person cannot doubt the existence of God, when he draws his higher life

12. Golubinskii, *Lektsii filosofii, umozritel'noe bogoslovie*, 4:61–65.

13. Golubinskii, *Lektsii filosofii, umozritel'noe bogoslovie*, 4:74.

from God."[14] As we will see in the next section, this important point will be developed by Golubinskii's follower, Viktor Kudriavtsev-Platonov, into an account of spiritual perception.

Having considered the arguments for the existence of God, Golubinskii turned to the discussion of divine properties, making an important attempt at integrating patristic insights into the framework of Western natural theology. Addressing the question of the knowability of God, the Russian philosopher chose the middle ground between the extreme apophaticism of Pseudo-Dionysius and Kant on the one hand and the rationalistic assurance of Eunomius and Hegel on the other hand.[15] As an example, let us consider how Golubinskii approached a distinction between the vulgar and subtle forms of anthropomorphism. Vulgar anthropomorphism consists in ascribing human traits and limitations, such as face or hands, to God. Subtle anthropomorphism consists in ascribing to God human perfections, such as perfect goodness or omnipotence. For radical apophaticism, associated with Pseudo-Dionysius and Kant,[16] both forms of anthropomorphism are problematic, and the subtle form was even more dangerous, as it was easier to confuse God with a mental concept (such as goodness or power) than with a physical image (such as face or hand). Golubinskii rejected radical apophaticism, but accepted subtle anthropomorphism, maintaining that human perfections were to be ascribed to God analogically, not literally. For the justification of the inevitability of subtle anthropomorphism, the Russian philosopher turned to the following statement of Jacobi: "It is necessary for man to anthropomorphize God because God, creating man, theomorphized him; that is, man necessarily represents God anthropomorphically by ascribing to God the essential aspects of his spirit because God made man in his image."[17] This insight would be developed by other Russian religious philosophers, such as Viktor Nesmelov and Sergius Bulgakov.

Golubinskii gives an account of the following divine properties: necessary being, aseity (uncaused existence), immutability, eternity (understood as timelessness), incorporeality, impassibility, omnipresence, omnipotence, omniscience, and so on. These are all attributes of the God of classical theism, which he carefully differentiates from pantheism and deism. His discussion of divine omniscience and foreknowledge is especially detailed.

14. Golubinskii, *Lektsii filosofii, umozritel'noe bogoslovie*, 4:75.

15. Golubinskii, *Lektsii filosofii, umozritel'noe bogoslovie*, 4:80–84.

16. Immanuel Kant, *Lectures on Philosophical Theology*, trans. Allen W. Wood and Gertrude M. Clark (Ithaca, NY: Cornell University Press, 1978), 79.

17. Golubinskii, *Lektsii filosofii, umozritel'noe bogoslovie*, 4:89–90.

God knows changeable things in an unchangeable way; he foreknows the future without predetermining free human actions. God's omniscience also includes his wisdom, which is "the eternal prototype of the world and of the order of all things."[18] This important element of Christian Platonism would receive further development in Russian sophiology.

Golubinskii's discussion of divine agency focuses especially on the creation of the world. He defends a classical theistic account of divine agency against the Spinozist and Hegelian versions of pantheism. The creation of the world is not a necessary unfolding of the divine being, but a free act of the divine will. The world is not eternally contained in God, but is created out of nothing in time.[19]

Golubinskii's presentation of classical natural theology is neither purely derivative, nor particularly original. He is a classical theist, uninterested in the metaphysical revisionism characteristic of German Idealism. However, it would be a mistake to characterize his synthesis of Western natural theology as eclectic. On the contrary, his thought possesses great clarity, unity, and elegance. As a builder of a philosophical culture in Russian theological academies he was among the pioneers, as far as the exposition of classical natural theology was concerned. His philosophical legacy at the Moscow Theological Academy was continued by his most gifted student, Viktor Kudriavtsev-Platonov.

Viktor Kudriavtsev-Platonov: cumulative case argument and religious experience

Upon his retirement from the Moscow Theological Academy in 1854, Golubinskii recommended as his successor his former student, Viktor Kudriavtsev.[20] Similar to Golubinskii, Kudriavtsev was born into a family of an Orthodox priest, received church-affiliated secondary education, and stud-

18. Golubinskii, *Lektsii filosofii, umozritel'noe bogoslovie*, 4:132.

19. Golubinskii, *Lektsii filosofii, umozritel'noe bogoslovie*, 4:169. Golubinskii's critique of Hegelian pantheism drew on the work of the German theistic philosopher Hermann Ulrici, who was also important for Kudriavtsev-Platonov. See Viktoriia E. Lutsenko, "Dukhovno-akademicheskaia filosofiia v Rossii i evropeiskii filosofskii teizm vtoroi poloviny XIX veka" (doctoral dissertation [abstract], Ussuriiskii Gosudarstvennyi Pedagogicheskii Institut, 2008), 12.

20. I. N. Korsunskii, "Biograficheskii ocherk," in Kudriavtsev-Platonov, *Sochineniia*, 3 vols. (Sergiev Posad: Tipografiia A. I. Snegirevoi, 1893), 1:15.

ied at the Moscow Theological Academy from 1848 to 1852. Kudriavtsev's second last name, "Platonov," was given to him at the Academy in honor of the fellowship of Metropolitan Platon (d. 1812), which Kudriavtsev received for academic excellence. Upon graduation, Kudriavtsev accepted an offer to teach at the Academy, a task to which he remained dedicated for nearly four decades, until his death in 1891. His studies in metaphysics, psychology, and natural theology were published in his collected works posthumously in the 1890s and enjoyed a relatively wide readership.

The main significance of Kudriavtsev's work was to make natural theology (he uses the exact Russian equivalent of this expression, *estestvennoe bogolsovie*) broadly acceptable and well-established in nineteenth-century Russian Orthodox theology.[21] Natural theology has a twofold purpose of elucidating theological beliefs and defending those beliefs against the criticism of skeptics and unbelievers. In Kudriavtsev's time, a formidable challenge to religious faith was presented by the reductionist materialism of the natural sciences and positivism, especially as articulated by Auguste Comte.[22] Kudriavtsev's general strategy is to question the limitations of rationalism and empiricism in the study of religion. Specifically, against narrow empiricism, Kudriavtsev argues that the method within a particular domain of knowledge has to be aligned with the object of investigation. The empirical method, appropriate in the natural sciences, does not apply to the study of mathematical or philosophical objects, which transcend experience. The natural sciences themselves are not methodologically self-sufficient, since they operate with assumptions, such as the sufficiency of the empirical method, which themselves are not empirical. Hence, even the natural sciences require the aid of philosophy.[23]

Kudriavtsev endorses the post-Cartesian assumption that metaphysics must be preceded by epistemology. He rejects Kantian objective idealism in favor of critical realism, which locates truth in the correspondence between mental objects and external reality. Kudriavtsev distinguishes critical realism from naïve realism, which holds that mind-independent objects have exactly the same features as humans perceive them to have. In contrast, critical real-

21. See G. D. Pankov, *Filosofskaia apologetika religii: iz istorii pravoslavno-akademicheskoi mysli XIX—nachala XX stoletiia: opyt filosofsko-teologicheskogo obosnovaniia religii: V. D. Kudriavtsev-Platonov, P. Ia. Svetlov, V. I. Nesmelov, M. M. Tareev* (Khar'kov: KhGAK, 2005).

22. Kudriavtsev-Platonov, "Nuzhna li filosofiia?," in *Sochineniia*, 1:120.

23. Kudriavtsev-Platonov, "Metod v filosofii," in *Sochineniia*, 1:204.

ism holds that humans accurately perceive some features of external objects, but not all features.[24]

Kudriavtsev's doctoral dissertation, *The Essence and Origin of Religion* (1871), was a response to the reductionist explanations of religion, especially that of Ludwig Feuerbach and his influential work *The Essence of Christianity* (1841). Having responded to the ancient accounts of religion as a function of human fear or self-interest, Kudriavtsev turned to Feuerbach's theory, which interpreted belief in God as a projection of the human ideal of perfection. Feuerbach noted that divine attributes—perfect goodness, wisdom, omnipotence, and so on—looked suspiciously like infinitely magnified human virtues. As a materialist, Feuerbach accepted only the existence of matter and objects of sense-experience as real. Given these limitations, a god described as a perfect being cannot be real; such a deity must be a figment of the human imagination. Feuerbach concluded that the object of religion was nothing but an idealized human self. Religion is motivated by egotistical desire for self-glorification.[25]

Kudriavtsev responds that Feuerbach's account of religion ignores such crucial religious motivations as self-denial and fear of divine judgment. Feuerbach's theory attributes to humanity a longstanding collective delusion, which renders humans less rational than animals. The fact that a particular object satisfies a strong desire (e.g., that bread satisfies human hunger) does not render this object a mere projection of desire (e.g., hunger cannot be really satisfied by merely imagining bread). On the contrary, the satisfaction of desire must have a cause outside of the human imagination.[26] When we imagine things under normal circumstances (say, without narcotic substances), we have a concomitant awareness of such things as merely imagined, not real. In contrast, throughout history, the object of religion was understood to be real and provided strong incentives for human actions, shaping human societies and institutions.

Kudriavtsev also comments that Feuerbach's presentation of all divine attributes as anthropomorphic does not do justice to classical theism. Such attributes as primary cause, eternity, and infinity are not anthropomorphic. As Descartes noted, the idea of infinity is not a property of any physical or mental object; the human imagination can handle potential infinity (such

24. Kudriavtsev-Platonov, "Metod v filosofii," in *Sochineniia*, 1:218.

25. Kudriavtsev-Platonov, *Religiia, ee sushchnost' i proiskhozhdenie* (Moscow: Katkov and Co., 1871), 28.

26. Kudriavtsev-Platonov, *Religiia, ee sushchnost' i proiskhozhdenie*, 32–33.

as an endless sequence of numbers), but it cannot represent actual infinity. Hence, the source of the idea of actual infinity in our mind is quite mysterious; Descartes argued that this source could only be the infinite God himself, who implanted in humans an innate idea of himself.[27]

Kudriavtsev concurs that the idea of God is found in the depth of the human soul.[28] As evidence for this claim, he notes that religious rituals have been a part of human life since the dawn of humanity. However, human representations of the divine realm are too variegated across cultures to conclude that a clear and distinct idea of divine perfection is innate (as Descartes and his followers would have it). Instead, Kudriavtsev postulates that human awareness of God is a result of God's direct impact upon the human spirit. He jettisons the Kantian limitation that God cannot appear as a subject of any experience. Kudriavtsev accepts Jacobi's contention that the divine Spirit may directly act upon the human spirit or mind. Following Kant and Jacobi, the Russian philosopher distinguishes between reason (German: *Verstand*; Russian: *rassudok*) involved in discursive thinking, and mind (German: *Vernunft*; Russian: *razum*) engaged in rational contemplation. For Jacobi, God is an object of rational contemplation, which he also renders as "spiritual feeling" (*Geistes-Gefühl*).[29] As Jacobi puts it: "We believe in God because we *see* him, although certainly not with our bodily eyes."[30] Following Jacobi, Kudriavtsev also postulates a distinct faculty of the human mind, akin to perception, which is responsible for the direct apprehension of divine reality.

Kudriavtsev is the first Russian philosopher to develop an account of spiritual or inner perception. He was not aware of premodern accounts of spiritual perception and drew primarily on Jacobi and Schleiermacher, although he rejected their versions of fideism.[31] According to Jacobi, since human consciousness can only access things as they appear, not as they are in themselves, the existence of things independent of the human mind is a matter of *faith* rather than rational investigation. Hence, there is a parity between the existence of the objects of sense-perception and the existence of God, who is the object of spiritual perception. Human belief in the existence

27. Kudriavtsev-Platonov, *Religiia, ee sushchnost' i proiskhozhdenie*, 44.

28. Kudriavtsev-Platonov, *Iz chtenii po filosofii religii*, in *Sochineniia*, 2:14.

29. Kudriavtsev-Platonov, *Religiia, ee sushchnost' i proiskhozhdenie*, 133–34.

30. Kudriavtsev-Platonov, *Religiia, ee sushchnost' i proiskhozhdenie*, 126.

31. See Paul Gavrilyuk and Sarah Coakley, eds., *The Spiritual Senses: Perceiving God in Western Christianity* (Cambridge, UK: Cambridge University Press, 2012) and Frederick D. Aquino and Paul Gavrilyuk, eds., *Perceiving Things Divine* (Oxford: Oxford University Press, forthcoming in 2021).

of any object of perception, whether bodily or spiritual, is a matter of faith. As an epistemological realist, Kudriavtsev did not accept an idealist theory of mind. Hence, Kudriavtsev did not see any need to extend the function of faith, which indicated acceptance of the supernatural, to belief in the existence of any external object.

The negative motivation for Jacobi's fideism was Kant's demolition of the classical arguments for the existence of God in *The Critique of Pure Reason*. In his natural theology, Kudriavtsev also grapples with the Kantian objections at great length. While the Russian philosopher concedes that the classical arguments are not deductively valid, he nevertheless insists that when taken cumulatively, the classical arguments play a central role in the rational justification of Christian belief. Kudriavtsev concludes his discussion of the arguments for the existence of God as follows: "While each argument had its faults, when taken together, developed sequentially and considered as mutually complementary, they may be regarded as quite sufficient for the rational justification of the truth of the existence of God as a supremely perfect being, distinct from the world to the extent to which such a justification is possible for human reason."[32]

In what precise sense does Kudriavtsev take the arguments for the existence of God to be complementary? The main reason for complementarity has to do with the fact that the classical arguments are not deductively valid, since their conclusions do not follow from their premises with logical necessity, but are at best inductively valid, since the premises render their conclusions probable, rather than logically necessary. In other words, the conclusion of a classical argument explains its premises in a manner analogous to how a *hypothesis* explains the relevant data. Probability enters the picture either because the data is disputed (e.g., the dispute over whether natural processes are indeed purposeful in the classical argument from design), or because of the explanatory force of rival hypotheses (e.g., materialism vs. theism, or chance vs. intelligent designer).[33] The classical arguments are also complementary because their premises warrant *some* properties of a perfect being, but do not rule out the metaphysical alternatives to classical theism. For example, the premise of the cosmological argument (contingency or change) warrants a conclusion that for there to be anything at all, there has

32. Kudriavtsev-Platonov, "Znachenie dokazatel'stv bytiia Bozhiia," in *Sochineniia*, 2:485–86.

33. Kudriavtsev-Platonov, *Issledovaniia i stat'i po estestvennomu bogosloviiu*, in *Sochineniia*, 2:257.

to be a necessary being. However, such a necessary being could be identified with the world as a whole or with the impersonal ground of the world, thereby leading to pantheism rather than perfect being theism. Kudriavtsev concludes that the cosmological argument needs to be complemented with and followed by the teleological argument, which adds the property of intelligent designer to the property of necessary being. The latter property rules out the metaphysical option of pantheism, which was not ruled out by the premises of the cosmological argument.

Like Golubinskii, Kudriavtsev divides the classical arguments into two main groups: those grounded in outer and inner experience. The cosmological and teleological arguments appeal to the features of the external world or to outer experience; the ontological, epistemological, psychological, and historical arguments appeal to the features of human consciousness or to inner experience. According to Kudriavtsev, the arguments from inner experience are closely connected and build upon each other. As he explains:

> The idea of God, considered in itself and independently, gives us the *ontological* argument; when we turn our attention to the significance of this idea for knowledge, this gives us the *epistemological* argument; the idea's origination in our mind gives us the *psychological* argument; the idea's universality gives us the *historical* argument; and the idea's connection with moral consciousness gives us the *moral* argument for the existence of God. As we shall see, all of these proofs are closely and organically connected, representing proper degrees of increasingly precise definition and understanding of God.[34]

The ontological argument begins with the idea of God as infinite perfection and concludes that such an idea has to exist both in the mind and in reality, if it is not to be contradictory. The epistemological argument starts with the premise that the operation of cognition necessarily includes the acquisition of true beliefs. Such acquisition, in turn, depends on reliable cognitive capacities. In the Cartesian form of this argument, epistemological skepticism concerning our cognitive capacities (e.g., that our senses may deceive us or, more precisely, lead reason to form false beliefs) is addressed by postulating that God, who created both ourselves and the external world, cannot deceive us. The existence of *one* creator of human consciousness and

34. Kudriavtsev-Platonov, *Issledovaniia i stat'i po estestvennomu bogosloviiu*, in *Sochineniia*, 2:257 (emphasis in the original).

the external world explains why the structure of consciousness corresponds to the structure of reality.[35] Kudriavtsev notes that if the idea of God is nothing but a result of a rational argument, then radical skepticism will subject to doubt such conclusions as a part of the same unreliable process of cognition. However, if the idea of God is a result of God's direct action upon the human mind, then radical skepticism is avoided. Thus, Kudriavtsev's theory of spiritual perception plays a crucial explanatory role in his version of the epistemological argument.[36]

To strengthen the case for the possibility of God's direct action upon the human mind, Kudriavtsev turns to the psychological argument. As originally formulated by Descartes, the argument starts with a premise that is nearly identical with the first premise of the ontological argument: We find in the human mind a concept of infinite and perfect being. Such a concept is not a mere negation of limitation and imperfection. No finite thing in the external world and no feature of consciousness, such as imagination, could cause such an idea in us, since all external things and powers of the self are finite. Hence the concept of the infinite being in human consciousness had to be formed by the infinite being itself. This conclusion of the psychological argument makes room for the hypothesis that God can directly act upon the human mind.

The historical argument or the argument from the universal consensus of humankind is, by Kudriavtsev's admission, the weakest. The reason for this is that it is difficult to verify whether such a consensus exists and even more difficult to ascertain, given the variety of religious beliefs and practices, just what is it that all people agree upon concerning religion.

Kudriavtsev considers the moral argument for the existence of God at great length. He finds the Kantian version of the argument—postulating the existence of God, the immortal soul, and eternal life as a way of reconciling a virtuous life with a happy life—unpersuasive. Instead, Kudriavtsev replaces the Kantian form of the argument with an argument from degrees of perfection. Humans find themselves striving for truth, goodness, and happiness. This striving could otherwise be described as an aspiration to attain perfection. This aspiration, unattainable in this life, would remain a fantasy

35. Kudriavtsev-Platonov, *Issledovaniia i stat'i po estestvennomu bogosloviiu*, in *Sochineniia*, 2:321. Kudriavtsev notes that the existence of truth as an evaluation of true/false propositions is inexplicable in materialism, according to which cognition is a chemical material process indistinguishable from any other chemical process in nature (323–24).

36. Kudriavtsev-Platonov, *Issledovaniia i stat'i po estestvennomu bogosloviiu*, in *Sochineniia*, 2:312.

in the absence of a reality to which this aspiration could correspond. This reality is a perfect being in whose properties humans can participate. While the premise renders the conclusion probable rather than necessary, taken together with the rest of the arguments, the moral argument offers sufficient rational justification for the existence of God.

What is the cumulative payoff of the arguments for the existence of God? Kudriavtsev's conclusions are remarkably modest. He accepts the general agreement of post-Kantian natural theology that none of the arguments are deductively valid. He also concedes that the conclusion—the existence of the perfect being—is in different ways "contained in" or assumed by the premises. Kudriavtsev concludes:

> It follows that the first and foundational proof of the existence of God is, in essence, empirical, based on the immediate perception of divine action. Since it is the first, this proof has to be the ground of and precede all other possible proofs of this truth [of God's existence]. As we pointed out, this explains why the concept of God is the hidden presupposition of all proofs of the existence of God. As empirical, this proof possesses immediate force of persuasiveness, which increases in proportion to the vividness and liveliness of the perception of the divine and according to the measure of our development of the awareness of God.[37]

Kudriavtsev clarifies that, strictly speaking, is it more appropriate to speak of the content of spiritual perception as the ground for belief in God rather than the proof of God.[38] The reason for this is because typically perceptual beliefs do not involve formal inference. Belief in God, on his account, is basic, because it is grounded in God's direct action upon the human mind and in the sense that it undergirds our beliefs about the general features of the world. While Kudriavtsev builds on Jacobi, he does not share the German philosopher's fideism or his disparagement of all attempts to justify the existence of God by means of rational inference as opposed to direct perception.

What is, then, the point of the rest of the arguments, if direct spiritual

37. Kudriavtsev-Platonov, *Issledovaniia i stat'i po estestvennomu bogosloviiu*, in *Sochineniia*, 2:498.

38. Kudriavtsev's account of religious experience and spiritual perception elicits comparison with Alvin Plantinga's version of philosophical theism in "Is Belief in God Properly Basic?," *Nous* 15, no. 1 (1981): 41–51 and his account of *sensus divinitatis* in *Warranted Christian Belief* (Oxford: Oxford University Press, 2000), 245–46.

perception is all that seems to be required? Kudriavtsev answers that for many people and in many circumstances such a perception is opaque and often does not match the vividness of sensory perception of physical objects. In addition, the rational justification of the truth of religion requires that we move from representations (or qualia of perception) to the concept of God, which is clarified and established by the classical arguments. We need the proofs of the existence of God in the same way that we need a rational account and clarification of the first principles of knowledge.

Kudriavtsev's perfect being theism shaped the training of the Russian Orthodox clergy who studied at the Academy for nearly four decades. Outside the Academy, his works were read by a relatively limited number of people because they tended to be published in ecclesiastical journals. Kudriavtsev remains untranslated and mostly unknown in the West.[39]

Viktor Nesmelov's psychological argument

Another important representative of Russian academic natural theology is Viktor Ivanovich Nesmelov. Born into a family of a village priest in the Saratov region, Nesmelov studied at the Kazan Theological Academy, where he defended his master's thesis on the dogmatic theology of St. Gregory of Nyssa in 1888. In the same year, Nesmelov received a teaching position at the Academy, which he occupied for the next three decades. When the Bolsheviks came to power, the Academy was forced to close and Nesmelov lost his job. Due to his opposition to the Soviet regime, he became unemployable. In 1931, he was arrested on suspicions of counterrevolutionary activity and condemned to a three-year exile. Remarkably, he was released without serving his time on the grounds that he was a father of a "revolutionary hero." (His eldest son, Valentin, became a member of the Soviet secret police, the dreaded "Cheka," and was killed while attempting to loot a local monastery.) During the time of the Stalinist purges, the aging Nesmelov died of a natural cause: chronic pneumonia.

39. One exception is Sean Gillen, "V. D. Kudriavtsev-Platonov and the Making of Russian Orthodox Theism," in Patrick Lally Michelson and Judith Deutsch Kornblatt, eds., *Thinking Orthodox in Modern Russia: Culture, History, Context* (Madison, WI: University of Wisconsin Press, 2014), 111–30. In Russian scholarship, see Irina Tsvyk, "Philosophy in the Russian Academies: The Case of Viktor Kudryavtsev-Platonov," in David Bradshaw, ed., *Philosophical Theology and the Christian Tradition: Russian and Western Perspectives* (Washington, DC: Council for Research in Values and Philosophy, 2012), 161–75.

In the Kazan Theological Academy, Nesmelov studied under Veniamin Alekseevich Snegirev (1841–1889). In his study of psychology and theory of consciousness, Snegirev analyzed moral perception and religious feeling. Engaging the work of Schleiermacher and Hegel, the Russian philosopher postulated the existence in human consciousness of the "innate idea" of the Highest Personality. According to Snegirev, this idea typically evokes the feelings of trust and peace, as contrasted with Schleiermacher's feeling of absolute dependence. Snegirev held that humans find the idea of the Highest Personality congenial because they are made in God's image and likeness.

In his magnum opus *The Science of Man* (*Nauka o cheloveke*, 1905), Nesmelov developed his teacher's psychological insights in a deeply original manner. He rejects the existence of "innate ideas" as discrete concepts planted in consciousness. Nesmelov also engages and rejects Kudriavtsev's hypothesis that the idea of a perfect being is the result of God's direct supersensory impact upon the human spirit. Calling such an explanation "fantastical," Nesmelov denies the possibility of supersensory or spiritual perception as a distinct conscious event.[40] He proposes instead—and this is his central insight—that "the image of the unconditional being is not a mental abstraction created by humans, rather, this image is given in the nature of personality."[41] This central insight requires some unpacking.

For Nesmelov, the concept of God is not a discrete thought lodged in consciousness. Rather, the idea of God is disclosed in human consciousness as the living image of God. We conceive of ourselves in a twofold manner: as embodied beings, we share our existence with other physical beings and things; as centers of consciousness, we possess ideal existence that consists in first-person experiences (feelings, volitions, thoughts), rational thinking, free will, moral decisions, and creativity. Each human consciousness brings these interconnected operations together in an unrepeatable manner, constituting a unique personality. Each personality is conscious of its uniqueness; this concrete, living experience of personal uniqueness constitutes the image of the perfect Person, or God. Nesmelov writes:

> Being aware of oneself as the real image of God, man discovers his true life in the life according to his divine image, that is, in living out a life that develops in the confines and conditions of the physical world, but

40. Viktor Nesmelov, *Nauka o cheloveke*, 2nd ed., 2 vols. (Kazan': Tipolitografiia imperatorskogo universiteta, 1898, 1905; reprinted in St. Petersburg, 2000), 1.7.2 (pp. 231–32).

41. Nesmelov, *Nauka o cheloveke*, 1.7.1 (p. 228).

> nevertheless tends toward the likeness of God's own life. For man, this life expresses the sole meaning of his physical existence as a free and rational person . . . ; thus, upon becoming aware of oneself as the real image of God, man does not merely think of God as of truly existing and does not merely see in God the genuine reality of every person, but also seeks to fulfill himself in the world as the true image of the truly existing God.[42]

Unfortunately, instead of reflecting the likeness of God, man ends up reflecting the likeness of this world. This failure to fulfill the divine likeness leads to a sense of fear, guilt, and alienation from God. However, the very fact that humans experience those feelings testifies to the fact that the voice of conscience speaks in us as a part of the image and likeness of God.[43]

Nesmelov does not precisely offer a formal argument for the existence of God, although he makes these reflections a part of the discussion of the classical arguments for the existence of God, which he rejects one by one. According to Nesmelov, the teleological argument assumes circular logic: in order to recognize the creative activity of the transcendent divine Mind behind the mechanical purposefulness of nature, one has to assume that such a perfect being exists. Otherwise, no instance of finite order in the world warrants an inference to the existence of an infinite divine Designer. Likewise, the cosmological argument on its own does not yield an inference that God as the first cause is distinct from the world. On the contrary, the more likely inference is that the totality of the world itself is the first cause and this totality is God. In other words, if the existence of the transcendent primary cause of theism is not already presupposed in the premise, the cosmological argument leads either to atheism (nothing but the world exists) or to pantheism (the world and God are identical).

Having rejected the classical arguments for the existence of God, Nesmelov offers a set of "psychological" considerations that are at once less and more than an argument. They are less than an argument, because Nesmelov never makes it clear how the existence of God follows from the following premises: (1) each human person is both a thing among things of the physical world and also more; (2) this "more" consists in human aware-

42. Nesmelov, *Nauka o cheloveke*, 1.7.4 (p. 254).

43. Unlike some authorities in the patristic tradition, Nesmelov does not distinguish consistently between the image of God, as a part of the original endowment of human creatures, and the likeness of God, as a feature of the transformed eschatological state.

ness of personal uniqueness; (3) personal uniqueness consists in the manner in which each human person combines such powers as rational thinking, free choice, moral decision-making, first-person experiences, and the like; (4) the awareness of personal uniqueness is identical with the awareness of being unlike anything in the physical world and therefore being like the non-physical perfect person, God; (5) this awareness also brings about the awareness of imperfection and falling short of fully instantiating the image of God; (6) which in turns brings about the desire to attain the image and likeness of God, to the extent to which such attainment is possible for humans. Thus, Nesmelov stops short of providing a logical link to the proposition that God exists. He deliberately eschews such a method, because for him the existence of God cannot be reached as a result of a particular chain of reasoning. According to Nesmelov, to be able to reason at all is to "perform" the image of God, so to speak. An inferential argument based on Nesmelov's principles might be summarized as follows: (a) human beings are both thing-like (e.g., they have bodies) and not thing-like (e.g., they think); (b) humans are both a part of the physical world and not a part of the physical world; (c) that which is not a part of the physical world is either nothing or God, who transcends the world; (d) choosing to believe in nothing beyond the physical world (materialism) does not resolve the puzzle (Russian: *zagadka*) of human existence, which points to our twofold nature; (e) a more rationally satisfactory explanation is to postulate a perfect person, God. Cast in this form, this is an inference to the best explanation.

Nesmelov's reflections on the image of God are also *more* than a classical argument, because he quickly moves beyond establishing the existence of God. Human awareness of being in the image of God generates a desire to conform to God, accompanied by a frustration of this desire by ending up conformed to the world instead. In the second part of *The Science of Man*, Nesmelov no longer finds the Promethean efforts of natural theology effective and moves into the realm of revealed theology in order to offer an Orthodox account of salvation.

Following a central theme of patristic theology, Nesmelov construes the divine incarnation as a restoration of the image of God in humanity. The image of God was perishing due to sin and death. By assuming human nature and undergoing suffering, death, and resurrection, the divine Logos reclaims in Christ what belongs to him, namely, his image. The divine incarnation provides an answer to the central "puzzle" of human existence: the contradiction between God-like dignity disclosed in human consciousness and the empirical reality of human wretchedness is resolved in the union of divine and human natures in Christ. Nesmelov was the first among Orthodox "academic" theists to connect explicitly the findings of his metaphysical psychology with the central tenet of revealed theology, namely, God's becoming man.

While the tradition of natural theology that was produced in Russian theological academies was often ignored by philosophers not associated with church-affiliated institutions, the originality of Nesmelov's psychological argument was noted and valorized by his far better-known contemporary, Nikolai Berdyaev (1874–1948).[44] Hence, we should expand Berdyaev's notion of the Russian "religious-philosophical renaissance" of the 1890s–1930s to include the outstanding representatives of Orthodox academic theism, such as Kudriavtsev and Nesmelov, even if this philosophical trend did not become as influential in Russian religious thought as that associated with Vladimir Solovyov and his followers.

Solovyov's metaphysics of all-unity

Vladimir Solovyov was born into the family of a prominent Russian historian, Sergei Mikhailovich Solovyov, whose own father was an Orthodox priest. Vladimir studied natural sciences and philosophy at Moscow University (1869–1873). Concomitantly, he also audited lectures at the Moscow Theological Academy, while Viktor Kudriavtsev taught philosophy of religion there. After defending his master's thesis in 1874, Solovyov briefly lectured in philosophy at Moscow and St. Petersburg Universities. In 1881, he resigned from his university post permanently in order to pursue a life of the mind unencumbered by routine teaching and committee work. In addition to being a philosopher, Solovyov was a poet, mystic, polemicist, political commentator, and a prominent public intellectual.

Solovyov's comprehensive epistemological, metaphysical, ethical, aesthetic, and theo-political vision does not afford a straightforward comparison with classical natural theology, which assumes a form of epistemological

44. See Nikolai Berdiaev, "Opyt filosofskogo opravdaniia khristianstva (o knige Nesmelova *Nauka o cheloveke*)," in *Dukhovnyi krizis intelligentsii* (Moscow: Kanon, 2009), 269–92, first published in 1909; see also Florovsky, *Puti russkogo bogosloviia*, 445–50. Florovsky notes that Nesmelov compartmentalized his early study of the Church Fathers, especially the dogmatic theology of Gregory of Nyssa and his philosophical theism. More recently, see A. Iu. Berdnikova, "Problema psikhologicheskogo dokazatel'stva bytiia Boga V. I. Nesmelova v kontekste ego khristianskoi antropologii: 'Za' i 'protiv,'" *Vestnik RUDN* 23, no. 1 (2019): 19–31.

realism and involves inferential reasoning from generally accepted features of the world to the existence and properties of God. It is more accurate to describe Solovyov's work as a religious philosophy of nature, which assumes the existence of God (based on general revelation, the incarnation of God in Christ, and mystical experience) and proceeds to explain natural processes in light of this assumption, summarized in the concept of Godmanhood.

Solovyov's ambitious theory of integral knowledge offered a synthesis of scientific, philosophical, and religious domains of knowledge. In his doctoral dissertation, *The Critique of Abstract Principles* (1880), Solovyov criticized the one-sidedness of Western empiricism and rationalism. Sense-perception and conceptual apprehension of objects are mental acts, internal to consciousness. No mental act may establish that the objects of sense-perception and rational apprehension exist independently of consciousness. Drawing on Jacobi, Solovyov concludes that our belief in the existence of the external world must be a matter of faith. Such a faith (as a conviction that accompanies any experience of the external world) must be based on the underlying unity of the subjects and objects of experience. This underlying unity is not given in ordinary sense-experience or thought, but rather has to be postulated in order to render subject-object relations possible. Thus, in addition to empirical and rational forms of knowledge, Solovyov postulates the third type of knowledge, namely, mystical.[45] Mystical knowledge consists in the awareness of the inner connection between the consciousness of the knower and the external object. While mystical knowledge also discloses the unity of all things, it would be inaccurate to confuse it with absorption mysticism, where the difference between the subject and the object disappears. While critics often point out pantheistic tendencies in Solovyov's metaphysics of all-unity, it should be stressed that the Russian philosopher himself was at pains to distance himself from pantheism.

In his mature work *The Justification of the Good* (1897), Solovyov developed a comprehensive ethical theory, grounded in human nature and in God. According to Solovyov, the anthropological foundations of ethics are the feelings of shame, compassion, and awe. Shame indicates human desire to transcend the limitations of animal nature; compassion signals equality and unity with fellow humans; and awe is a feeling characterizing human relations to that which surpasses them. Following Jacobi and Schleiermacher, Solovyov asserts that the reality of God is given in religious feeling. The

45. Solovyov, *Kritika otvlechennykh nachal*, in *Sochineniia*, 2 vols. (Moscow: Mysl', 1990), 1:724–25.

Russian philosopher states: "The reality of the deity is not an *inference* from religious perception, but is the *content* of religious perception, it is *that which is being perceived*. . . . God is in us, therefore, God exists."[46] It may be objected that some people do not experience religious awe or do not seem to be attuned to God. Solovyov dismisses this objection by noting that the existence of blind people who cannot see the sun is not a good reason for doubting the sun's existence.

In Solovyov's epistemology, the existence of God as a unity underlying all things and the condition of subject-object relation is more basic than the existence of the external world. In his ethics, the existence of God is the content of religious perception. In the *Lectures on Godmanhood* (1881), Solovyov summarily dismisses the classical arguments for the existence of God on the grounds that their premises are based on the existence of the external world, which itself is hypothetical and based on faith. While Solovyov was sympathetic to Jacobi's fideism in his epistemology, his religious philosophy also makes positive use of the arguments to the best explanation. For example, he develops what one might call an axiological argument for the existence of God. He observes that epistemic, moral, and aesthetic judgments involve a distinction between how things appear to be and how things ought to be. As a Christian Platonist, Solovyov held that such normative judgments assume the existence of an *a priori* norm of the true, the good, and the beautiful. Since such a norm exists, it is very likely that there exists an unconditional principle that gives rise to this norm. This unconditional principle is God.[47]

In his philosophy of nature, Solovyov considered the evolution of life-forms from simple organisms, like mollusks, to more complex organisms, such as birds and mammals. The development of the physical world exhibits growth in the degrees of perfection. This growth culminates in the human form, which is uniquely endowed with the awareness of its imperfection and the desire to reach perfection. The history of humanity is the development from animal-like humanity to divine-like humanity.[48] The growth of all life-forms toward perfection is possible because God himself is perfection and does not grow or change. One might discern the contours of the Thomistic

46. Solovyov, *Opravdanie dobra*, in *Sochineniia* (1990), 1:251. English translation by Boris Jakim, *The Justification of the Good: An Essay on Moral Philosophy* (Grand Rapids, MI: Eerdmans, 2005) (emphasis in the original).

47. Solovyov, "Chteniia o Bogochelovechestve," in *Sochineniia*, 2 vols. (Moscow: Pravda, 1989), 2:32–33. English translation by Boris Jakim, *Lectures on Divine Humanity* (Hudson, NY: Lindisfarne Press, 1995).

48. Solovyov, *Opravdanie dobra*, in *Sochineniia* (1990), 1:255–57.

argument from the degrees of perfection in Solovyov's reasoning, although the Russian philosopher himself does not offer a formal argument.

Solovyov's followers: Sergius Bulgakov and others

In the spirit of *The Critique of Abstract Principles*, Solovyov's followers argued for extending the boundaries of experience in order to include religious and mystical experience. Nikolai Lossky (1870–1965) called Solovyov's epistemology "mystical empiricism" and developed it in the direction of intuitivism. Nikolai Berdyaev also insisted on the irreducibility and centrality of religious experience for the knowledge of God, emphasized intuition, and treated faith as a form of knowledge that was more foundational than discursive reasoning. He held that if the existence of God is proven, God can no longer be an object of free act of faith and love.[49] For Berdyaev, all attempts at proving the existence of God are futile; it is only possible to proceed *from* God, having discovered God in the depth of one's own being.[50] Berdyaev moved further away from the rationalist elements of Solovyov's system in the direction of existentialism, personalism, intuitivism, and mysticism. It was the mystical dimension of Solovyov's philosophy and poetry, especially his mysterious personal encounters with the figure of the divine Sophia, not the rationalist elements of his system, that attracted his followers at the turn of the century.

No Russian thinker was more impacted by Solovyov than Sergius Bulgakov. In *Unfading Light* (1917), Bulgakov provided a subtle literary imitation of Solovyov's three encounters with Sophia, by weaving deeply personal reminiscences of experiencing God through the beauty of nature, religious art, and church architecture into a philosophical account of religious experience. As Bulgakov insists, religious experience is not reducible to any other type of experience. Humans, especially those who are religiously gifted, possess a special "eye of contemplative vision."[51] When God speaks, humans are capable of "listening to God and hearing him, although not with a physical ear."[52] According to Bulgakov, humans perceive God with a "religious or-

49. Nikolai Berdyaev, *Filosofiia svobody* (Moscow: Pravda, 1989), 51–53.

50. Berdyaev, *Filosofiia svobody*, 78.

51. Sergius Bulgakov, *Svet Nevechernii* (Moscow: Respublika, 1994), 13. English translation by Thomas Allan Smith, *Unfading Light: Contemplations and Speculations* (Grand Rapids, MI: Eerdmans, 2013).

52. Bulgakov, *Svet Nevechernii*, 17.

gan,"[53] which he associates with the heart. He sketches out a rudimentary theory of spiritual perception without elaborating it.

Bulgakov questions Jacobi's extension of the operation of faith to include belief in the existence of the external world. Bulgakov holds that our belief in the independent existence of the objects of perception is based on intuition. He is not prepared to equate this intuition with an act of faith, which he reserves exclusively for the reception of divine revelation. Such a reception is not purely passive but requires an active search and an open and pure heart. As created in the image and likeness of God, humans have a divinely established basis for the reception of revelation. However, revelation is also supra-rational in the sense that its truths cannot be discovered as logical deductions of pure reason.[54] Bulgakov points out that there is a difference between believing in God and knowing the Pythagorean Theorem. The former is a free act of trust, the latter is knowledge to which the mind is compelled by logical necessity. It is futile to inquire about the proofs of the existence of God, since God presents himself immediately, without any inferential or causal chain, in religious experience. Moreover, to analyze contingent causal chains in order to establish the reality of a necessary being or the Absolute is a category mistake: it is an attempt to prove that which is most certain by means of that which is merely probable. At best, the classical proofs are disguised postulates of God's existence or elucidations of the philosophical concept of God.[55] Bulgakov maintained that religious experience provided direct awareness of God, thereby rendering the arguments of classical theism superfluous.[56]

The central impulse of Bulgakov's *Tragedy of Philosophy* (1920) was reminiscent of Solovyov's *Critique of Abstract Principles*. Like Solovyov before him, Bulgakov argued that the nineteenth-century idealist and materialist philosophical systems suffered from reductionistic monism. Bulgakov went

53. Bulgakov, *Svet Nevechernii*, 19.

54. Bulgakov, "Glavy o troichnosti," in *Trudy o troichnosti* (Moscow: OGI, 2001), 63.

55. Bulgakov, *Svet Nevechernii*, 20. Bulgakov conflates the order of being with the order of knowing.

56. For further analysis and critique of Bulgakov's position, see Travis Dumsday's chapter. For a contemporary defense of religious experience, see William P. Alston, *Perceiving God: The Epistemology of Religious Experience* (Ithaca, NY: Cornell University Press, 1991) and Alvin Plantinga, *Warranted Christian Belief.* For discussion of the shift from internalism to externalism, and the corresponding rejection of classical foundationalism, see John Greco, "Knowledge of God," in William J. Abraham and Frederick D. Aquino, eds., *The Oxford Handbook of the Epistemology of Theology* (Oxford: Oxford University Press, 2017), 9–29.

on to argue that Fichtean and Hegelian "absolute systems" were Christian "heresies," taking this term to mean one-sided rationalistic reductionism of the antinomic relationship between being and consciousness to a single principle.[57] The one-sidedness of philosophical heresies could be overcome through the acceptance of the Trinitarian dogma, which while grounded in revelation, provided fertile ground for philosophical speculation, particularly in the sphere of analogies between the human image of God and its divine prototype. Here Bulgakov set aside the traditional analogies based on impersonal simultaneous relations between the three aspects of one entity (e.g., the sun, its rays, and light) and criticized, somewhat tendentiously, Augustine's psychological analogies (e.g., mind, self-knowledge, and will). The Russian theologian insisted instead that any adequate analogy had to capture the tri-hypostatic nature of the Trinity and developed original linguistic and Social Trinitarian analogies. Criticizing the monistic tendencies of German Idealism, Bulgakov maintained that in the final analysis the structure of reality was triune rather than monistic. Only a Trinitarian metaphysic, accepted as a revealed postulate, could free philosophy from its tendency toward monistic reductionism. In this sense, philosophy depends on the revealed truth of religion, and the revealed truth, in turn, invites and requires philosophical speculation.

Despite the strongly speculative character of his metaphysics, Bulgakov remained opposed to natural theology. While such a view was generally shared by Solovyov's followers, Semen Frank's reformulation of the ontological argument provided an important exception.

Semen Frank's version of the ontological argument

Born into a Jewish family, as a young boy Semen Frank attended a synagogue in Moscow with his grandfather. Like many in his generation, he experienced a crisis of faith in his teenage years and became interested in socialism. Frank went on to study law and economics at Moscow University (1894–1898). Like Berdyaev, Bulgakov, and others, he was disillusioned with Marxism, and in the early 1900s turned to religiously colored philosophical idealism and eventually converted to Christianity, developing his own ver-

57. Bulgakov, *Tragediia filosofii*, in *Sochineniia*, 2 vols. (Moscow: Nauka, 1993), 1:312–28. English translation by Stephen Churchyard, *The Tragedy of Philosophy (Philosophy and Dogma)* (Brooklyn, NY: Angelico Press, 2020).

sion of the Solovyovan metaphysics of all-unity. After a period of literary activity and research trips abroad, he taught philosophy at St. Petersburg University (1912–1917), a post that he had to leave during the revolutionary upheaval. In 1922, he was arrested and banished from the Soviet Russia on a "Philosophy Steamer," together with other outstanding religious thinkers. In exile, he first settled in Germany, where he taught Russian intellectual history at the University of Berlin. When Hitler's government came to power in 1933, as a person of Jewish descent, Frank was removed from his post. Frank left Germany and continued to give lectures at various European universities. He lived in France during the prewar period and then spent the final years of his life in Great Britain.

Frank saw himself as a successor to the *philosophia perennis* of Christian Platonism associated with the names of Plotinus, Augustine, Pseudo-Dionysius the Areopagite, Franz Baader, and Vladimir Solovyov.[58] Frank's metaphysics begins with the observation that the existence of finite objects is saturated with and surrounded by unknowable being, which can never be rationally exhausted. Mental states and external objects are a part of rationally inexhaustible potentiality of being. As a condition of everything real, the Unknowable itself is unconditional; as that which encompasses all reality, it is all-unity; as that which manifests itself as the power of being, it is God.[59]

Frank's philosophy of religion accords a uniquely central place to the ontological argument for the existence of God, which he discussed at different stages of his philosophical career, from his early epistemological treatise *The Object of Knowledge* (1915), continuing in his monographic essay "The Ontological Argument for the Existence of God" (1930), and culminating in his magnum opus, *The Unknowable* (1938).[60] Frank begins "The Ontological Argument for the Existence of God" by observing that the classical theistic arguments have been discredited among unbelievers and believers alike. For believers, the arguments seem to take away the freedom to doubt and to

58. Frank, *Nepostizhimoe* (Moscow: Ast, 2000), 248. English translation by Boris Jakim, *The Unknowable: The Ontological Introduction to the Philosophy of Religion* (Athens, OH: Ohio University Press, 1984).

59. Frank, *Nepostizhimoe*, 353–400.

60. For the historiography of Frank's work on the issue, see Paweł Rojek, "God and *Cogito:* Semen Frank on the Ontological Argument," *Studies in Eastern European Thought* 71 (2019): 119–40. Frank formulated a preliminary sketch of the history of the ontological argument in the addendum to *The Object of Knowledge*. He originally wrote *The Unknowable* in German. When the publication of the book became impossible in Nazi Germany, he rewrote the book in Russian. See *Nepostizhimoe*, 249.

trust in revelation. Even if such arguments are sound, their conclusions do not coincide with the God of religious faith. The ontological argument has been discredited not only on general fideist grounds, but also by thinkers as diverse as Gaunilo, Aquinas, Gassendi, Locke, and Kant.[61] In Anselm's classical formulation, the ontological argument is a deduction from the concept of an object to the object's reality. Frank concedes that in this formulation the argument is indefensible.

However, the ontological argument could be, in Frank's words, "rehabilitated." The main point to grasp is that the logical distinction between "concept" and "reality" does not apply to God. To demonstrate that this is so, Frank turns to the Cartesian *cogito ergo sum* ("I think, therefore I am," which itself, as he points out, goes back to Augustine[62]). The Cartesian cogito is not an inference from thinking to existence, but a claim that the "I" that is being thought exists in the very act of thinking. The thinking "I" is not an object. Unlike external objects, the existence of the thinking self does not require a demonstration. On the contrary, the thinking self is self-evident and self-manifest. Hence, there is at least one entity—namely, the inner world of human consciousness—whose mental content is inseparable from its existence.[63]

Frank suggests that this peculiarity of human consciousness could also be analogically applied to God. For God is not an average-sized external object among other objects. Rather, God is that light which allows us to relate to and understand any object. However, God is more than simply a "pure subject" or the Fichtean "I." God as the Absolute is prior to everything that is relative and limited; God is ontologically prior to the subject-object distinction, or the distinction between thought and being (in this formulation, notes Frank, the ontological proof goes back to Plotinus rather than Anselm). The ontological argument is, strictly speaking, not an argument at all, but a train of thought that engenders a recognition that God, as the all-encompassing unity of the mental and extra-mental worlds, exists necessarily. To be more precise, God is the living, self-authenticating foundation of every kind of necessity.[64]

Drawing on Descartes, Frank argues from the idea of infinity in the hu-

61. Frank, "Ontologicheskoe dokazatel'stvo bytiia Boga," in *Po tu storonu pravogo i levogo: Sbornik statei*, ed. V. S. Frank (Paris: YMCA Press, 1972), 109–51, at 109–12.

62. Frank, "Ontologicheskoe dokazatel'stvo bytiia Boga," 141. See Augustine, *De trinitate* 10.14 and *De civitate Dei* 11.26.

63. Frank, "Ontologicheskoe dokazatel'stvo bytiia Boga," 113–17.

64. Frank, "Ontologicheskoe dokazatel'stvo bytiia Boga," 120–29.

man mind to the reality of the infinite being. The concept of the finite being is obtained by imposing a limit on an indefinite or infinite being; it is the marking out of the known, or at least the comprehensible, in the ocean of the unknowable. Thus, the infinite, as unknowable, must be ontologically prior to the finite.

Frank develops his version of the ontological argument further by drawing on Nicholas of Cusa, whom he considered "my only teacher in philosophy."[65] God contains everything, as the condition of any possible being and any possible thought.[66] To deny the existence of anything is to exclude it from the content of being, which presupposes that something (other than that which is denied) exists. But God is the very condition of the possibility of any existent thing. Hence, in denying a particular reality, we are still affirming the existence of the necessary condition of any reality, which is God.[67] The move to God as the ground or cause of all things appears to be a peculiar combination of the ontological argument with the cosmological argument, although Frank himself would not have accepted such a connection.[68]

Strictly speaking, then, the ontological argument is "the recognition of the self-evidence of the Absolute."[69] As such, it is not an argument that involves reasoning from established true premises to less certain conclusions. It is an expression of a fundamental mystical intuition: we cannot have a proper concept of God that is separate from God's existence. If this is so, then the fideist objections to using inferential reasoning to prove the existence of God may be set aside. But what relation does such a "God" have to the God of religious faith, the "God of Abraham, Isaac, and Jacob"? Frank answers this question by pointing out that the presentation of God as the unknowable being that transcends the distinction between human persons and imper-

65. Frank, *Nepostizhimoe*, 248. There is a measure of rhetorical exaggeration in this claim. It would be more accurate to say that Nicholas of Cusa was his major philosophical influence.

66. In this formulation, Frank's train of thought anticipates Karl Barth's *Anselm: Fides Querens Intellectum; Anselm's Proof of the Existence of God in the Context of His Theological Scheme* (1931), which is summarized by Matthew Levering thus: "God's existence provides the ground for the concept of existence, which God transcends." See Levering, *Proofs of God: Classical Arguments from Tertullian to Barth* (Grand Rapids, MI: Baker Academic, 2016), 196. It must be stressed, however, that the parallel does not extend to Barth's theological fideism and his rejection of natural theology in *Church Dogmatics*.

67. Frank, "Ontologicheskoe dokazatel'stvo bytiia Boga," 132; *Nepostizhimoe*, 634.

68. Frank, "Ontologicheskoe dokazatel'stvo bytiia Boga," 133. Frank treats all other arguments as "empirical" and claims that the existence of evil invalidates them. See p. 146.

69. Frank, "Ontologicheskoe dokazatel'stvo bytiia Boga," 136.

sonal things is compatible with the presentation of the divine transcendence in Scripture and tradition.

If the existence of God is intuitively true and self-evident, then what place is left for the freedom of faith and doubt? According to Frank, freedom consists in "turning the eyes of the soul" (Plato) from the outward to the inward, in other words, in focusing spiritual attention on the reality of God as distinct from the reality of particular things in the world.

We may conclude that Frank "rehabilitated" the ontological argument in order to make it the cornerstone of his philosophical system. Since Frank's publications that dealt with the ontological argument appeared only in Russian, his contribution to natural theology remained unnoticed in the West.[70] As for his Russian émigré contemporaries, Vasily Zenkovsky praised Frank as the most outstanding of Russian religious philosophers, and Boris Vysheslavtsev (1877–1854) drew on his work. In *The Ethics of a Transfigured Eros* (1931), Vysheslavtsev followed Frank's reformulations of the ontological argument.[71] The structural role that the ontological argument played in the philosophical theisms of Frank and Vysheslavtsev indicates their unease with Jacobi's fideism, although they distanced themselves in equal measure from the evidentialism of classical natural theology. The followers of Solovyov often "began" with a version of philosophical idealism and its distinct epistemological preoccupations; however, the general thrust of their philosophical project was in the direction of realism, which accorded foundational significance to the reality of God.

Conclusion

Two main trajectories of philosophical theism may be identified in Russian religious thought. The first trajectory was primarily associated with the nineteenth-century graduate Orthodox theological schools or "academies." The most outstanding representatives of this strand were Golubinskii, Kudriavtsev, and Nesmelov. Grounded in the liturgical life of Orthodoxy and operating within the institutional structures of the Russian Orthodox

70. Today, Frank's works are studied by a modest, but growing number of specialists. For a monographic study in English, see Philip Boobbyer, *S. L. Frank: The Life and Work of a Russian Philosopher, 1877–1950* (Athens, OH: Ohio University Press, 1995).

71. See Boris Vysheslavtsev, *Etika preobrazhennogo erosa* (Moscow: Respublika, 1994), 131–52. He explores two Cartesian forms of the ontological argument, which we discussed in connection with Frank.

Church, these philosophers also engaged a tradition of Western natural theology. They were versed in the eighteenth–nineteenth century critiques of classical natural theology, especially as developed by Kant and Feuerbach. They responded to Kant's demolition of classical natural theology with philosophical rigor and without abandoning epistemological realism. Golubinskii played a pioneering role in establishing natural theology as a part of the Orthodox graduate educational system. Kudriavtsev developed a cumulative case for the existence of God and a theory of spiritual perception. Golubinskii and Kudriavtsev considered arguments based on the general features of the external world, but their emphasis lies elsewhere, namely, in the investigation of inner experience. In Nesmelov's natural theology, the inner God-like structure of human consciousness is the main ground for believing in the existence of God.

The second trajectory of philosophical theism is represented by Solovyov and his followers, especially Bulgakov and Frank. Metaphysically, this tradition builds on Christian Platonism with a German Idealist update, especially in the work of late Schelling. With the important exceptions of Frank and Vysheslavtsev, this tradition takes the Kantian critique of the classical arguments for the existence of God to be successful and shows ambivalence vis-à-vis epistemological realism. Solovyov's metaphysics of all-unity was based on "mystical empiricism," which established a parity between the belief in the existence of the external world and the belief in the existence of God. In his philosophy of nature and ethics, the Russian philosopher postulates the existence of God and then uses inference to the best explanation to offer reasons for this postulate. To be clear, Solovyov is not engaged in classical natural theology, which starts from the general features of nature and concludes to the existence and properties of God. Nevertheless, his metaphysics of all-unity offers a comprehensive theological account of nature, proceeding from the assumption that there is a God and then moving back and forth between nature's development toward perfection and God's actual perfection, in a manner reminiscent of but not identical to the Thomistic argument from the degrees of perfection, as well as to Pierre Teilhard de Chardin's hypothesis of the evolutionary development of the cosmos toward ultimate unity with Christ.

In his work in philosophy of religion, Sergius Bulgakov insists upon the priority of religious experience and draws on Solovyov's mystical empiricism. He also gestures in the direction of a theory of spiritual perception, but unlike Kudriavtsev, does not develop it. Following Solovyov, Bulgakov rejects classical natural theology in favor of a speculative theological vision, which extends the historical divine incarnation into a general metaphysical principle of Godmanhood.

Operating within the framework of the metaphysics of all-unity, Frank refashions the ontological argument. God is the condition of any possible thought and any possible being. As such, to deny the existence of God is to deny the very possibility of thought and being, which is absurd. Thus, the ontological argument expresses the intuitive truth that the concept of God is inseparable from God's existence. As the incomprehensible One, God underlies and conditions any possible encounter between the mind and being, and discloses himself partially in that encounter. In the metaphysics of all-unity, the ontological argument is turned into a mystical awareness that the divine power of being undergirds any encounter with specific beings.

As we can see, the followers of Solovyov showed profound ambivalence toward classical natural theology, and either saw no value in the arguments for the existence of God at all (Bulgakov), or proposed a considerable revision of classical arguments (Frank). Additionally, Russian sophiology was characterized by metaphysical revisionism of classical theism in the direction of panentheism. In contrast, academic philosophers (Golubinskii and Kudriavtsev) defended classical theism. While they recognized the importance of direct perception of God for the life of faith, they were equally insistent on the value and significance of cumulative case arguments for the rational defense and elucidation of Orthodox Christian theism.

The vicissitudes of philosophical theism in Russian religious thought should not obscure the fact that there was an original, influential, and well-developed tradition of classical natural theology in the Orthodox prerevolutionary academies. This tradition made no attempt to barricade itself mentally in the "Eastern" Christian world alone. On the contrary, this tradition robustly engaged the main proponents and critics of natural theology in the West and developed its own authoritative voice. While the work of Golubinskii is of largely historical interest, the work of Nesmelov and especially Kudriavtsev is eminently worthy of further philosophical engagement. Kudriavtsev's cumulative case for theism is an especially promising point of departure, given the prominence of similarly structured arguments in the contemporary philosophy of religion owing especially to the work of Richard Swinburne and Basil Mitchell.[72]

72. See Richard Swinburne, *The Existence of God*, 2nd ed. (Oxford: Clarendon Press, 2014), *Faith and Reason*, 2nd ed. (Oxford: Clarendon Press, 2005); Basil Mitchell, *The Justification of Religious Belief* (New York: Oxford University Press, 1981).

Unfortunately, Kudriavtsev's natural theology, as also the works of other Orthodox pre-revolutionary theists, remain understudied. Since these authors remain untranslated, the general lack of awareness about them in Western scholarship is understandable. But Orthodox theologians who perceive natural theology as something foreign to the Orthodox tradition should know better. This tradition cannot be dismissed as a quaint remnant of Western scholasticism. Sheer ignorance of our own rich nineteenth-century tradition of natural theology is a poor foundation for historical judgment. Whatever doubts and objections one might have about the methods and findings of this tradition, one historical fact cannot be doubted and denied: namely, that this tradition flourished in pre-revolutionary Russian Orthodoxy.

Unscientific postscript

What is, then, the place of natural theology in the history of Russian religious thought and, more broadly, in Russian intellectual history? Perhaps it could be compared to Atlantis, the ancient island with a highly advanced civilization, which sunk to the bottom of the ocean as a result of an earthquake. Similarly, before the Bolshevik coup of 1917, the main educational institutions of the Russian Orthodox Church boasted a lively tradition of philosophical theism. Despite its spiritual vigor and intellectual fecundity, this rich tradition was swallowed up by the sea of history and nearly perished in the "earthquake" of the Bolshevik Revolution.

After the Revolution, the living carriers of this tradition either lost their means of livelihood and were harassed by the state (Nesmelov), or were packed onto the "Philosophy Steamers" and shipped out of Soviet Russia on Lenin's direct orders (Bulgakov, Frank), or in the worst-case scenario were sent to the Gulag, where they eventually perished.[73] The only form of natural theology that remained permissible behind the Iron Curtain was natural a-theology or "scientific atheism," as the Soviet authorities preferred to call it. For scientific atheism, any argument, no matter how bad, was recyclable, as long as it led to the conclusion that there was no God. In fact, the cruder the argument, the more useful it could be for the propaganda machine of the Soviet state.

73. The third category includes Pavel Florenskii (1882–1937) and Lev Karsavin (1882–1952), whose contributions to natural theology cannot be covered in this essay due to space limitations.

Growing up in the Soviet Union of the 1970s–1980s, I distinctly remember *The Agitator* magazine, which was a compulsory (sic!) subscription for any citizen who wished to subscribe to other, somewhat less ideologically loaded periodicals. *The Agitator* published political propaganda and "agitated" the Soviet population "under the banner of Marxism-Leninism" to cast aside all doubts about state-imposed atheism. In the pages of *The Agitator* one could read, for example, that since the Soviet astronauts failed to encounter God in outer space, the deity's celestial absenteeism was a clear sign of its non-existence. Even more popular was the claim that surfaces in Mikhail Bulgakov's novel *The Master and Margarita*, with which our essay began: "scholarship has proven" that the Gospels are pure fiction.

It is this claim that scandalizes Satan who in M. Bulgakov's story arrives in interwar Moscow in the guise of a German professor, Woland. The Devil proceeds to challenge educated Soviet unbelievers by offering his own account of the Gospel events. In order to make his case, the Prince of Darkness has to establish his own existence and identity first. As a sign of his preternatural powers, Woland causes people to discover various embarrassing truths about themselves and foretells the future, involving a few rather grotesque accidents. He also lets his band play tricks on unsuspecting Muscovites and, more generally, wreak havoc in the city. But since Satan happens to visits Russia during the reign of Stalin, the unspoken message is that there is not much for the poor Devil left to do, since humanity's own efforts at multiplying evil are so obvious. Hence, tragicomically, while the novel's characters who encounter a new version of Mephistopheles are variously affected, often to their own embarrassment or even ruin, the vast majority of Soviet citizens continue their business as usual. Satan's pathetic attempt to offer an impressive proof of his authority fails, but only because there are humans competing for the same role.

In my parents' household *The Master and Margarita* was read, custom-bound, and copied, as one of the great treasures of that sunken Atlantis, the very memory of which the Soviet system had attempted to erase. With the arrival of Perestroika in the mid-1980s, diving expeditions to the lost treasures of Atlantis were now permitted and encouraged, and the works of Russian religious philosophers were being reprinted and were in demand. Meanwhile, *The Agitator*, no longer required for purchase, lost its readership and went straight into the wastebasket of history.

5. Reactions of Modern Greek Theologians to Natural Theology

DIONYSIOS SKLIRIS

This chapters surveys the stances of Greek Orthodox theologians of the twentieth and twenty-first centuries toward natural theology. After a period in the early twentieth century when natural theology was traditionally included in works of systematic theology and dogmatics, there was an innovative current which is generally termed the "Theology of the Sixties," since its main adherents started developing their thought in the 1960s by differentiating themselves from the style of nineteenth- and early twentieth century Greek Orthodox theology. This was not a homogenous "school" of thought and its various representatives have developed different stances. Among its subcurrents one could name, for example, the "theology of personhood," as well as novel interpretations of Maximus the Confessor (c. 580–662) and Gregory Palamas (1296–1359), some of which were favorable toward natural theology, since they highlighted the continuity and complementarity between nature and supernatural grace or revelation. However, the mainstream current of the Theology of the Sixties was characterized by distrust toward natural theology. After considering objections to it from theologians who were mainly inspired by the continental tradition, I will briefly consider whether there can be a fruitful dialogue between Orthodoxy and natural theology as it is practiced within contemporary analytic philosophy. I will particularly examine some characteristics of the natural theology of Richard Swinburne (b. 1934) that arguably make it compatible with an Orthodox worldview. I will conclude by formulating some questions about the fruitfulness of natural theology today for Orthodoxy in view of the theological stances that will have been discussed.

The theology of "complementarity": a positive stance toward natural theology in the thought of twentieth-century Greek theologians

Greek theologians of the first half of the twentieth century usually included natural theology in their works of systematic and dogmatic theology, referring not only to the patristic tradition, but also to the Western tradition from Aquinas to Kant. This was the case with Christos Androutsos (1869–1935), a scholar who was born in Asia Minor and wrote a thesis on "The Logical Validity of the Arguments for the Existence of God" in 1892 while studying at the Theological School on the island of Halki near Constantinople. After completing his studies in Leipzig, he became an influential professor at the University of Athens (1912–1935). Androutsos accepted the ontological argument and tried to clarify the concept of God as an eminent identification of essence, existence, and attributes. Human reason constitutes for him the formal assimilation of divine truth, while faith is the subjective one.[1] Panayiotis Trembelas (1886–1977), known for his involvement in the religious organizations Zoi and Sotir, followed Androutsos in an argument from the concept of God to his necessary properties and attributes, while placing more emphasis on the moral feeling of the faithful, which arises from the perception of moral and spiritual properties of the world as created by God.[2]

In the decade of the 1960s, a new postwar generation of innovative theologians broke with the previous tradition and promoted a new current of theology that tended to focus more on Orthodox particularity and Orthodoxy's difference from the West. This took place in the context of a wider effort to reinvigorate modern Greek self-consciousness, which arguably continued the project of the generation of the 1930s in literature and art (e.g., Giorgos Seferis, Odysseas Elytis, Giannis Ritsos, Angelos Sikelianos, Nikos Kazantzakis, Giorgos Theotokas, Andreas Empeirikos, Zisimos Lorentzatos, Giannis Tsarouchis, Giannis Moralis, Nikos Hadjikyriakos-Ghikas). In the postwar period, theologians tried to resume this effort in order to establish "Greek particularity" in theology as well.[3]

However, this did not mean a uniform stance toward natural theology.

1. Christos Androutsos, *Δογματική* [*Dogmatics*] (Athens: 1956), 13–17.

2. See Panayiotis Trembelas, *Dogmatique de l'Église Orthodoxe Catholique,* vol. 1., trans. Pierre Dumont (Bruges: Chevetogne and Desclée de Brouwer, 1966), 58. Originally published as *Δογματική της Ορθοδόξου Καθολικής Εκκλησίας,* 3 vols. (Athens: Zoi, Sotiras, 1959–1961).

3. See Christos Yannaras, *Orthodoxy and the West: Hellenic Self-Identity in the Modern Age,* trans. Peter Chamberas and Norman Russell (Brookline, MA: Holy Cross Orthodox Press,

As the Theology of the Sixties tended to emphasize the particularity of Orthodox theology, it focused on the Eastern patristic use of natural theology in contradistinction to that of the Thomist tradition. The main patristic distinction that was highlighted was the triple one between (i) the "that" (ὅτι), i.e., the simple fact *that* God exists, *that* there is a God; (ii) the "what" (τί) of God, i.e., his super-substantial substance; and (iii) the "how" (πῶς) of God, i.e., God's mode of existence or subsistence. The question of "how" refers to the fact that according to specifically Christian theology, the (super-substantial) substance of God has a Trinitarian mode of existence as the hypostases of the Father, the Son, and the Spirit. In Greek "hypostasis" can also signify the act of subsisting; the question of "how" thus refers to the particular mode of subsisting which is considered as hypostatic. This mode of subsisting is related to personal causation, i.e., to "how" a hypostasis is caused to be a personal existence. For this reason, in the Eastern terminology, the personal properties (ἰδιώματα) of the Trinity tend to emphasize the mode of personal causality rather than just the relations of origin. The personal properties that have prevailed in the East as characteristic of the Trinity are the "unbegottenness" (ἀγέννητον) of the Father (and not just "paternity"/πατρότης, which denotes a relation), "being begotten" (γεννητόν) for the Son (and not just the relation of "filiation"/υἱότης), and "being brought forth" (ἐκπορευτόν) of the Spirit (and not just the Spirit's characteristic property of "sanctification"/ ἁγιότης, according to the initial formulation of Basil of Caesarea[4] that was gradually overshadowed in the Eastern tradition by other terms indicating causality). In other words, the prevailing Eastern tradition understands the personal properties mainly as modes of subsisting and personal causation, in contradistinction to the Thomistic view that regards them as relations. For this reason, the question of "how" is considered as more important than that of "what," or of the relations that could be developed regarding this "what" of the substance as in the Thomist tradition.

The question of "how" can be extended to how God reveals himself in creation through his energies/activities (ἐνέργειαι). These maintain a personal mode of manifestation, the Father having the "good will" (εὐδοκία) for creation and salvation, the Son being the creator par excellence (i.e., possessing αὐτουργία) due to the Incarnation, and the Spirit leading to eschatological fulfillment (τελείωσις). These are personal modes of activity

---

2006), 258–71. Originally published as *Ορθοδοξία και Δύση στη Νεώτερη Ελλάδα* (Athens: Domos, 1992).

4. Basil of Caesarea, *On the Holy Spirit* 19.48 (PG 32, 156B).

that echo the personal modes of eternal subsistence without, however, being identified with them. (Indeed, the prevailing Orthodox theology stresses the real distinction between the eternal Trinity *ad intra* and its manifestation *ad extra* toward the contingent world, criticizing Thomism for an excessive and unfortunate identification of divine essence and act.) The divine activity is of course common to the three persons, but it is articulated in the divine economy through different personal modes. In the worship of the Church, we relate to these different personal modes; for example, we pray to the Father through the incarnate Son in the Spirit. These distinct personal modes constitute the answer to the question of the "how."

Of course, in patristic thought the three questions of "that," "what," and "how" are complementary. The "what" of the divine (super-substantial) substance is unknowable, but it is communicated to the faithful through the energies. These have a personal mode ("how") of manifestation, which echoes the fact that in the eternal Trinity the "what" of the substance only subsists through the "how" of the Trinitarian hypostases or modes of subsistence. And the "that" of God's existence is implied in the revelation of the "how" in the Church as the locus of revelation of the Trinity. However, various theologians might adopt different stances toward this complementarity. Proponents of natural theology could note that the Greek-speaking Fathers did engage in natural theology in a positive manner, even though they thought that it concerned only the "that" of God, which was not their primary preoccupation. According to this stance, the question of the existence of God has a value of its own and could be regarded as a preliminary issue that helps us to ascend to the revelation of the Trinity. However, critics of natural theology could emphasize the contrast between the question of "how" and the questions of "that" and "what," thus leading to a negative or even dismissive stance toward natural theology. On such a view one should absolutely not start from the question of "that" and then proceed to "how," but the other way round: God is first revealed as Trinity and his existence ("that") is only implied in the fact that we come to know him in the Church as a Trinity of persons.

Both sides agree that for Eastern apophatic theology the "what-ness" of the divine substance is absolutely unknown and its investigation could even be considered blasphemous. They also agree that the "how" of God is revealed in the Church through the personal modes of activity that reflect the eternal modes of the personal hypostatic subsistence of the divine nature. The issue concerns the question of the "that." Proponents of natural theology could rightly claim that it belongs to the realm of the "known" according to both Eastern and Western patristic tradition. Orthodox critics of natural theology would emphasize that we only know the existence of God through his personal manifestation as the Trinity, and that natural theology should therefore be subordinated to Trinitarian theology and not stand as an independent preliminary "introduction."

One eminent thinker of the Theology of the Sixties who had a positive stance toward natural theology was Panayiotis Nellas (1936–1986). Nellas emphasized the continuity between the natural and the supernatural, in accord with his interpretation of the theory of the *logoi* by Maximus the Confessor[5] and the cosmological ecclesiology of Nicholas Cabasilas.[6] In this Neo-Maximian approach, the *logoi* express the rationality of the universe that points to the existence of a God who is the source of rationality. This view of complementarity between natural and supernatural revelation echoes the stance of the Romanian theologian Fr. Dumitru Staniloae, who had been very influential in Greece initially through his scholarship on Maximus the Confessor.[7] Staniloae highlighted the importance of natural revelation at the very beginning of his dogmatics. Natural revelation is the manifestation of God through nature that can be perceived by human beings who are spiritually purified and thus open to divine illumination. While natural revelation is distinct from an argument from design in natural theology, natural revelation is nevertheless in the vicinity of natural theology, as it may include a short informal inference from perceived features of the world to the existence of God.

Among the achievements of Staniloae's neopatristic synthesis one can note the use of modern science (quantum mechanics, theory of relativity, Darwinism) in a constructive way that does not always focus on the break with the medieval worldview.[8] Staniloae followed the Maximian theory of motion and evolution, which is a novel Christian interpretation of Aristo-

5. Panayiotis Nellas, *Deification in Christ: Orthodox Perspectives on the Nature of the Human Person* (Crestwood, NY: St. Vladimir's Seminary Press, 1987), 229–37. Originally published as *Ζώον Θεούμενον: Προοπτικές για μια Ορθόδοξη Κατανόηση του Ανθρώπου* (Athens: Epopteia, 1979).

6. Nellas, *Deification in Christ*, 141–45.

7. See Dumitru Staniloae, *Η* Μυσταγωγία *του Αγίου Μαξίμου του Ομολογητού: Εισαγωγή, Σχόλια* [*The* Mystagogy *of St. Maximus the Confessor with Introduction and Notes*] (Athens: Apostoliki Diakonia, 1973).

8. See the thorough analysis in Doru Costache, "A Theology of the World: Dumitru Stăniloae, the Traditional Worldview, and Contemporary Cosmology," in *Orthodox Christianity and Modern Science: Tensions, Ambiguities, Potential*, ed. Vasilios Makrides and Gayle Woloschak (Turnhout: Brepols, 2019), 205–22.

telian teleology, not stressing the fact that teleology has been questioned in many ways in modernity, especially by Darwinian evolutionism. Staniloae saw the patristic view of nature as dynamic and evolving as a result of a continuing divine action.[9] Panayiotis Nellas followed Staniloae in regarding the patristic view of nature as one of contingency and perpetual motion toward its eschatological fulfillment.[10] The element of natural theology here is that one could argue from the existence of human consciousness and relationality to the existence of God. Following Maximus the Confessor,[11] Nellas valued human intellection as a means of detecting the divine intentionality within creation, bringing the traditional argument from design into dialogue with modern versions of the anthropic principle.[12] The main line of this Orthodox natural theology followed by Staniloae and Nellas is that God has a plan for nature through the *logoi* of beings. This plan can be grasped by the human intellect, if the latter is purified. The observation of the "logical" character of the universe can serve as an indication for God's existence, which is then disclosed through the divine economy of revelation, the latter not contradicting but completing natural revelation. This Orthodox way of theology of nature does not consist in abstract reasoning and argumentation, but in the approach to God through the logical structure that is inherent in nature. The latter is affirmed and assumed by Christ who is the Logos par excellence, but it is also approachable rationally, including through inference from design. In other words, even though the patristic notion of rationality that is based on the *logoi* of beings mainly involves perception and spiritual discernment, it also includes inference, and so is in the vicinity of natural theology. The perception of the rationality of the cosmos and of its teleological design could thus serve as potentially broadly accessible grounds for believing in the existence of God.

9. Dumitru Staniloae, *The Experience of God: Orthodox Dogmatic Theology*, vol. 1, *Revelation and Knowledge of the Triune God*, trans. Ioan Ionita and Robert Barringer (Brookline, MA: Holy Cross Orthodox Press, 1994), 125–40. Originally published as *Teologia Dogmatica Ortodoxa I.* (Bucharest: Editura Institutului Biblic şi de Misiune al Bisericii Ortodoxe Române, 1978).

10. Nellas, *Deification in Christ*, 157–59.

11. Nellas, *Deification in Christ*, 211–21.

12. For a thorough analysis of the dialogue between the notion of the anthropic principle in St. Maximus the Confessor and contemporary versions of the anthropic principle, see Costache, "A Theology of the World," 217–21.

The "communitarian fideism" of trust in the thought of Christos Yannaras

The main current of the Theology of the Sixties was, however, highly critical of natural theology for a number of reasons that were related to the core commitments of its fundamental project. This strand was rather influenced by continental philosophy and more specifically by existentialism, personalism, and in different ways by phenomenology and hermeneutics, seeking and in many ways achieving an original synthesis with the premodern thought of the Byzantine Fathers. Most of the basic tenets of the project of the "theology of personhood" were hostile to natural theology, tending to work within the framework of sharp polarities such as person and nature, ontology and psychology, ontology and morality, freedom and necessity, and eschatology and history. From the standpoint of these oppositions, natural theology appears as a project of Western modernity, rooted in scholastic philosophy and centered on the notion of the necessity of divine being and the approach to it through human consciousness.[13] Since the Theology of the Sixties tended to link nature with necessity in a quasi-existentialist way, the emphasis on the necessity of divine being was criticized as "physiocratic" in the sense given to this term by Yannaras: namely, as an approach to God through the capacities of rational human nature, at the expense of the ontological gap between the created and the uncreated that is only bridged by personal freedom in Christ. The philosophical presupposition of this peculiar use of the term "physiocracy" (φυσιοκρατία) is a double equation of nature with necessity and of personhood with freedom from necessity. According to this view, an approach to God through natural reason, including inference, would be a menace to personal freedom. While the fundamentally critical stance of this movement toward natural theology is undeniable, let me also highlight some interesting similarities between the movement's basic tenets and some themes that we find in contemporary natural theology, particularly in the thought of Richard Swinburne.

First, it should be noted that there are important differences among the thinkers of the Theology of the Sixties. Despite using similar terminology and admitting some fundamental oppositions, as I have highlighted, the var-

13. For the critique of scholastic philosophy and its continuation in early modernity, see, for example: Christos Yannaras, *The Schism in Philosophy: The Hellenic Perspective and Its Western Reversal*, trans. Norman Russell (Brookline, MA: Holy Cross Orthodox Press, 2013), 95–112. Originally published as *Σχεδίασμα Εισαγωγής στη Φιλοσοφία* (Athens: Ikaros, 2013).

ious thinkers employed them with very different meanings and methodologies. For the purposes of this chapter, I will focus on the two most prominent representatives of the Theology of the Sixties who engaged philosophical problems, Christos Yannaras and John Zizioulas. In their thought, which differs in many ways despite the use of similar terminology, one can find a consistent critique of natural theology as well as some elements that could trigger a fruitful dialogue with its contemporary exponents.

The critique of natural theology by Christos Yannaras (b. 1935) is based on the experience of faith as personal trust.[14] In ancient Greek the word for faith (πίστις) had the connotation of "trust" in a person, even in the sense of commercial or financial credibility.[15] Yannaras follows the trend of fideism that was popular in continental theology after Karl Barth, but he gives it a specifically communal and communitarian meaning that is arguably more distinctively Orthodox than the more individualistic Protestant version.[16] The locus of trust in God is the whole community that has experienced God's personal acts of love and thus has faith in his future interventions.[17] One might speak of a "communal" or "communitarian fideism"[18] in the thought of Yannaras, in the sense that for Yannaras the community of the ecclesia also has a cosmological and metaphysical dimension, after the Eastern patristic tradition as one finds, for example, in the *Mystagogy* of St. Maximus the Confessor.[19] This sort of fideism is thus not only about a voluntaristic decision of the community, but about the community functioning as a "microcosm" of creation in reference to the Creator.

In order to understand the tensions in Yannaras's thought, one should note that Yannaras is against the reduction of God to the rational powers of human nature, which he often characterizes as "physiocracy,"[20] but at

14. Christos Yannaras, *Elements of Faith: Introduction to Orthodox Theology*, trans. Keith Schram (Edinburgh: T&T Clark, 1991), 7–14. Originally published as *Αλφαβητάρι της Πίστης* (Athens: Domos, 1983).

15. Yannaras, *Elements of Faith*, 11–12.

16. Yannaras, *Elements of Faith*, 30–31.

17. Metropolitan John of Pergamon (Zizioulas) is critical of what he conceives as a Protestant emphasis on faith as trust. See John Zizioulas, *Communion and Otherness: Further Studies in Personhood and the Church* (London: T&T Clark, 2006), 98.

18. For the biblical roots of this "communitarian fideism" in the Abrahamic community, see Yannaras, *Elements of Faith*, 8–9.

19. See Christos Yannaras, *The Freedom of Morality*, trans. Elizabeth Briere (Crestwood, NY: St. Vladimir's Seminary Press, 1984), 85–88. Originally published as *Η Ελευθερία του Ἠθους* (Athens: Grigoris, 1979).

20. For a critique of the ideological basis of physiocracy on the subject of relationality,

the same time he maintains that the Church is the consummation of a cosmological project in the sense that it both assumes the natural cosmos and manifests its metaphysical background in the logoi of beings which have a Christological reference.[21] For this reason, Yannaras's stance toward natural theology is more complex than one might initially think due to his explicit denunciation of physiocratic religiosity.[22] On the one hand, Yannaras is critical of natural theology, because he holds that it makes faith and trust superfluous. If someone can prove the existence of God through natural reasoning, then she does not need to have a personal relationship of trust with God. In a way that is characteristic of the Theology of the Sixties, the freedom of personhood is opposed both to the necessity associated with nature and to rationalism. Reason and faith are not seen as complementary. On the other hand, in Yannaras faith and reason are not seen as radically opposed or mutually exclusive,[23] as is arguably the case in fideist critics of rationalism from Tertullian to Blaise Pascal and Lev Shestov, who are sometimes considered as having elements of irrationalism in their thought. The reason for this is that Yannaras's thought could be described as "anti-naturalist metaphysics," a notion that stands in need of some clarification.

Yannaras is one of the few representatives of the Theology of the Sixties who accepts both the philosophical project of ontology and that of metaphysics.[24] His ambition is to assume the ancient Greek tradition and way of philosophizing as it was inherited by the Byzantine Fathers.[25] At the same time, he wishes to come into dialogue with philosophical modernism by also assuming a phenomenological method of thinking. The result is a paradoxical hybrid in his method that could be termed a "phenomenological metaphysics." Of course, the revival of metaphysics goes against the mainstream phenomenological current in which phenomenology is conceived exactly as the abolition and deconstruction of metaphysics. But Yannaras rather engages in a radical reinterpretation of metaphysics through a phe-

---

see Christos Yannaras, *Relational Ontology*, trans. Norman Russell (Brookline, MA: Holy Cross Orthodox Press, 2011), 26–30. Originally published as *Οντολογία της Σχέσης* (Athens: Ikaros, 2004).

21. Yannaras, *The Freedom of Morality*, 85–88.

22. Christos Yannaras, *Against Religion: The Alienation of the Ecclesial Event*, trans. Norman Russell (Brookline, MA: Holy Cross Orthodox Press, 2013), 1–20. Originally published as *Ενάντια στη Θρησκεία* (Athens: Ikaros, 2006).

23. Yannaras develops his methodology in Yannaras, *Relational Ontology*, 4–9.

24. Yannaras, *Elements of Faith*, 3.

25. Yannaras, *Elements of Faith*, 18–19.

nomenological method of philosophizing that could be called bottom-up, i.e., starting from the concrete experience of the human personal subject (phenomenology) and proceeding to the grounding of this experience of nature that transcends nature.[26] Yannaras's theory of subjectivity has modern personalistic and phenomenological elements, which he combines with the theology of personhood in the Fathers: he regards the person as relational and extrovert subjectivity and not as a dominant Cartesian thinking substance or a post-Kantian introvert idealistic container of categories.[27] Unlike Zizioulas, Yannaras speaks about personhood as self-consciousness, but he hastens to add that it is a "relational self-consciousness" and not an individualistic one.[28] One could argue that this combination of phenomenology with metaphysics allows a certain place for natural theology in Yannaras's thought, even though Yannaras denounces the excessively rationalistic character of natural theology in the scholastic tradition and its modern heirs. If one could speak about natural theology in the thought of Yannaras, then its starting point would be the "natural contemplation" (φυσικὴ θεωρία) of the Fathers.[29] In a novel interpretation of Maximus the Confessor, the person as a whole (i.e., not the detached intellect as in medieval philosophy) can experience nature in the extroverted way of post-Brentano and post-Husserlian phenomenology. The person contemplates in this experience the *logoi* of divine presence[30] through which one can also participate in the divine *energeia* in a Palamite way.[31]

Yannaras also has a place for a certain kind of teleology,[32] which might seem strange given his strong anti-Thomist stance. He admits that not only efficient but also final causality are part of metaphysics and human reason[33]

26. Yannaras, *Elements of Faith*, 2.

27. For Yannaras's critique of interiority, see Yannaras, *Against Religion*, 147.

28. Yannaras, *Elements of Faith*, 29–30, 36.

29. Yannaras, *Elements of Faith*, 46.

30. See Christos Yannaras, *Person and Eros*, trans. Norman Russell (Brookline, MA: Holy Cross Orthodox Press, 2007), 73–100. Originally published as *Το Πρόσωπο και ο Έρως* (Athens: Domos, 1987).

31. Yannaras, *Person and Eros*, 171–72.

32. Yannaras, *Elements of Faith*, 2, 4.

33. In the terminology of the Greek speaking Fathers and especially in that of Maximus the Confessor, who is the main inspiration for Yannaras, there are different sets of terms for human reason. The terms νοῦς and νόησις, which are often translated as "intellect" and "intellection," denote on the one hand the contemplation of God's "logoi" in creation and, on the other, an approach to God's simplicity without images, especially in the case of the "intellectual prayer" (νοερὰ προσευχή). The term λόγος, which could be translated as either "reason" or "speech"

functions with these categories in its metaphysical investigation. By accepting the importance of teleology—in contrast to Zizioulas, who totally rejects teleology in favor of non-teleological eschatology—Yannaras embraces the Aristotelian tradition as it was inherited by the Byzantine Fathers. To sum up, on the one hand the point of departure of Yannaras's methodology is a phenomenological one based on extrovert personhood. On the other hand, on the way to approaching God as the efficient and final goal of the experienced nature, as its Logos that is manifested through the energies, Yannaras would wish to assume the achievements of ancient Greek and Byzantine metaphysical thought.[34] In the latter, one could arguably detect a certain form of natural theology focused on the contemplation of nature (φυσικὴ θεωρία).[35] In other words, Yannaras would not reject the sense that the human person can arrive at God as both efficient and final cause through the contemplation of nature; he would accept a meta-physical "extension" of the experience of the *physis*.[36] This possibility to elevate oneself from the physical to the meta-physical could be considered as a divine gift bestowed by God upon man's "logical" character, i.e., upon his ability to apprehend[37] the final causality that is manifest in nature. In this sense, natural theology could focus on the inference to the existence of God from design, which is linked to the observation of the rationality of the cosmos in a Maximian and Palamite sense.[38]

Having made these remarks about how a certain sort of natural theology could be preserved as an aspect of Yannaras's philosophical approach, it is equally important to note that he rejects a great part of the tradition of natural theology as it was formulated in the scholastic and modern West. This rejection has to be understood in the context of Yannaras's wider cultural project. Yannaras wishes to make extensive use of modern science (e.g.,

---

depending on the context, denotes man's rational response to the "logoi" of beings that are contemplated by the human νοῦς and consequently the manifestation of this response through speech. Finally, the term διάνοια denotes different types of discursive reasoning, including inference.

34. Yannaras, *Elements of Faith*, 6–7.

35. Yannaras, *Person and Eros*, 188–90.

36. See Christos Yannaras, *Post-Modern Metaphysics*, trans. Norman Russell (Brookline, MA: Holy Cross Orthodox Press, 2004), 83–182. Originally published as *Μετανεωτερική Μεταφυσική* (Athens: Domos, 1993).

37. The Greek verb used for this "apprehension" is συλλέγειν, which usually means "to collect." In this sense, the apprehension of final causality in nature is metaphorically compared to a "collection" (συλλογή) of the divine logoi of beings by the human intellect (νοῦς).

38. Yannaras, *Person and Eros*, 55–65.

quantum mechanics, the theory of relativity, the Darwinian theory of evolution) in order to show the collapse of the Western medieval worldview and hence the importance of Orthodox apophaticism.[39] His general plan is to regard the modernism of the late nineteenth and twentieth centuries (including phenomenology and existentialism, but also Marxist materialism and Freudian and Lacanian psychoanalysis[40]) as the witness to the failure of the medieval and early modern Western worldview, while postmodernity is viewed as a potential opening to alternative worldviews in which the Eastern metaphysical tradition could have a fruitful role through its apophaticism.[41] This is obviously a philosophical program that is placed inside the continental philosophical tradition, using a peculiar reading of Martin Heidegger, and as such rejects natural theology.

One may highlight some fundamental objections against natural theology in the thought of Yannaras:

(i) Natural theology is regarded as "onto-theological," after Heidegger's famous critique.[42] In other words, the God of natural theology is one being among many, even if he is regarded as the first efficient cause or the absolute final cause. It is true that Yannaras has space for a contemplation of God's efficient and final causality in his neo-metaphysical thought, but he regards the latter as an openness of personhood to radical otherness. In Yannaras's phenomenological metaphysics, the human person can approach the rationality of the cosmos that is caused by God without however "grasping" and "conceiving" (after the Latin etymology of *concipere* from *con* and *capio*, grasp) God's being as a divine reified substance in an onto-theological way.

(ii) In a similar way, Yannaras criticizes the rationalism of natural theology. He denounces natural theology as an effort to conquer and objectify God in order to acquire individual certainty.[43] The latter could be considered as a sort of epistemological "egoism,"[44] since certainty is for Yannaras tantamount to a "fortification" of the individual to oneself as well as to the objectification and "consumption" of otherness, be it human or divine.[45]

39. See Yannaras, *Post-Modern Metaphysics*, 1–46, 73–140.

40. Christos Yannaras, *The Meaning of Reality: Essays on Existence and Communion, Eros and History* (Los Angeles: Sebastian Press and Indiktos, 2011), 51–59.

41. Yannaras, *Elements of Faith*, 15–19.

42. For Yannaras's comprehension of the Heideggerian distinction between the "ontic" and the "ontological," see Yannaras, *Person and Eros*, 28–30.

43. Yannaras, *Elements of Faith*, 155.

44. Yannaras, *Elements of Faith*, 1.

45. Yannaras, *Against Religion*, 54.

What is denounced is thus natural theology as a sort of "epistemological imperialism."

(iii) Yannaras has an existentialist view of rationality as necessity that is opposed to personal freedom. Natural theology would thus be regarded as "unfree" or as undermining the risk of the personal encounter with otherness. Again, this is a part of his critique of the rationalist character of natural theology.[46]

(iv) Yannaras gives an original interpretation of the patristic distinction between the "that" (ὅτι), the "what" (τί), and the "how" (πῶς). For Yannaras, the opposition is rather a dual one between the "what" and the "how." The "what" is regarded as tantamount to objective data and information about the substantial content of a being, whereas the "how" can refer to one's personal mode of existence in the case of persons, or to substance as the dynamic product of interpersonal interaction in the case of non-personal natures.[47] It is to be noted that for Yannaras even non-personal nature is seen as the dynamic "deed" of personal intervention.[48] Yannaras thus conflates the "what" and the "how," considering that in reality even the "what" of nature is a "how." As a matter of fact, the "what" arises only from an inauthentic human epistemological stance that objectifies nature. In this context, natural theology could perhaps offer some information about the fact of God's existence, even though this is not certain in view of late modern objections. But in any case, this information is irrelevant for what theology really is, namely, an encounter with the mode of God as personal Trinity.[49] According to Yannaras, natural theology could be seen as an inauthentic epistemological stance in an existentialist sense, i.e., an abstraction of the "that/what" from the "how." For Yannaras this abstraction is impossible in reality and is only a fiction created by the human mind.

(v) Yannaras is also critical of Western "apologetics" that constitute for him an "arrière-garde" combat.[50] Modern natural theology would thus be regarded as fundamentally conservative in character, since it engages in dialogue with modern science, logic, and epistemology mostly in order to reaffirm or at best to reformulate the Western medieval worldview. But

46. Yannaras, *Elements of Faith*, 31.

47. Yannaras, *Person and Eros*, 73–81.

48. Yannaras, *Elements of Faith*, 42–45.

49. This encounter takes place through the corresponding mode of the ecclesial tradition, See Yannaras, *Against Religion*, 51–52.

50. For Yannaras's views on apologetics, see Yannaras, *Η Απολογητική* [*Apologetics*] (Athens: Grigoris, 1975).

Yannaras's project is exactly the opposite, namely to celebrate some of the achievements of modern science and epistemology in order to deconstruct the medieval and early modern Western worldview (roughly from Augustine to the idealist-materialist divide of the nineteenth century).[51] Yannaras thus rather wishes to engage in an "avant-garde" combat to reformulate the Hellenic apophatic tradition in dialogue with the new "uncertainties" and "unlearning" that late modernity and postmodernity have brought.[52] Thus, for Yannaras denouncing natural theology would be part of this late modern or postmodern "un-learning" that could be brought into fruitful dialogue with the Eastern tradition of apophatic participation (*methexis*).[53]

(vi) Finally, Yannaras makes a stark contrast between ecclesia and religion, following but also reinterpreting Karl Barth and Dietrich Bonhoeffer in a novel Orthodox way.[54] In this context, on the one hand natural theology would be part of religion, that is, according to Yannaras's definition of it, of the effort of the individual to acquire objective certainty[55] and thus increase his epistemic credentials.[56] On the other hand, genuine ecclesial experience is viewed as a communal and intra-personal openness to the risk and the surprise of the encounter with a non-objectified divine otherness.[57]

Yannaras's dismissive stance toward natural theology has been quite influential in modern Greek theology. At the same time, as we have observed, Yannaras's thought presents some interesting tensions that can only be labeled paradoxically, such as "communitarian fideism" and "phenomenological metaphysics." In this respect, Yannaras's thought might prove fruitful for showing what a distinctively Orthodox natural theology would look like. For example, it recognizes man's possibility to approach divine efficient and final causality through the patristic notions of *logoi* and *energeiai*, the latter being experienced through a holistic *methexis* of human persons in communion.[58] In this sense, there might be space for natural theology as the contemplation of nature (φυσικὴ θεωρία) and the divine presence in it, as long as this divine

51. Yannaras, *Post-Modern Metaphysics*, 1–46.

52. Yannaras, *Elements of Faith*, 37–42.

53. Yannaras, *Post-Modern Metaphysics*, 83–140, 171–82.

54. See Yannaras, *Against Religion*.

55. Yannaras, *Against Religion*, 16–20.

56. Yannaras, *Elements of Faith*, 5–6.

57. Yannaras, *Against Religion*, 21–48.

58. Christos Yannaras, *On the Absence and Unknowability of God: Heidegger and the Areopagite*, trans. Charalambos Ventis (London: T&T Clark, 2005), 83–110. Originally published as *Χάιντεγγερ και Αρεοπαγίτης* (Athens: Domos, 1988).

presence is not objectified and nature is itself regarded as a dynamic mode (πῶς) of interaction between divine and human personhood.[59]

The "hermeneutics of the Resurrection" in the thought of John Zizioulas

In the thought of Metropolitan John of Pergamon (b. 1931) one finds a different non-phenomenological understanding of personhood that does not include consciousness even in a relational sense, but is focused mainly on otherness.[60] Zizioulas makes theological use of Darwinism and Freudian psychoanalysis in order to question the post-Cartesian priority of the individual consciousness, thus being opposed to any kind of natural theology that posits the independent reasoning of the individual consciousness as its point of departure.[61] Even though Zizioulas rejects phenomenology,[62] he follows a hermeneutical method which is eschatological in character since the end explains the beginning. This is not a metaphysical teleology as in Yannaras; in fact, Zizioulas rejects metaphysics and only assumes a non-metaphysical ontology of personhood.[63] For Metropolitan John final causes are neither natural/biological nor metaphysical in the sense of an extension of *physis* to its grounding. Final causation might take place inside history, but it is a free divine intervention that moves from the future to the past. Zizioulas does not conflate philosophy and theology as Yannaras does; philosophy might provide the significant questions and existential demands, but the role of the theologian is to reinterpret the theological truth in order to cater to these philosophical demands, according to an original version of Paul Tillich's method of correlation.[64] The role of the theologian is thus an interpretation of history based on insights coming from the future of eschatological salvation. It seems, then, that there is not much space in Zizioulas's thought for independent reasoning such as that found in natural theology. However, one could note some interesting points of contact with natural

59. Yannaras, *Elements of Faith*, 46.

60. Zizioulas, *Communion and Otherness*, 46.

61. Zizioulas, *Communion and Otherness*, 39, 211.

62. Zizioulas, *Communion and Otherness*, 44.

63. Zizioulas, *Communion and Otherness*, 99–112.

64. This is the fundamental principle in John Zizioulas, *Ελληνισμός και Χριστιανισμός: Η συνάντηση των δύο κόσμων* [*Hellenism and Christianity: The Meeting of the Two Worlds*] (Athens: Apostoliki Diakonia, 2003).

theology, provided that the hermeneutical character of his theology is taken into account.

Metropolitan John emphasizes the patristic distinction between the "that" (ὅτι), the "what" (τί), and the "how" (πῶς) in God. While Yannaras tends to conflate them and reduce everything to the "how," identifying the *logos* and the *tropos* of beings, Zizioulas is more careful to articulate a genuine contrast between them.[65] For Zizioulas, modern atheism is restricted to the question of the "that," which was considered as too preliminary by the Fathers. In other words, God is regarded solely as a divine substance and the question is whether this substance exists or not. But for Zizioulas true theology really begins only when the question of "how" emerges, that is the question of God's personal, living relationship with man.[66] In this sense, one could say that both atheism and a part of natural theology are beside the point, since they try to give different answers to a question that is irrelevant for genuine theology. An Orthodox theologian should not engage with the atheist in a debate about the question of "that," but should reply with an answer about the Trinitarian "how" of God, thus giving an answer about the "that" only implicitly. In the experience of the Church the "what" of God, i.e., his super-essential essence, remains unknown, but the "how," i.e., the personal mode of existence of the Trinity, which also constitutes God's "image" in man, is revealed in the communion of the Eucharist.[67] If the question of "how" is answered in an experiential way, then the question of "that" is superfluous and the question of "what" might remain unanswered. For Zizioulas, atheism could thus be regarded as emerging exactly due to the wrong questions put by the substantialist theology of the Augustinian and Thomist tradition.[68] On the other hand, the emphasis on the "how" of the Trinity is regarded by Zizioulas as offering valuable insights for the concept of "relationality" that is very important in the philosophy of nature, after the scientific revolution brought by quantum mechanics.[69]

The eschatological event that functions as the hermeneutical key for every

65. For Zizioulas the importance of the question of the unknown "what" of God is to guarantee the otherness between the created and the Uncreated: "The real—and perhaps the only—issue behind the use of the notion of the substance in theology was to safeguard . . . the dialectic between created and uncreated," Zizioulas, *Communion and Otherness*, 183.

66. John Zizioulas, *Being as Communion: Studies in Personhood and the Church* (London: Darton, Longman and Todd, 1985), 16–17.

67. Zizioulas, *Communion and Otherness*, 165–66.

68. Zizioulas, *Communion and Otherness*, 97–98, 151.

69. John Zizioulas, "Relational Ontology: Insights from the Patristic Thought," in *The*

interpretation is par excellence the Resurrection of Christ, which entails the resurrection of all mankind and creation. For Zizioulas this event could even become a principle of deduction from which every Christian dogma could follow. Dogmatics is then the consequence of an event that is both historical and eschatological in character.[70] It is interesting that Zizioulas might follow lines of reasoning that sometimes resemble the project of Richard Swinburne; the main difference is that for Zizioulas the point of departure is the Resurrection, which explains everything, rather than the other way round, i.e., starting from natural reason and then approaching tenets of the Christian faith through induction and probabilism. For Zizioulas all theology is already included in the exclamation "Christ is risen." It will suffice to note here some main points of his reasoning. The salvation entailed by the Resurrection implies two different full natures, since the one saved must be fully human; but the unity of the two natures can be achieved only by a single person that unites them in the hypostatic union. And since the Resurrection is not an individual but a relational event, a plurality of divine Persons is implied in it, since the Father resurrects the Son in the Spirit. One could arguably proceed to more complex dogmas, such as the virgin birth of Christ in its patristic understanding as a *prolepsis* of the eschatological abolition of sexual reproduction. What is important to note is the double historical and eschatological character of the Resurrection of Christ: The Resurrection is a particular historical event that happened at a certain time to Jesus of Nazareth. But at the same time, the resurrected Christ eschatologically bears in his person the totality of human nature or even of the whole of creation.[71] The Resurrection is thus also the inbreaking of the eschatological mode of being into history. In a sense, the Resurrection of Christ comes from the future and not from the past, since its full consequences will be manifested only in the eschaton and are now offered proleptically through communion in the Eucharist.[72]

This deduction of dogmatics from a historical/eschatological event is of course very far from natural theology. But what I would like to point out is Zizioulas's insistence on sound reasoning (even though in his case mostly deductive rather than inductive, as is the case with Richard Swinburne).

Trinity and an Entangled World, ed. John Polkinghorne (Grand Rapids, MI: Eerdmans, 2010), 146–56.

70. For the relation between history and eschatology, see John Zizioulas, "Eschatology and History," in *Cultures in Dialogue: Documents from a Symposium in Honor of Philip A. Potter*, ed. Thomas Wieser (Geneva: World Council of Churches, 1985), 30–39.

71. Zizioulas, *Communion and Otherness*, 243–44.

72. Zizioulas, *Communion and Otherness*, 227.

The latter is also due to the fact that Zizioulas has had an Anglo-Saxon philosophical education and he insists on the values of clarity, simplicity, and coherence, even though he does not employ them in an analytical framework. Zizioulas's method would seem to start from eschatology and eschatological Christology, then perform a "hermeneutics of the Resurrection," through which dogmatics is deduced, finally approaching anthropology and natural theology toward the end of the deductive process. Zizioulas understands the *logoi* of creation as God's personal wills that lead nature toward its eschatological fulfillment in the Person of the Logos.[73] It is notable that Zizioulas's dogmatics is not "dogmatic" in character, since it is an offspring of hermeneutics. In other words, it does not constitute initial axiomatic tenets, but is more like a vision for what future salvation might be.

While discussing the latter, Zizioulas engages in a type of reasoning that arguably resembles that of philosophers like Richard Swinburne, who uses the methods of analytic philosophy. Regarding Trinitarian theology, both thinkers develop consistent Social Trinitarianism by employing simple and gradual arguments. Zizioulas's argument starts from the fact that in Christianity salvation is linked to love, hence God must be love in his own being and not only in relation to the world.[74] There is thus need for a plurality of divine persons. The "Christian cogito" therefore would not only be an *amo ergo sum* (I love therefore I am),[75] but a more complex *amamur ergo sunt* (we are loved, therefore they are, i.e., we, as an ecclesial community, are loved by God, who cannot but be a plurality of persons).[76] An important difference between Zizioulas's and Swinburne's Social Trinitarianism is that for Zizioulas there is a certain logical and *quoad nos* (though not of course ontological and *per se*) contingency in God being *three* Persons,[77] whereas Swinburne has developed Richard of St. Victor's position in the direction of demonstrating that God can be neither less *nor more* than three Persons.[78]

73. Zizioulas, *Communion and Otherness*, 64.

74. Zizioulas, *Being as Communion*, 46.

75. The *amo ergo sum* is regarded by Zizioulas as offering ontological priority to selfhood in an unfortunate way. It should be completed by the *amar ergo sum* ("I am loved, therefore I am"). See Zizioulas, *Communion and Otherness*, 89.

76. Metropolitan John formulates his own "cogito" as "I am loved, therefore I am" and as "We are loved, therefore he [God] exists." See Zizioulas, *Communion and Otherness*, 89, 98.

77. For Zizioulas the image of God in man is rather an *imago Trinitatis*, i.e., the image of a plurality of Divine Persons; see Zizioulas, *Communion and Otherness*, 249. However, Zizioulas refuses to establish logically necessary reasons for the Threeness of the divine persons.

78. Richard Swinburne, "The Social Theory of the Trinity," *Religious Studies* 54 (2018): 419–37; *The Christian God* (Oxford: Oxford University Press, 1994), 170–91.

Notably, while Swinburne uses cumulative and probabilistic arguments in order to show the existence of God, in his argumentation for God being a Trinity of persons he employs arguments that have a necessary character. In this sense, Swinburne's project entails a very bold form of natural theology which uses probabilistic arguments to make a cumulative case for the existence of God and then continues with necessary arguments in order to show his Trinitarian character, the latter resulting from God's definition as love.

For the needs of this chapter I would like to stress two complementary views: On the one hand, Zizioulas's project is just the opposite of natural theology, or, to be more precise, it is the *inverse way* of theologizing: it is a top-down theology,[79] moving from the eschaton to the anterior, from eschatological Christology through hermeneutics to dogmatics and then to anthropology and theology of nature.[80] (In this Zizioulas's way of theologizing is also opposite to that of Yannaras, who often starts from phenomenology and then proceeds with metaphysics before arriving at theology proper.) The project of natural theology, as exemplified in modern thinkers like Richard Swinburne, usually follows the inverse way, starting from rational argumentation based on nature and then proceeding mostly through inductive, probabilistic, and cumulative arguments to the existence of God, then to Christian soteriology proper as well as to God as Trinity and to Christology. In some cases, such as in Trinitarian theology, there might be a recourse to deductive arguments. This is a very bold project, in which natural theology is not only a prolegomenon to revealed theology, but its main foundation. It is to be noted, however, that both thinkers have a similar *ethos* of reasoning. They are committed to step-by-step reasoning with simplicity and coherence, building in the end a very impressive all-encompassing theoretical construction. One could note that the main difference is the *direction* of this reasoning, top-down in the case of Zizioulas,[81] bottom-up in the case of Swinburne.

79. See for example the top-down approach to anthropology in Zizioulas, *Communion and Otherness*, 206–49.

80. The most characteristic example is that the notion of personhood is drawn from Trinitarian theology and eschatological Christology and is then applied to anthropology. It is for this reason that Zizioulas distinguishes between the person and the individual, since the latter is rejected in Trinitarian theology and eschatological Christology. See Zizioulas, *Communion and Otherness*, 175–77.

81. Zizioulas's "top-down" methodology is best exemplified in Zizioulas, *Communion and Otherness*, 171–77.

"God's detectives": a dialogue between the Orthodox theology of the *logoi* of beings and Richard Swinburne's natural theology

The aforementioned critique of natural theology has been exercised by Greek scholars who are steeped in the continental philosophical tradition. But in order to achieve fruitful progress in the twenty-first century, a deeper dialogue should be pursued between Christian thinkers in the analytic and continental traditions. Following the linguistic turn of philosophy with Ludwig Wittgenstein,[82] there has been a certain stabilization of the split between the continental and analytic thought in the English-speaking countries. What characterizes "analytic philosophy" is that it believes in careful rigorous argument leading to conclusions about metaphysics, epistemology, or ethics, starting from premises which are of various kinds but are very sensitive to the discoveries of modern science. In the beginning, analytic philosophy was very antagonistic to natural theology, its two main currents being: (i) "ordinary language philosophy," which held that one could not talk about God, and that to talk apparently about God involved using words in highly misleading ways; (ii) logical positivism, which held that religious utterances did not conform to positivistic criteria of meaningfulness and were therefore nonsensical.[83] Logical positivism claimed that metaphysical, religious, or even moral statements were not even false: they were nonsense, deprived of meaningful content, as they could be neither confirmed nor disconfirmed.

However, even though analytic philosophy initially had a very hostile attitude toward metaphysics, its shift of emphasis to semiotics has led to an interest in accounting for the way we use words, including those that denote religious experience. In this analytic philosophy has to some extent repeated the stance of British empiricism. While empiricist epistemology often led to a deconstruction of traditional metaphysics, its very emphasis on the study of any experience meant that religious or mystical experiences could also be discussed as part of the general engagement in the study of experience. In the same way, even though analytic philosophy originally meant an emphasis on logical rigor deconstructing obsolete metaphysics, its very emphasis on the construction of meaning meant that eventually any meaning could or

82. For the reception of Ludwig Wittgenstein by modern Greek Orthodox thought, see Michalis Paraskevopoulos, *Wittgenstein και Θεολογία: Η υποδοχή της φιλοσοφίας της θρησκείας του Wittgenstein από τη νεοελληνική θεολογία* [*Wittgenstein and Theology: The Reception of Wittgenstein's Philosophy of Religion by Modern Greek Theology*] (Athens: Grigoris, 2017).

83. See A. J. Ayer, *Language, Truth and Logic* (London: Victor Gollancz, 1936).

should be discussed, including the meaning of religious signifiers, provided that this discussion is performed with rigor.

What is ironic is that it is mainly in the Anglophone world that we find a flourishing of natural theology, particularly after the 1970s. In continental philosophy the post-Enlightenment anti-metaphysical stance has led to an almost permanent burial of natural theology. The main way out for religious subjects in continental philosophy has been the current of phenomenology, in its eventual relationship with personalism and hermeneutics. But phenomenology is usually hostile to natural theology and sometimes (but not always) lacks rigor in its construction of arguments. It has sometimes been sensitive to the presence of the divine Otherness inside the world of experience, but its stance has usually been that of bracketing, according to the Husserlian "epoche," what can be objectively known in order to encounter its pure contingent presence in our consciousness. For such reasons natural theology was underdeveloped in continental thought, and such influences partly account for the distrust we have observed of Orthodox theologians towards natural theology. In the beginning of the twenty-first century, there has been among Greek Orthodox religious thinkers a renewed interest in analytical philosophy, which might bring a revival of natural theology in novel terms.[84] The dialogue between traditional Orthodox theology and new forms of natural theology is thus very promising.

What changed after the 1970s in analytic philosophy was a renewed interest in the semiotics of religious meanings, in the epistemology of religious knowledge, and, largely thanks to Richard Swinburne, in the validity of arguments for the existence of God. A further change was the so-called "metaphysical turn" from linguistic analysis to a renewed form of contemporary metaphysics. The latter occurred because philosophy had to take account of science as the modern paradigm of knowledge as well as the development of modern logic after Gottlob Frege. Since science was now picturing a reality that lay behind the observable physical world, philosophers realized they had to share that aim and take it further by producing theories of everything. Hence most analytic philosophers came to acknowledge the centrality of metaphysics in philosophy. Of course, this often meant a metaphysics that was closer to an atheist worldview, but sometimes it did not. If one makes a

84. See for example, Stelios Virvidakis and Michalis Philippou, eds., *Επιχειρήματα για την Ύπαρξη του Θεού και άλλα δοκίμια Αναλυτικής Φιλοσοφίας της Θρησκείας* [*Arguments for the Existence of God and Other Essays in Analytical Philosophy of Religion*] (Athens: Artos Zois, 2018).

comparison with the continental philosophy that inspired Greek Orthodox thinkers of the late twentieth century, one could note that the project of phenomenology had entailed a deconstruction of traditional metaphysics, which was continued by other post-phenomenological continental currents, such as structuralism or post-structuralism. The options offered to Orthodox thinkers inspired by continental thought were either to reject metaphysics, thus becoming alienated from a great part of the Byzantine tradition, or to make a radical reinterpretation of metaphysics, thus risking the creation of a hybrid philosophy that would be paradoxical to the detriment of its plausibility. What analytic philosophy has to offer to Orthodox thinkers is its late modern revival of metaphysics that is attuned to the scientific worldview. This new form of metaphysics takes into account the achievements of modern logic and science. However, at the same time it allows Christian thinkers to retain some of the best insights of medieval Christian philosophers. For this reason, a dialogue between Orthodox theology and analytic philosophy might prove fruitful in showing a way out of some of the impasses provoked by a perhaps too one-sided dependence on the continental tradition.

The relevant project of Richard Swinburne can be summarized under the following points.[85] (i) It relies primarily on inductive rather than deductive reasoning, particularly that with an empirical foundation. It is based on probable arguments and not necessary ones (probabilism). (ii) The arguments are cumulative: theism is not proved by a single decisive argument (such as the ontological argument, for example), but by the accumulation of a series of probable arguments. Some of their starting points are as follows: the existence of a complex world; the existence of laws of nature that present a certain permanence, reliability, and rational structure; the emergence of conscious beings that can conceive of moral and aesthetic values, progress morally, or succumb to evil; and, finally, the fact that the natural world responds to the demands of such conscious beings. (iii) Despite the accumulation of such arguments, they do not provide decisive grounds to move beyond agnosticism. However, a decisive leap in this direction is provided by the religious and mystical experience of religious believers. This is usually some sort of transcendent experience that has, however, the nature

85. See the trilogy: Richard Swinburne, *Faith and Reason* (Oxford: Oxford University Press, 1981); *The Existence of God*, 2nd ed. (Oxford: Oxford University Press, 2004); *The Coherence of Theism*, 2nd ed. (Oxford: Oxford University Press, 2016). For an evaluation of Swinburne's natural theology in relation to Orthodox theology, see Michalis Philippou, "Αναλυτικά επιχειρήματα για την ύπαρξη του Θεού" ["Analytical Arguments for the Existence of God"], in Virvidakis and Philippou, *Επιχειρήματα για την Ύπαρξη του Θεού*, 224–318.

of a concrete perception of the divine. (iv) When the hypothesis that would explain all these phenomena is introduced, there are certain criteria for its adoption. One of them is simplicity.[86] (v) Another criterion is its being in tune with what is already known, i.e., its coherence. (vi) A final criterion is its explanatory power, i.e., its ability to explain as many phenomena as possible. (vii) The theistic hypothesis, which posits God as the personal type of cause, fulfills all these criteria. God has the greatest interpretative range, being both coherent with what is known and the simplest possible cause.

In light of our subject in this chapter, we may well ask whether this line of highly technical argumentation could indeed be regarded as an Orthodox natural theology (apart from the fact that Swinburne is an Oxford philosopher who is also an Orthodox believer), or, at the least, whether it can be the basis for a fruitful dialogue with Orthodox thinkers. In many respects Swinburne's endeavor constitutes a contemporary revival of Thomas Aquinas's thought in particular and of medieval scholasticism in general. One could claim that Swinburne's conversion to Orthodoxy has not entailed a change in his beliefs. However, some of Swinburne's views are more at home in the Orthodox Church, as for example, his emphasis on free will, which has been maintained vigorously by Orthodox theology, but not always by all branches of Protestant thought. Similarly, his views on the problem of evil, namely that it is valuable for the choices that it gives us as a reaction to it, is also more at home in the Orthodox tradition and its view on theodicy.[87] More concretely, his setting aside of the ontological argument for more inductive and probabilistic ones is in tune with the empiricism that is characteristic of the Orthodox tradition. After all, the cumulative probabilistic arguments are crowned by an appeal to the experience of people who have had a mystical and ecstatic experience of God, something that recalls the Orthodox emphasis on participation in the divine energies as a means of direct knowledge of God. On the other hand, in some cases Swinburne complements the Orthodox stance with elements that are less native to it, such as a stance of intense intellectual curiosity, and also a valorization of scientific research and progress as one means among many by which men respond to the challenge of evil, following God's incentive.

86. See also Richard Swinburne, *Simplicity as Evidence of Truth* (Milwaukee, WI: Marquette University Press, 1997).

87. See Richard Swinburne, *Providence and the Problem of Evil* (Oxford: Oxford University Press, 1998).

A possible objection to natural theology is that it makes faith superfluous. It is to be noted that this is not the case in Swinburne's thought. Swinburne's probabilism leaves plenty of room for faith, since human reason offers only probable arguments for the existence of God and not necessary ones. The full psycho-corporeal participation in the energies of God that is rendered possible thanks to the Incarnation of Christ is considered the pinnacle of testimonies for his existence. The Christian, according to Swinburne, resembles a detective who searches for probable evidence of God's existence everywhere, with an outstanding intellectual curiosity (a feature that, alas, is not shared by many Orthodox) and finds it in inductive thoughts about nature, but most of all in ecstatic experience. Moreover, Swinburne's use of analytic thought, which is in many ways a foreign element for most Orthodox, leads to great syntheses and to an appeal to God as the One who guarantees simplicity. Analysis is, for Swinburne, a point of departure, which ends in the favoring of simplicity and wide synthetic interpretative range over a futile *a priori* insistence on pluralism and relativism. For such reasons, one could claim that Swinburne's natural theology is indeed an Orthodox natural theology of the twentieth and twenty-first centuries, as it constitutes a fruitful combination of Orthodox empiricism with the British tradition of empiricism. Swinburne's probabilism could be rendered compatible with the Orthodox emphasis on apophaticism, since God's hiddenness inside creation is an incentive for investigation, in the same way that in traditional Eastern theology the wise man searches for the *logoi* of God in the cosmos.

An open question for this dialogue between natural theology and a properly Orthodox theology is whether it is possible for natural theology to be reconciled with a traditional ecclesial understanding of knowledge, in which purification (κάθαρσις) is needed for the knowledge of God.[88] In patristic theology, the wise man is also a sort of "detective," since he tries to detect God's traces in beings. He is in fact a detective who, like Oedipus, gains self-consciousness in the process of inquiring into the truth: by searching for God's *logoi* for beings, the wise man is equally searching for his own true nature and relational selfhood as it will be revealed in the future. For this reason, he needs to purify his cognitive capacities through a better relationship with his environment. In this reinterpretation of its traditional sense, natural theology could be conceived as a first analogical step in the open historical trajectory of the meeting with God, which will culminate in the eschatological integration of the many *logoi* in the One Logos of Christ.

88. Yannaras, *Elements of Faith*, 49–50.

6. Experiential Objections against Natural Theology in Some Recent Orthodox Thinkers

TRAVIS DUMSDAY

Introduction

The practice of employing philosophical argumentation to explicate and defend the doctrinal commitments of the Church has a distinguished pedigree, going back to the early patristic era. The label "natural theology" is sometimes employed broadly to refer to that practice; others use it more narrowly, to refer to the use of philosophy in explicating and defending those doctrinal commitments in principle[1] accessible to human reason independently of special revelation. For present purposes I will adhere to the latter, more common usage.

Natural theology constitutes a noteworthy part of the intellectual heritage of Christianity, both East and West. Yet, despite the many examples of it on display within Eastern thinkers historically (sometimes fairly sophisticated),[2] and despite the fact that there are today quite a few Orthodox scholars making valuable contributions to the field, natural theology is widely viewed as being more characteristic of the West than of the East. This is not a mistaken impression, as natural theology has in fact enjoyed greater prominence in the West. That prominence waned somewhat during the post-Enlightenment period, when such influences as Kantianism, pos-

1. The "in principle" is needed in order to bracket (for now) debates about what was accessible to pre-lapsarian reason versus what is accessible to our actual rational faculties as they function today, and also debates about alleged differences in what is accessible today to those who reason from within the Church versus those outside it.

2. Consult for instance the teleological and cosmological arguments for theism deployed by Maximus the Confessor, *On Difficulties in the Church Fathers: The Ambigua (Volume I)*, ed. and trans. Maximos Constas (Cambridge, MA: Harvard University Press, 2014), 283–99.

itivism, and theological liberalism combined to render widespread the belief that the entire enterprise was inherently doomed to failure; but the latter half of the twentieth century up through the present has seen a radical shift in its status in the West, at least outside liberal theological circles (where the nineteenth century never dies) and the continental tradition. In fact it is no exaggeration to say that natural theology has experienced a renaissance. There are a number of partially intersecting reasons for this, including: the implosion of positivism as a philosophical movement in the 1950s and 1960s, with the attendant revival of metaphysics as a respectable subdiscipline within analytic philosophy (followed closely by the revival of philosophy of religion);[3] scientific developments from the 1950s through the 1970s that were seen (rightly or wrongly) as lending a boost to some theistic arguments, such as the confirmation of the big bang theory and new discoveries concerning apparent cosmic fine-tuning;[4] a whole raft of new findings in biblical archaeology that served to undermine core claims of eighteenth- and-nineteenth century higher biblical criticism, itself so central to modern liberal theology;[5] the refinement of CPR techniques in the 1960s, leading to the unprecedented situation of millions being brought back from clinical death over the succeeding decades, hundreds of thousands of whom (at least) came back with shockingly consistent stories of what they experienced while clinically dead (a development whose broad cultural impact has been persistently underestimated);[6] the gradual realization in some quarters

3. For instance, Craig and Moreland write: "The collapse of positivism and its attendant verification principle of meaning was undoubtedly the most important philosophical event of the twentieth century. Their demise heralded a resurgence of metaphysics, along with other traditional problems of philosophy that verificationism had suppressed. Accompanying this resurgence has come something new and altogether unanticipated: a renaissance in Christian philosophy. The face of Anglo-American philosophy has been transformed as a result. . . . The renaissance of Christian philosophy over the last half century has served to reinvigorate natural theology." William Lane Craig and J. P. Moreland, "Introduction," in *The Blackwell Companion to Natural Theology*, eds. William Lane Craig and J. P. Moreland (Oxford: Wiley-Blackwell, 2009), ix.

4. A fine introduction to these developments may be found in Jeffrey Koperski, *The Physics of Theism: God, Physics, and the Philosophy of Science* (Oxford: Wiley-Blackwell, 2015).

5. For a starting point on these see J. Randall Price and H. Wayne House, *Zondervan Handbook of Biblical Archaeology* (Grand Rapids, MI: Zondervan, 2017).

6. See for instance Raymond Moody, *Life After Life* (Covington, GA: Mockingbird Books, 1975) and *Reflections on Life After Life* (New York: Bantam, 1977); Melvin Morse and Paul Perry, *Closer to the Light: Learning from the Near-Death Experiences of Children* (New York: Ballantine, 1990); Michael Sabom, *Recollections of Death: A Medical Investigation* (New York: Harper and Rowe, 1982) and *Light and Death: One Doctor's Fascinating Account of Near-Death*

that advancements in medicine were making many claims to miraculous cures *less* rather than more amenable to naturalistic explanation;[7] et cetera.

That renaissance has had an impact on Orthodox scholarship, though to a lesser degree than within Evangelicalism and conservative Catholicism. Why the delayed and diminished effect? Again there are multiple reasons, but it is likely due at least in part to the ambivalent or even openly skeptical attitudes taken towards natural theology by a diverse set of influential Orthodox thinkers, among them Sergius Bulgakov, Olivier Clément, H. Tristram Engelhardt Jr., Vladimir Lossky, and Christos Yannaras. Each of these has expressed reservations (more or less severe) about natural theology. And despite some relevant differences between them concerning the larger relationship between philosophy and theology, and some important differences in detail, all five of these thinkers are united in their affirmation of at least one general line of critique: natural theology is problematic (whether redundant or a distraction or positively misleading, depending on who is framing the point), and God is more truly known (or *only* truly known) *experientially*. In other words, they claim that the Church directs us towards the achievement of a knowledge of God by way of a direct *encounter* with God (in his energies, not his essence), which encounter is in turn to be gained via the ascetic and mystical practices laid down by Church tradition rather than by humanly-constructed philosophical reasoning.[8] My counter-claim is that, while there is an important insight embedded in their objection, it is not ultimately persuasive as a complaint against the entire enterprise of natural

Experiences (Grand Rapids, MI: Zondervan, 1998); Pim van Lommel, *Consciousness Beyond Life: The Science of Near-Death Experience* (New York: HarperOne, 2010).

7. See especially the discussions of contemporary medical miracles in Craig S. Keener, *Miracles: The Credibility of the New Testament Accounts*, 2 vols. (Grand Rapids, MI: Baker Academic, 2011).

8. By way of clarification at the outset (especially for readers with a background in religious epistemology): there are different senses of "knowing God." One can know (or just rationally believe) *that* there is a God (i.e., that theism is true) without necessarily having any devotion to God or a personal relationship with God. Alternatively, one can know God in the latter sense, where there is more than merely factual knowledge. This is a commonplace distinction, familiar from everyday life. (E.g., knowing *that* you have a spouse is different from knowing your spouse personally.) The Orthodox authors examined here are certainly aware of the distinction, and of the fact that natural theology claims to provide only the first sort of knowledge (i.e., both supporters and detractors of natural theology are aware that coming up with a proof for theism would not by itself bestow a relationship with God). As we shall see, however, some of these authors at least are concerned that the natural theologian's quest for knowledge of God in the first sense (and achieved using reason alone) could impede the quest for knowledge of God in the second sense.

theology, which functions as a useful (and for some, perhaps even *necessary*) partner in the pursuit of the experiential path.

The remainder of this paper is divided as follows: In the next section I lay out in more detail the somewhat different experiential objections against natural theology laid out by each of the above-cited Orthodox thinkers. Then in the final section I develop and defend my counter-objection, which in turn draws on some of the recent literature in the epistemology of religious experience.

The experiential objections

In the interests of space and on the assumption that most readers will have at least a passing familiarity with these five authors, I will dispense with any preliminary biographical remarks or observations about their larger theological views.[9] Likewise in the interests of space, I will limit my attention to one work from each author.

Let us begin with Clément's brief and somewhat allusive statement of the experiential objection, put forward in the context of a wider defense of the value of monasticism in the modern world:

> In a society in love with wisdom as well as power we should expect to find not only laboratories for scientific research, but spiritual laboratories dedicated to the more important "research into God." Eventually we see that squabbling about the existence of God is ridiculous. Better to pay close attention to those who know God from experience, whose humanity is evidently not degraded, but rather enhanced, by their faith and the integrated knowledge which results from it. We need spiritual people who can be our spiritual fathers. . . . Monks are indispensable![10]

I take it the idea here is that the pursuit of natural theology is an unhelpful distraction; it is silly to spend our time wading through abstruse philosophical arguments for theism, whether for our own supposed benefit or that of our atheist interlocutors, because there is a better option available for acquiring a knowledge of God: Ask the professionals. Make inquiries among

9. Those desirous of such background are encouraged to consult Louth, who provides a treatment of all but Engelhardt: Andrew Louth, *Modern Orthodox Thinkers: From the* Philokalia *to the Present* (Downers Grove, IL: InterVarsity Press Academic, 2015).

10. Olivier Clément, *On Human Being: A Spiritual Anthropology*, trans. Jeremy Hummerstone (Hyde Park, NY: New City Press, 2000), 74.

those who have dedicated their lives to the pursuit of direct experiential contact with God. Orthodox monasticism is the most hallowed and efficacious route towards this contact; those of us not called to that vocation (or who *are* called but prove unworthy or otherwise unsuited to it) can and should still benefit from the example, testimony, and instruction of those who are. And while Clément's point is directed primarily at Christians seeking to strengthen their faith and deepen their knowledge of God, he seems inclined to extend its applicability to atheists and agnostics. Most of those sincerely seeking to learn whether there is a God would do better to visit a monastery than to read the latest tome on the Kalam argument.

Engelhardt presents the experiential objection in many writings authored over several decades. Of the scholars under discussion here, his is the most pessimistic perspective about the place of natural theology (and indeed of philosophical reasoning more generally) within Orthodoxy. Here I will make use of a relatively recent piece in which he concisely lays out his thinking on the matter and also summarizes how his views evolved over time.

His suspicions of natural theology began early in his scholarly career, while he was still a Roman Catholic:

> As I came to study philosophy in 1959, it became clear to me that the Scholastic philosophical project that had taken shape in the 13th century and that up until the late 1960s had provided an intellectual framework for Roman Catholicism was not sustainable. The general metaphysics on which this intellectual edifice rested presupposed a consanguinity between a set of intellectual distinctions and being itself. These connections were unsecured. That is, the distinctions on which this philosophical project rested, though capable of organizing reflection about reality, could not be shown to reflect the actual structures of reality. The same was the case with regard to its special metaphysics: rational cosmology and rational psychology. . . . The five Thomistic proofs for the existence of God, the *quinque viae*, assumed that human thought could ascend by discursive argument from the finite to the infinite. These arguments presupposed that, from the evidence about reality as experienced within the horizon of the finite and the immanent, one could discursively conclude to the existence of an infinite, transcendent God.[11]

11. H. Tristram Engelhardt Jr., "A Journey to the East: Coming to Right Worship and Right

Later on, partly through an analysis of the historical currents of post-Humean Western philosophy, Engelhardt became convinced that any attempt to do substantive work in metaphysics or ethics without the prior assumption of a broadly theistic framework (i.e., theism viewed as at least a possibility) was doomed to failure—failure eventuating in a radical pluralism in which there is no way to use objective reason to convince opposed parties of much of anything:

> Once morality and reality are approached in the shadow of an atheistic or at least agnostic assumption and/or methodological postulate, there is no final perspective beyond particular social constructions. Within such accounts, one can no longer invoke the reference point of an unconditioned knower in terms of whom one could at least in principle presume a rooting of morality in reality. Again, the claim is *not* that agreement exists or ever existed concerning God as the unconditioned knower or final perspective. Rather, the claim is that without being able in principle to reference an unconditioned knower, one loses a standpoint from which one can in principle envisage setting aside a moral pluralism and the plurality of narratives regarding the nature of reality. Absent that perspective, moral pluralism and the protean character of accounts of reality take on a foundationally intractable, indeed an in-principle-fragmented character. Once God is no longer envisaged even as a theoretical possibility, even as a heuristic for moral and metaphysical reflection, moral pluralism and a plurality of visions of reality gain a canonical standing. . . . In eschewing reference to God, one is left with a principled plurality of moralities, as well as of narratives concerning reality.[12]

Engelhardt then discovered that he had been preceded in this realization by some key Eastern patristic figures, such as John Chrysostom, who likewise understood that philosophy is unable to make any significant progress on matters of real importance. Reason independent of revelation cannot provide a shared foundation on which to ground a rational ethic or natural theology.

What Chrysostom and company then added to that pessimistic analysis

---

Belief," in *Turning East: Contemporary Philosophers and the Ancient Christian Faith*, ed. Rico Vitz (Yonkers, NY: St. Vladimir's Seminary Press, 2012), 216.

12. Engelhardt, "A Journey to the East," 230.

was a solution, a way forward out of a seemingly obdurate pluralism by way of a prior commitment to the Christian moral life and the divine encounter that can flow from it:

> It is theology as the experience of God, not theology as an academic discipline, that can directly know truth. The fathers understood that the philosophical project could not disclose a canonical account of morality or of reality. Only theology achieved through rightly-directed prayer leads to the Truth who is not a proposition but the Persons of the Trinity. Without right worship and right belief, one is left with a plurality of orderings of basic human goods.[13]

Engelhardt reached a fuller grasp of this, and a fuller appropriation of Chrysostom's insight, after his own conversion to Orthodoxy:

> After my baptism, I found myself in a new relationship with philosophy. Philosophy was surely essential to an appreciation of the history of thought. It could crucially aid in assessing the validity of arguments. It could analyze concepts and make plain the implications of positions taken. However, it could not discover non-formal truths, whether these were truths of the empirical sensible world, of morality, of metaphysics, or of theology. . . . After becoming Orthodox, I was confronted with the circumstance that I had entered a place I never imagined existed, but which I knew in my heart, however dimly, was always there. This became apparent only gradually during my first decade as an Orthodox. Yet the reality of this circumstance came home with force in the fall of 1997 when I visited Mount Athos for the first time. Through the great love of God, I met a monk at the monastery of Vatopaidi who subsequently intervened a number of times in the life of my family. As the years passed, I was confronted by one miracle after another. The result was that I could no longer say that I believed in God. In the face of God's power, given the grace of his presence, I had come to know that he exists. It was now as inappropriate to contemplate giving five proofs for God's existence as it would be for my wife to give five proofs for my existence. . . . The impact of the philosophical turn of the Western High Middle Ages was now much clearer to me. It represented a turn away from an experience of truth available through an encounter with God

13. Engelhardt, "A Journey to the East," 232–33.

> gained in the traditional Christian ascetic life. It represented instead an attempt through discursive reflection to argue one's way to the truth.[14]

Engelhardt's version of the experiential objection against natural theology can thus be seen to be not only more thoroughly developed than Clément's, but also more thoroughly antipathetic to the enterprise. He would surely agree with Clément's assessment of natural theology as a distraction, an opportunity cost leeching away from a more efficacious, experiential approach to God. Unlike Clément he also sees it as bound up with hopelessly optimistic attitudes about the capacity of human reason to reach substantive demonstrative truths, especially when operating outside a theistic frame of reference. By extension, any attempt by Orthodox to argue in favor of God's existence (or in favor of Christian moral teachings) using "neutral" tools of reason and premises supposedly shared with secularists is likely to leave the latter unmoved (if not offended), and to leave the former frustrated and saddled with a dangerously mistaken idea of how faith and reason actually relate in our fallen world.

The version of the experiential objection developed by Sergius Bulgakov in his important 1917 book *Unfading Light* bears some similarity to Engelhardt's, while leaving more room for the productive pairing of philosophy (*qua* informed by revelation) and theology. Bulgakov begins to lay out his version in the context of a discussion of the nature and origins of religion. He sees religious experience as being at the core of both, and as itself rooted in a special faculty of the human person. The genuine pursuit of religion must involve the pursuit of experiential contact with transcendent reality, and, pending that, an immersion in learning about the religious experiences of the saints (prefiguring Clément's point about the vital witness of monastics). He writes:

> [There is an] eye of noetic knowing that penetrates higher reality where neither the mental nor physical eye reaches. Religious experience assures the human being of the reality of another, divine world, not so as to demonstrate its existence or by various conclusions to convince him of its necessity, but so as to lead him to a living, immediate bond with religious reality, and show it to him. Only the human being who really has encountered divinity on his life's journey, who has been overtaken by it and on whom it has been poured out with its prevailing force

14. Engelhardt, "A Journey to the East," 238–39.

> has embarked on an authentically religious path. Religious experience in its immediacy is not scientific, philosophical, aesthetic, or ethical, and in the same way as it is impossible to know beauty with the mind (one can only think about it) so too only a pallid representation of the scorching fire of religious experience is given by thought. In order to comprehend religion, to fathom the *specificum* of the religious in its distinctiveness, one needs to study the life of those who are *geniuses* in religion. . . . The life of saints, ascetics, prophets and founders of religions . . . here side by side with the personal experience of each person, is what leads more reliably to cognition in the domain of religion than abstract philosophizing about it.[15]

The *authentic* religious seeker must therefore pursue experience of the divine—others' *and* one's own. This experience transcends one's cognitive faculty and convinces one of the reality of the divine without supplying rational proof. By analogy, really *seeing* beauty inevitably convinces one of the reality of the beautiful, but not by supplying the first premise of a modus ponens that demonstrates its existence rationally. Transcending normal cognition as it does, the conviction resulting from authentic religious experience is also immune to rational disproof: "The fundamental experience of religion, the encounter with God, possesses (at least at its summits) the sort of conquering power and ardent persuasiveness that leaves every other evidence far behind. One can forget or lose it, but one cannot refute it."[16] Bulgakov has not wholly dismissed the potential value of abstract reason in this context; but a different faculty is employed when philosophizing as opposed to directly communing, and the latter provides more trustworthy access to religious truth.

He comes closer to an outright dismissal of natural theology in the following passage, which bears some similarity to Engelhardt's stance:

> And so in religious experience an immediate contact with other worlds *is given*. . . . In the face of this . . . the so-called "proofs for the existence of God" fall short. They can have a certain significance (whatever that might be) in philosophy, in speculative theology, in general outside the proper domain of religion; in this latter the joyous immediate YOU

15. Sergius Bulgakov, *Unfading Light: Contemplations and Speculations*, trans. Thomas Allan Smith (Grand Rapids, MI: Eerdmans, 2012), 7 (emphasis in the original).

16. Bulgakov, *Unfading Light*, 13.

> ARE reigns. On the whole, proofs for the existence of God by their very appearance attest to an approaching crisis in religious consciousness, when for one reason or another the sources of religious inspiration, which is immediately conscious of itself as revelation, run dry or are covered with sand, but that faith which is called upon to say to the mountain "move into the sea" seems to have absolutely no relationship with the proofs. Of course even on purely speculative grounds one should refute the idea of *proofs* for the existence of God, for here, obviously, there is an internal contradiction in the very formulation of the problem: the existence of the absolute which towers above the relative and is free of causality is affirmed by relative notions based on the law of causality and the analysis of causal series. Obviously, we will not encounter God in the field of Kantian experience, for "God is an entirely unnecessary hypothesis for science" (Laplace), and the so-called proofs for the existence of God only lead to a more or less successful postulation of God or to a disclosure from the various aspects of the philosophical concept of God. Religious experience remains the sole path for a real, living comprehension of God.[17]

Here he maintains the stronger claims that experience is the *only* route to a live knowledge of God, such that the prominence of natural theology as an intellectual pursuit is actually evidence of a decline in authentic religion rooted in such experience. Moreover, for standard Kantian reasons the proofs don't work anyway, or at least not in the way they were originally intended. They might succeed in providing rational grounds for accepting theism as a posit within some larger system (Kant himself affirmed theism in this fashion as part of the grounding of morality, though the status of his own actual religious belief remains a matter of contention), and might be useful in clarifying what philosophers mean by "God," but their concrete spiritual value is negligible (if not negative). There can be no bottom-up, creation-to-Creator proofs in the strict sense of "proof." For Bulgakov, the so-called proofs of natural theology are both religiously unhelpful and fail to provide certainty as to their conclusions—distinct but related problems, in his eyes.

On the other hand, once one has been granted a profound religious experience by God, top-down arguments become feasible. Once one knows God is there, one can see his creation with a new set of eyes and rationally

17. Bulgakov, *Unfading Light*, 17–18 (emphasis in the original).

discern its design and his presence. Something akin to natural theology becomes possible, but as an addendum to faith rather than a prolegomenon:

> However, only the Transcendent recognized in religious experience and existing above the world opens one's eyes to the transcendent in the world; in other words, only an immediate sense of God grants one to see the divine in the world, to come to know the world as a revelation of God; it alone teaches how to grasp the transcendent in the immanent. . . . One and the same world stands before us at one time like a mechanism, monstrous in its bad infinity, blankly keeping silent about its meaning, at another time like a revelation of the mysteries of Divinity or the source of cognition of God. And cognition of the world—be it natural science (in the broadest all-embracing sense of the word) or "spiritual knowledge"—in the light of faith in God receives a completely new meaning. The decisive moment remains the encounter with God in the human spirit.[18]

When faith, properly grounded in experience (one's own or others'), is in place, one can then use philosophy to inquire into theological concepts. Provided that the distinction between philosophy and theology is always kept in mind, and their mutual autonomy safeguarded, there is actually nothing wrong with the development of self-consciously Christian philosophical systems: "Is religious philosophy of a definite type possible, for example, a Christian philosophy (or even more particularly, an Orthodox, a Catholic, or a Protestant philosophy)? The question is resolved without any difficulty in an affirmative sense."[19] This is in part because even the philosopher who has accepted the faith on experiential grounds will then wish to apply philosophical methods in reflecting on the content of Church doctrine, something Bulgakov sees as inevitable and entirely proper: "That which a human knows as religious dogma he wants to fathom as a philosophical, theoretical truth too. . . . Christian philosophy is the philosophizing of Christians who strive philosophically to realize their religious existence."[20] Secular philosophers have no grounds for resentment here, provided the Christian thinker is genuinely seeking truth, and maintains a distance between real philosophy and mere apologetics, which differ fundamentally in their aims:

18. Bulgakov, *Unfading Light*, 23–24.
19. Bulgakov, *Unfading Light*, 91.
20. Bulgakov, *Unfading Light*, 93–94.

> One always philosophizes on a definite theme, and only a conscious or unconscious animosity towards Christianity forces one to exclude Christian dogmas from the number of possible themes of philosophizing. . . . The opponents stubbornly and persistently lump together "apologetics" or dogmatics with Christian philosophy. The first is completely deprived of philosophical Eros and with quasi-philosophical means strives to the attainment of a goal that is religious-practical and not at all philosophical. For that reason it is not philosophical but polemical and pragmatic in its very essence. . . . Philosophy is the art of concepts that has its own artists, and the chosen servants of this art cannot lie artistically, which would be inevitable with a premeditated, unphilosophical dogmatism in philosophizing; this would be first of all a manifestation of bad taste, and aesthetic sin. They readily allow that a Christian artist can be sincere in his artistic quests no less than an artist who does not choose religious themes; why then do they have any difficulty allowing this with respect to an artist of concepts, i.e., a religious philosopher?[21]

Though Bulgakov is not actually opposed to apologetics *per se*, provided it knows its place: "Of course, religious philosophy can also have an 'apologetic' use; more precisely, it is a powerful means for religious enlightenment, but only when it does not set this as its immediate practical goal."[22]

Bringing the point back to our central theme, it is not immediately clear how that last passage coheres with his earlier complaint against natural theology. Granted, the field of apologetics is wider than that of natural theology—still, their close association makes one wonder whether Bulgakov is not here tempering somewhat the severity of his earlier critique. At any rate, even if he shares Engelhardt's pessimism about the efficacy of natural theology considered as a pre-experiential exercise of neutral reason, Bulgakov is more optimistic about what philosophy can achieve when conducted in light of revelation; in fact both in *Unfading Light* and in his later, larger corpus, he himself indulges in a great deal of speculative metaphysics.

More could be said about Bulgakov's views concerning the right relationship between theology and philosophy, but the preceding suffices to show that he was an advocate of the experiential objection against natural theology. Vladimir Lossky is too, though like Bulgakov he is willing to grant a

21. Bulgakov, *Unfading Light*, 92.
22. Bulgakov, *Unfading Light*, 94.

place for philosophy within Orthodoxy, provided it is a philosophy informed by Church doctrine and grounded ultimately in a personal encounter with God.

That personal encounter is key to Lossky's notion of faith: "And since the object of contemplation is a personal existence and presence, true gnosis implies encounter, reciprocity, *faith* as a personal adherence to the personal presence of God Who reveals Himself."[23] He distinguishes between this sense of "faith" and that often employed in ordinary language, which lacks this sense of personal engagement:

> Certainly, faith is present in all walks, in all sciences of the human spirit, but as supposition, as working hypothesis: here, the moment of faith remains burdened with an uncertainty which proof alone could clear. Christian faith, on the contrary, is adherence to a presence which confers certitude, in such a way that certitude, here, is first. . . . Thus faith allows us to think, it gives us true intelligence. Knowledge is given to us by faith, that is to say, by our participatory adherence to the presence of Him Who reveals Himself. Faith is therefore not a psychological attitude, a mere fidelity. It is an ontological relationship between man and God . . .[24]

That notion of faith as itself a form of encounter becomes the basis for understanding both the nature of theology and how it relates to philosophy:

> Faith mortifies and vivifies the intellect, it makes the intelligence bear fruit through an altogether new ontological relationship with God, a relationship proper to the Christian and which is the criterion within us of truth. . . . To think theologically is not to think of this revelation, but to think by means of it. The Fathers often invoke "our philosophy." In fact, the method of this "philosophy" (which properly denotes theology) is based on an approach opposite to that of speculation. Theology starts from a fact: revelation. . . . The philosophy which speculates on God starts, on the contrary, from an idea. For the theologian, the point of departure is Christ, and it is also the point of arrival. The philosopher

23. Vladimir Lossky, *Orthodox Theology: An Introduction*, trans. Ian Kesarcodi-Watson and Ihita Kesarcodi-Watson (Crestwood, NY: St. Vladimir's Seminary Press, 1978), 13 (emphasis in the original).

24. Lossky, *Orthodox Theology*, 16.

> raises himself to an idea from another idea or from a group of generalized facts according to an idea. For certain philosophers, the search for God corresponds to an inherent necessity in their thought: God must exist so that their conception of the universe might be coherent. There follows the search for arguments to demonstrate the existence of this necessary God—whence these "proofs for the existence of God," "proofs" which the theologian can well do without.[25]

So faith is an adherence to God resulting from God's revelation of his presence (in some way) to the individual in that individual's personal experience; this results in a knowledge that supplies a criterion of truth, and which enables and empowers the now faith-informed intellect to reflect on the contents of revelation. The starting point for that reflection is not an abstract idea but Christ himself in his concrete historical manifestation, as handed down and divinely safeguarded within Church tradition. Philosophers as distinct from theologians—even if they be theists themselves—have a different starting point, in abstract ideas rather than concrete fact. They may succeed in coming up with arguments for theism that work within their own self-contained systems (and here Lossky is making much the same point as did Bulgakov above, regarding the "more or less successful postulation of God" within a system), but these arguments are simply superfluous from the perspective of the faith-informed theologian, who enjoys a superior starting point.

Philosophers operating independently of faith are thus operating the wrong way, a way which cannot but fail in its effort to bring about an authentic knowledge of God: "Philosophers construct an idea of God. For the theologian, God is someone Who reveals Himself and Who cannot be known outside of revelation. One must open oneself to this personal God, to encounter Him in a total involvement: that is the only way to know Him."[26]

As a further supporting argument for the necessary priority of experience-grounded faith over philosophical reflection, Lossky points out that even the staunchest advocates of natural theology typically grant that one cannot establish distinctively *Trinitarian* theism on the basis of rational proofs, but at best a mere generic monotheism. Yet this would be a decidedly unsatisfactory and potentially misleading result from a Christian's perspective, for whom reflection on God must always be reflection on the true God who is three in one:

25. Lossky, *Orthodox Theology*, 18–19.
26. Lossky, *Orthodox Theology*, 20.

> One has no right to start from a treatise *De deo uno*, from a God Who is a purely intellectual substance accessible to reason, possessing all perfections to an eminent degree, containing all ideas of all things, principle of every order and every reality. For then, to go from this God to the Trinity, one must juxtapose—for reasons of credibility, it will be said—the God of revelation with that of the philosophers. Now, in producing these reasons, one remains on the level of "natural theology," one continues to play the philosophers' game. A Christian has no right to separate, even in thought, the One and the Three when he speaks of God. To go, rationally so to speak, from the One to the Three, is a *tour de force*, an intellectual conjuring trick rather than a logical development. One must therefore start from faith—and that is the only way to save philosophy.[27]

So there is really no way to use reason alone to get from generic monotheism to Trinitarian monotheism, and that by itself suffices to wreck the enterprise of natural theology, at least conceived as a prolegomenon to faith.

Yet for Lossky, philosophy can still have a role to play in a person's journey towards faith; philosophical reflection undertaken honestly has a way of revealing the limits of reason to itself, and in doing so it can point beyond itself to other sources of knowledge. Philosophy is no substitute for mysticism, but it can point the way to mysticism and to the necessity of deep religious experience as the only way to complete the true philosophical journey:

> Philosophy itself, on its summits, demands the renunciation of speculation; questing God, it attains the moment of supreme ignorance: a negative way where the failure of human thought is acknowledged. Here, philosophy ends in a mysticism and dies in becoming the experience of an Unknown God Who can no longer even be named. . . . If the summit of philosophy is a question, theology must reply by bearing witness that transcendence is revealed in the immanence of the Incarnation.[28]

27. Lossky, *Orthodox Theology*, 20–21.

28. Lossky, *Orthodox Theology*, 21. Incidentally, this is essentially the argumentative strategy pursued by Seraphim Rose in the opening chapters of his well-known short work *Nihilism*; there, he uses philosophical arguments in an attempt to show that various intellectual movements (such as materialism, liberal humanism, nihilism, etc.) are self-referentially incoherent or otherwise rationally unacceptable or pragmatically unworkable. He then argues that the failures of secular movements point toward the need for a transcendent revelation that avoids their crippling deficiencies, with Orthodoxy of course being his candidate. It is not an exercise

Much more could again be said regarding Lossky's views of theology in relation to mysticism, and that last quote provides a hint of the central role played by apophaticism in his wider thinking in these areas. Still, the preceding provides a clear idea of his version of the experiential objection against natural theology: natural theology is redundant because genuine knowledge of God is and must be rooted in personal experience of Him and adherence to Him; moreover, from a Christian perspective any rational proofs for the reality of God are bound to be potentially misleading failures because they cannot attain to the Trinity. Yet faith-informed philosophy has its uses, and even secular philosophy can indirectly lead one to God by leading one to recognize the limits of philosophy itself and its need for completion by mysticism.

Let us turn now to our fifth and final proponent of the experiential objection, Christos Yannaras. He begins his critique by suggesting that natural theology's rationalistic sundering of the question of God from both history and personal experience left it open to disproof:

> Even as early as the ninth-century Carolingian "Renaissance," but especially with the radical distortion of Aristotelian epistemology by scholasticism,[29] European metaphysics has been built upon the presupposition of God's existence, while progressively excluding his presence from the world. God is either identified with the conceptual notion of an impersonal and abstract "first cause" of the universe (*causa prima*), or of an absolute "authority" in ethics (*principium auctoritatis*). In both cases the existence of God is a conceptual necessity, secured by demonstrative argument, but unrelated to historical experience and the existential condition of human beings. Precisely because it offers an absolutized rational affirmation of God, European metaphysics prepares for the possibility of its own rational refutation. The "death of God" is

---

in traditional, deductive natural theology, and he certainly gives no proofs for theism, but it is still an employment of philosophical argumentation in the service (if somewhat obliquely) of Church doctrine. See Seraphim Rose, *Nihilism: The Root of the Revolution of the Modern Age*, 2nd ed. (Platina, CA: St. Herman of Alaska Brotherhood, 2018).

29. This is a counterintuitive characterization of scholasticism, and Yannaras includes an endnote in which he directs readers to several other works of his in which he expands on the point (unfortunately, available only in Greek): "Ὁ ἀποφατικὸς Ἀριστοτέλης" ["The Apophatic Aristotle"], *Diabazo* 135 (1986): 14; *Ὀρθὸς λόγος καὶ κοινωνικὴ πρακτική* [*Right Reason and Social Practice*] (Athens: Domos, 1984), 205ff; *Σχεδίασμα Εἰσαγωγῆς στὴ Φιλοσοφία* [*Outline of an Introduction to Philosophy*] (Athens: Domos, 1980–1981), §§18, 25, 28.

> but the end-result of the historical unfolding of this absolutized and double-edged rationalism, which took place in the nations of Western Europe over the span of approximately a millennium.[30]

So by trying to secure basic dogmatic commitments via error-prone, fallible human reasoning rather than tradition and experience, Western theology made itself vulnerable to the errors of that very same fallible reasoning. No matter how convincing a bit of natural theology may seem, by playing the deduction game in the first place it exposes itself to a Judo-like reversal by the skeptic playing the same game with the same faulty tools.

A bit later he draws attention to another blind spot of scholastic (and later Cartesian) rationalism, namely the vital importance of the lived experience of personal relationships in grounding knowledge:

> In applying this deductive reasoning to establish God's existence, Descartes follows faithfully the scholastic tradition based on Augustine: he follows Campanella, Anselm of Canterbury, Hugh of Saint-Victor, Bonaventura and Thomas Aquinas. While the total work of each of the above figures differs in many respects from the work of the others, there nevertheless exists among them a common denominator, an underlying assumption shared by all alike, and pushed by Descartes to its ultimate consequences: it is the radical reversal of the Greek understanding of *logos*—the interpretation of *logos* as the means of reference and relation, the means of verifying knowledge through experienced relationship. . . . The God of the Scholastics and Descartes turns out to be, in the final analysis . . . outside or beyond the experience of reality or life, where everything is the experience of relationship.[31]

For Yannaras this insight about relationship is the key to a proper understanding of apophaticism. Western theologians are stuck in a mere "apophaticism of essence," in which they acknowledge that while we can know that God must exist (and so in a way *conceive* of his being), we cannot *comprehend* his essence. Characteristic of Orthodoxy, however, is the more profound "apophaticism of the person," in which the theologian realizes that a knowledge of God must occur within a personal relationship and that persons are

30. Christos Yannaras, *On the Absence and Unknowability of God: Heidegger and the Areopagite*, trans. Haralambos Ventis (London: Continuum, 2005), 22.

31. Yannaras, *On the Absence and Unknowability of God*, 23.

inherently unique and indefinable, and so beyond any possible conceptual definition. We can know God by experience but cannot define God rationally, precisely because God is a Trinity of persons who must be known by direct encounter:

> No intellectual definition (whether conceptual or verbal) can ever exhaust the knowledge afforded us by the immediacy of relationship, consequently the logical definition of *essence* (as the common principle of examples of the same form) follows and does not precede the otherness of each existent, which I know in immediate relationship with it. Thus, if God exists, he is primarily known as a person (*hypostasis*) in the immediacy of relationship, and not primarily as an essence with its conceptual definition.[32]

We know persons through experience, over the course of a personal relationship, and that is something which cannot adequately be captured in clearly definable concepts, let alone proven to others through rational argument. (One is reminded here of Engelhardt's quip above about his wife not resorting to any *quinque viae* to prove his existence.)

Interestingly, this emphasis on the need to know God personally and as a person provides Yannaras with the opportunity to press for the workability of something akin to natural theology—not deductive proofs of God's existence from premises self-evidently obvious to all (willing or unwilling), but rather a freely accepted intuition of the personal characteristics of the Creator on display in creation. I think he intends something rather like the top-down, faith-informed model of natural theology that came up in Bulgakov's discussion above. Yannaras presents it as follows:

> There remains then for humankind, as a way to knowledge of God in principle, the effect of the creative activity of God. . . . It is not through beings in themselves (as existent fact), nor through the Being of beings, but only through the manner—the way or mode—in which beings are, that one who *wishes* to advance with deductive judgements to apprehension of the cause of everything can be led to the testimony of God. This possibility refers to a possible choice and a direction of which we are capable . . . and not to an "objective" certainty. In the way in which "every house" bears witness to its having been made "by someone,"

32. Yannaras, *On the Absence and Unknowability of God*, 29.

> the care, the good taste, and love of the designer, his intelligence and capability—betraying, that is to say, *personal* attributes of the maker, but nothing of his nature or essence (since the thing made is of another, different essence from the maker)—in the same way, too, the things that are mirror the creator God.[33]

Seemingly even more optimistically, he writes later: "Causal reasoning may certainly lead us to the intellectual certainty of a first cause of beings, of a preeminent self-caused creator. Yet both the essence or nature, and the mode of existence of this first cause remain inaccessible to causal scrutiny."[34] That essence and that mode "remain inaccessible to causal scrutiny," and yet for Yannaras we can know something of the mode of God's existence via revelation and personal relationship.

And how does God reveal himself to communities within history, and to individuals in personal relationship? Since the divine essence is forever inscrutable to us, he must do so via the divine energies. Yannaras makes considerable use of the Palamite essence/energies distinction when laying out his full theological epistemology. For instance, he writes: "The distinction between *essence* and *energies* is the starting point and presupposition for the apophatic knowledge of God. We know nothing at all about *what* God *is*—his essence. However, God's *mode of being* is accessible to us in experience. And we can speak of the mode of existence of God, since we know the divine energies."[35] So ultimately, what a rationalist natural theology could not accomplish (and caused great harm in trying to accomplish), religious experience actually achieves (by God's grace), namely a genuine, personal knowledge of him. A bit later Yannaras puts the point even more starkly: "Apophaticism is, for the ecclesial consciousness, an utterly consistent empiricism, an unyielding adherence to the absolute priority of experience as the way to, and possibility of, knowledge. And in the case of God it is a matter not of an experience of objective assurance, but an experience of personal *relationship*, a relationship constituted by the event of an encounter . . ."[36]

That concludes our survey of experiential objections against natural theology in five prominent Orthodox thinkers. Clearly they are not all employing quite the same argument, and just as clearly they do not all share

33. Yannaras, *On the Absence and Unknowability of God*, 63–64 (emphasis in the original).
34. Yannaras, *On the Absence and Unknowability of God*, 68.
35. Yannaras, *On the Absence and Unknowability of God*, 83 (emphasis in the original).
36. Yannaras, *On the Absence and Unknowability of God*, 86.

the same views regarding the broader relationship between philosophy and theology. While all five authors worry that natural theology detracts from the pursuit of the experiential path to God, they see it as doing this in various ways or for different reasons. In particular, three distinct lines of critique of natural theology can be detected (though some of our authors affirm more than one): (a) There is the concern that the arguments of natural theology are objectively unsound. This concern was especially evident in Engelhardt, though present also, to a degree, in Bulgakov and Lossky. (b) There is the concern that the pursuit of natural theology is counterproductive religiously, in that it fails to lead to an experiential encounter with God and may even detract from the ability to achieve such an encounter. This concern appears most clearly in Lossky, who fears that proofs (or "proofs") could become a substitute for faith. It is also quite evident in Yannaras, for whom the development of natural theology in the West contributed to the rise of atheistic nihilism. (This despite the fact that Yannaras is actually more open than some of our other authors to the prospect of natural theology being a locus for objectively sound arguments.) Finally, (c) there is the concern that the arguments of natural theology are liable to be unconvincing to nonbelievers.

Let's proceed now to a critical examination of these experiential objections against natural theology.

A critique of the experiential objections against natural theology

An Orthodox proponent of natural theology might pursue several distinct lines of response. Beginning with the latter accusation that natural theology fails to convince nonbelievers, she might point out that this is simply false on empirical grounds; as a matter of fact, a great many nonbelievers have been persuaded of the truth of theism (and other basic doctrinal commitments of the Church, like the reality of the human soul) via rational argument, including traditional standbys like the Five Ways and their many variants, updates, and competitors. I know such people personally, some of whom are prominent philosophers. Similarly, a great many believers have had their faith strengthened and further informed by engaging with the literature on natural theology. I count myself as an example of the latter.

Of course it is always possible that the people who *think* that they were rationally persuaded by arguments were in fact being operated on by very different subconscious processes, or by the unseen grace of the Holy Spirit, or both. And the seemingly positive consequences (like conversions facilitated by natural theology) will be weighed against the alleged disastrous long-term societal consequences for the West of putting too much stock in rational arguments about God, to the neglect of the experiential path. The claims and counter-claims here are strictly unfalsifiable, so at best the dialectic would appear to reach a deadlock at this point.

Turning to the concern regarding soundness: the defender of natural theology could reply that some of the better arguments are in fact provably sound, proceeding as they do in a logically valid fashion from true premises that cannot plausibly be denied. In other words, she could argue that Engelhardt especially is too pessimistic in dismissing philosophy's capacity for reaching substantive, non-formal truths in the realms of metaphysics and ethics. Moreover, she could argue that some of those substantive truths are directly relevant to questions of Church doctrine. Relatedly, she could take up the task of addressing the more specific criticisms offered by Bulgakov, Lossky, and Yannaras, who are less pessimistic than Engelhardt regarding philosophy's general prospects for achieving substantive truths, yet still leery of natural theology (e.g., Lossky's concern about the allegedly unbridgeable and deceptive gap between arguments for generic monotheism and the Church's actual commitment to Trinitarian monotheism).

I think that task is actually quite doable. Still, I will not pursue those avenues of reply here, for the following reasons: (1) a full reply to Engelhardt's general critique would require delving into wider discussions concerning epistemology and philosophical method (e.g., anti-Kantian defenses of the possibility of metaphysics), which space does not permit here and which has been effectively presented by many others; (2) replying to some of the more specific points raised against natural theology by Bulgakov, Lossky, and Yannaras (in particular the Trinitarianism issue) would take us too far afield; and, most importantly, (3) amidst all their differences, what most unites these five thinkers in opposition to natural theology is their joint commitment to the idea that it interferes with a *better* path to God, namely the experiential path. This seems to imply a further claim, namely that the experiential path is always able effectively to operate *independently* of the philosophical path. That shared commitment is what I wish to target in my response here. In other words, I wish to show how natural theology can be a help rather than a hindrance to the experiential path (indeed may be *needed* as a help, at least for some people). Showing this will of course not defuse all of the concerns of all five authors (a complete reply to which would have to engage explicitly with the aforementioned (1) and (2)), but it should serve to undercut their shared idea that natural theology actually detracts from the experiential path.

So let's grant that religious experiences (at least of certain sorts, under certain circumstances) are evidentially significant both for those who undergo them and, by way of the experiencers' testimony, also for those who don't (whether believers or unbelievers).[37] Nevertheless, my claim is that this experiential path can still benefit from the enterprise of natural theology—the two are partners, not competitors. And because of this, the experiential objection against natural theology fails. The experiential path to knowledge need not (and perhaps for some *cannot*) be pursued to the exclusion of the philosophical path.

One reason why the practice of natural theology can benefit the experiential path (and in some cases, for some people, may even be *necessary to* the pursuit of that path) is simple: just as there are competing religious philosophies, there are competing experiential paths. It is all very well for Clément to counsel tossing theistic proofs overboard in favor of a long spell at Athos, but what is the well-intentioned open-minded agnostic to do when on the same day an offer is received to spend a few months at a Taoist hermitage, or Zen temple, or Hindu ashram, or some neo-Druidic compound in Appalachia? The Orthodox monastic's testimony to a direct encounter with the Uncreated Light may be riveting to the agnostic, but then the Thelemite's narrative of encountering angelic entities while chanting Enochian and cutting himself inside a well-drawn pentagram might also sound pretty compelling. The inquirer needs a decision procedure for weighing up the many, many options available, especially in contemporary Western culture with its smorgasbord of old and new religions accessible in person or online. (Thanks to the internet, rampant religious pluralism is no longer restricted to big cities.) Which competing experiential path should one devote substantial time and study and attention to? (And *all* serious experiential paths demand substantial time and study and attention, even the ones making use of partial shortcuts like mind-altering narcotics.) For those inquirers with the ability to work through the arguments, one factor that might productively be included in this assessment process is the rational plausibility of the larger religious philosophies with which the various experiential paths are associated. Inevitably some inquirers will want to ask (and surely *should* want to ask?) whether the Orthodox picture of creation, human nature, morality, and the

37. Theoretically one might critique the experiential objection by arguing that religious experiences are devoid of significant evidential value, and thus ought not to be preferred to natural theology as a path to knowledge of God. But that is hardly a critique that Orthodox Christians would have much sympathy for.

divine enjoys more rational support than does that of the Scientologist or Sethian or Sufi. For the sake of those inquirers we ought to hope that our tradition of natural theology has more to offer them than our five critics (especially Engelhardt) suppose.

And it is no good simply to say that the mystical experience of the Athonite is veridical and trustworthy because undergone within Christ's Church and in a manner consistent with its dogmas (which appears to be Lossky's reply to this sort of concern).[38] After all, the Hindu will make the analogous claim for the mystical experience of the sadhu: "Of *course* our mystical experiences are veridical and trustworthy, since they are undergone within Shiva's temple and in a manner consistent with the best and most reliable Shaivite teaching." Similarly but more ecumenically, the Athonite might defend his own experiential path to the agnostic on the grounds that it was undertaken after moral purification and pursued within an ancient and hallowed and time-tested mystical Tradition. But then the Taoist can say precisely the same for her own experiential path. Likewise, it will probably not help to claim that the authentic religious experience of the Orthodox bears certain internal phenomenological markers that distinguish it from lesser sorts of paranormal or occult experiences (which is Bulgakov's reply to this concern).[39] Even if true, the Buddhist can make much the same claim

38. "Far from being mutually opposed, theology and mysticism support and complete each other. If the mystical experience is a personal working out of the content of the common faith, theology is an expression, for the profit of all, of that which can be experienced by everyone. Outside the truth kept by the whole Church personal experience would be deprived of all certainty, of all objectivity. It would be a mingling of truth and falsehood, of reality and illusion: 'mysticism' in the bad sense of the word." Vladimir Lossky, *The Mystical Theology of the Eastern Church*, trans. Fellowship of St. Alban and St. Sergius (Crestwood, NY: St. Vladimir's Seminary Press, 1957), 8–9.

39. "A pair of correlative concepts, transcendent and immanent, plays a most substantial role in the definition of religion. . . . The transcendent is at the very least a certain frontier domain for the immanent, its boundary. . . . Are there other worlds? Does the transcendent exist? It is impossible to respond with speculation alone (as usually one is wont to think) or with an immanent experience; one can respond to this only with a new experience, with an expansion and transformation of experience, presupposing of course that our cosmic nature will know by means of a special sense, completely indefinable and reducible to nothing, the domain of a different world 'supernatural' for it. The domain of 'mysticism' begins here, as does the path of 'occultism' or 'the science of how to attain cognition of higher worlds' (Steiner). All occultism is the expansion of the immanent into the place of the heretofore transcendent, and by transforming himself a human being becomes an entity of the other world, namely of the one that he comes to know. . . . On the path of occult knowledge, and in general, of any type of knowledge, with its constant and endless delving deeper into the domain of the divine,

to the agnostic inquirer: "*Our* internal phenomenological markers are the right ones to look for." The inquirer won't know whom to believe—unless she starts looking beyond internal experiential criteria and begins assessing these experiences in other ways, such as by rationally judging between the competing religious philosophies (metaphysical teachings and moral commitments) with which the competing experiential paths are associated.

Relatedly, it is sometimes argued that certain sorts of religious experiences are self-authenticating, such that, for the person who has them, a truth or truths are then infallibly and irrefutably known.[40] There has been a great deal of dispute over whether any experience could ever be self-authenticating; but even if such experiences occur, and even if Orthodox mystical experiences fall within this category and those of other experiential paths do not, this fact will not help the open-minded agnostic inquirer, who is liable to be faced with (presumably false) claims to self-authenticating experiences by non-Orthodox, and who will need something beyond internal experiential criteria in order to figure out whom to believe and correspondingly which experiential path to pursue.

---

it is impossible to encounter God in this world; in this cognition there is an infinity that in the religious sense is bad, i.e., leading away from God, for it does not draw closer to him. Herein lies the profound difference of the occult and the religious paths, which can *in certain conditions* become an opposition; in any case it is impossible to lump them together or substitute them one for the other, as often happens now." Bulgakov, *Unfading Light*, 20–22 (emphasis in the original). Relatedly, later on he writes: "One ought to distinguish between the expansion of our experience which reveals new worlds to us (it makes no difference whether it is a world to be studied with a telescope or with astral clairvoyance) and the breach of our experience which is contact with the principle that transcends our world, i.e., with God. Entry into new planes of the world, of course, breaks the previous limitedness; it is destructive for *crass* materialism (although in its place it may perhaps put a more subtle materialism), but occultism can remain atheistic since by expanding the world it locks it up in itself all the more. In general the path of occult and even of mystical comprehension of the world is not necessarily at all a religious path, although it can be united with it. Theosophy (in its more open admissions) lays claim to being a *replacement* for religion, its Gnostic surrogate, and in such a case it changes into a vulgar pseudoscientific mythology. It exploits the mystical curiosity, the Luciferian inquisitiveness of a cold, unloving mind. Commerce with beings from other worlds, if it really is possible and actually takes place, in and of itself is not only incapable of bringing nearer to God but on the contrary even extinguishes religious faith in the soul." Bulgakov, *Unfading Light*, 37 (emphasis in the original).

40. Bulgakov seems to accept the reality of self-authenticating experiences—recall a passage quoted in the previous section: "The fundamental experience of religion, the encounter with God, possesses (at least at its summits) the sort of conquering power and ardent persuasiveness that leaves every other evidence far behind. One can forget or lose it, but one cannot refute it." Bulgakov, *Unfading Light*, 13.

The basic point I am making here is of course not original—it is just the well-worn problem of religious diversity as applied to the epistemology of religious experience, paired with an equally well-worn solution based on the need to address that diversity by reference to more than just experiential evidence. Among the lessons learned from the last several decades of literature within that subdiscipline of the philosophy of religion (so a sub-subdiscipline?) is the following: there is a variety of types of religious experience of genuine evidential value, and neither Christianity in general nor Orthodox Christianity in particular has a monopoly on evidentially significant religious experiences. That said, religious experiences with distinctively Christian content do bear special evidential significance, and Christianity possesses better conceptual and empirical resources for explaining *both* that unique evidential status *and* what is going on in religious experiences taking place within non-Christian contexts (better, that is, than the competing accounts available in other religions for explaining what is going on in distinctively *Christian* experiences). Those resources importantly include reference to the metaphysical and moral commitments embedded in Church doctrine, as well as facts concerning the metaphysical and moral commitments of competing religions. In other words, Christian religious experiences are rightly taken to provide significant evidence for the truth of the faith (as our five Orthodox authors all affirm), but that evidence, in order to be convincing (at least to the outside, non-Christian inquirer), requires additional rational defense—it should not stand alone, but should instead take its place within a larger cumulative case argument for the faith, one that can (and probably *must*) incorporate natural theology.

Again, that is hardly a novel insight. In fact that is precisely how Richard Swinburne,[41] Phillip Wiebe,[42] and Keith Yandell,[43] among others, have employed religious experiences as part of a wider case for Christian theism. For Swinburne and Wiebe, the main dialogue partner and opponent in all this is atheism and metaphysical naturalism, while Yandell has more to say regarding other world religions (for instance, he spends a good deal of time de-

41. Richard Swinburne, *The Existence of God*, 2nd ed. (Oxford: Oxford University Press, 2004), 293–327.

42. Phillip Wiebe, *Visions of Jesus: Direct Encounters from the New Testament to Today* (Oxford: Oxford University Press, 1997), and *God and Other Spirits: Intimations of Transcendence in Christian Experience* (Oxford: Oxford University Press, 2004).

43. Keith Yandell, *The Epistemology of Religious Experience* (Cambridge: Cambridge University Press, 1993), and *Philosophy of Religion: A Contemporary Introduction* (London: Routledge, 1999).

fending the rational trustworthiness of Christian mystical experiences over and against the enlightenment experiences of Buddhists, Jains, and Hindus). But all three employ a broadly similar, overarching abductive argumentative strategy, in which Christian religious experiences play an important role in defense of central Church teachings, but only in conjunction with other sources of rational support for the faith. For at least some inquirers, this multifaceted approach will function as a better, more persuasive strategy than trying to run a defense based *entirely* on experience, to the exclusion of the Church's wider base of resources (including natural theology). Hence the experiential objection against natural theology is unsound—an unoriginal conclusion, but one that has not yet been widely appreciated within contemporary Orthodox theology. Hopefully this chapter will help spread the good news: natural theology is as relevant as ever. And as naturalism continues its decline in the West, and the Church faces ever more competition from non-naturalist worldviews with their own established mystical practices, Orthodox philosophers and theologians can rightly draw on our own longstanding tradition of natural theology to engage with them.

7. Natural Theology for Today

RICHARD SWINBURNE

Kinds of Natural Theology

Different people come to believe that there is a God for different good reasons. Some people have had what seems to them a strong awareness of the presence of God. In virtue of a principle which I call the Principle of Credulity,[1] it is always rational to believe that things are as they seem to be, in the absence of counter-evidence. If it seems to you that you hear me lecturing to you, or that (as you seem to recall) you had dinner in a restaurant last night, or that you have a brother, it is rational to believe these things—in the absence of counter-evidence. And the more strongly it seems to you that these things are so, the more rational it is to believe them. By "counter-evidence" I mean evidence that things are not as they seemed to be—for example if several other people tell you that you had dinner at home last night, then it is no longer rational to believe that you had dinner in a restaurant last night. Likewise with an apparent awareness of God. In the absence of arguments to show that there is no God, it is rational for someone to whom it seems that he has a strong awareness of the presence of God, to believe that he does indeed have this awareness and so that there is a God.

Other people come to believe that there is a God on the basis of testimony. Someone whom they trust—their parents or the wisest person in the village—tells them that there is a God. In virtue of the principle which I call the Principle of Testimony, it is always rational to believe what you are

1. For a short defense of the Principle of Credulity (often called "phenomenal conservatism," "epistemic conservatism," or—using the word in a favourable sense—"dogmatism"), see my *Mind, Brain, and Free Will* (Oxford: Oxford University Press, 2013), 42–44.

told—in the absence of counter-evidence, either evidence that things are not as you are told or that your informant was in no position to know what he claims to know.[2]

But some people come to believe that there is a God on the basis of positive arguments for his existence. And in the twenty-first-century Western world, even those who have had strong apparent experiences of the presence of God, or been taught by their parents that there is a God, also need arguments to back up their belief. For they will be aware of counter-arguments—arguments purporting to show that their belief in a God is delusory; and they need (as well as arguments to show that these counter-arguments are not sound) positive arguments to show that there is a God. St. Paul famously claimed that pagans who did not worship God were "without excuse," because "ever since the creation of the world [God's] eternal power and divine nature, invisible though they are, have been understood and seen through the things which he has made" (Rom 1:20). Inspired by this text, very many Christian thinkers from the second to the eighteenth centuries produced arguments of natural theology. I shall understand by "natural theology" the construction of arguments, independent of any particular historical claims, for the existence of a single creator of the universe who has such divine properties as being eternal, omnipotent, omniscient, and perfectly good. On that definition, it is not merely arguments which explicitly claim to be arguments for the existence of God, but also arguments which claim to show that God has the traditional divine properties, which count as natural theology. As Alexey Fokin's paper in this volume shows, the writings of the Christian Fathers, East and West, contained much natural theology in that sense. So too, and at greater length, did the writings of Western scholastic theologians and Islamic and Jewish philosophers in the medieval and early modern centuries.[3]

Arguments begin from premises, that is, propositions which are taken for granted for the purpose of the argument; and natural theology claims to start from propositions which theist and atheist alike can recognize as obviously true. Kant distinguished three kinds of arguments for the existence of God—ontological arguments which start from some supposed truth

2. For a short defense of the Principle of Testimony, see my *Mind, Brain, and Free Will*, 56–57.

3. For a very clear exposition of the different kinds of argument adduced in medieval Islamic and Jewish philosophy, see Herbert A. Davidson, *Proofs for Eternity, Creation, and the Existence of God in Medieval Islamic and Jewish Philosophy* (Oxford: Oxford University Press, 1987).

of reason, cosmological arguments which start from the mere existence of the universe or of some object within it, and teleological arguments which start from some general feature of the universe. St. Paul claimed that the observable world showed that there was a God, and all arguments to the existence of God before the eleventh century started from something publicly observable or privately experienceable, and can be classified as either cosmological or teleological.[4] It is noteworthy that Christian thinkers of the first millennium put forward teleological arguments to a much greater extent than did non-Christian Greek philosophers or Islamic philosophers, whose arguments were mainly cosmological arguments.

Arguments move from their premises to their conclusion by either a deductive or an inductive route. A deductively valid argument is one in which the conclusion simply draws out something already implicit in it premises, so that it would be contradictory to affirm the premises but deny the conclusion. It is a not unreasonable interpretation of at least the first four of Aquinas's famous "five ways"[5] that he was seeking to provide there deductive arguments for the existence of God. But the enterprise of producing deductive arguments from the observable world for the existence of God is, I think, an enterprise doomed to failure. For if it could be achieved, then a proposition which was a conjunction of the evident premises together with "there is no God" would entail a self-contradiction. But propositions such as "there is a universe, but there is no God," though perhaps false, seem fairly evidently not to entail a contradiction. So my own preference is for the "inductive" form of natural theology. This begins from premises evident to the senses and claims that they make probable (though not certain) the existence of God. Thinkers were not very clear about the distinction between inductive and deductive arguments during the first thousand years

4. The arguments which Alexey Fokin discusses in section 2 of his paper in this volume under the heading of "*a priori*" arguments are not ontological arguments in Kant's sense of arguments "from pure concepts *a priori*," nor is the argument which he discusses in section 5 from an "ideal or formal cause." They all include a premise describing human observation or experience of some phenomenon such as the awareness of the presence of God, or the awareness of some concept. But that humans are aware of God or of some concept is a contingent *a posteriori* truth; whereas concepts themselves (if they exist) exist necessarily, and so an argument from the nature of the concept is *a priori*. And although Augustine gave the definition of God, quoted in Fokin's section "Argument from degrees of perfection," which is used by Anselm as a premise of his ontological argument, I do not yet see any reason to believe that anywhere in the patristic literature is there a premise similar to the crucial premise of Anselm's argument that something which exists in reality is greater than something which exists only in the mind.

5. Aquinas, *Summa Theologiae* I, q. 2, a. 3.

of the Christian era, and not much clearer until the eighteenth century. So it would be anachronistic to say that the patristic writers were explicitly seeking to give inductive, or alternatively, deductive arguments, but I consider that some patristic and later arguments do conform to an inductive pattern. Having exhibited this pattern by presenting my own natural theology, I shall then point out that one kind of argument discussed by Alexey Fokin is of exactly the same pattern.

What I have sought to do in my own natural theology is to give rigorous form to inductive arguments to the existence of God from premises reporting phenomena evident to the senses; and to bring out the close similarities between such arguments and arguments of historians or detectives to some particular person having done some deed, and arguments of physicists to some very general and fundamental theory such as Newton's theory of gravitation. Arguments for the existence of God can be ordered by the generality of their premises—the phenomena from which they begin. The most general phenomenon is that there is a physical universe; the argument from the physical universe to God is a cosmological argument. Then there are arguments of two main kinds from the order in the universe; these are teleological arguments. One is the argument from the universal operation of simple natural laws, which I call the argument from temporal order. The other is the argument from those laws being such as (given an early state of the universe) to lead to the existence of human bodies, which I call the argument from spatial order. Then there are arguments which are not naturally called "teleological" in Kant's sense. There is the argument from consciousness—that humans are not merely bodily organisms, but are conscious beings (having sensations and beliefs, thoughts, desires and purposes, and the ability to reason and to choose to bring about good or evil). Then there are arguments from particular miraculous events within history, and above all from the Resurrection of Jesus—or rather, since it is disputed whether these events happened, from the public evidence about them. And finally there are arguments from the very widespread reports of religious experiences. Like all inductive arguments from particular phenomena to some deep physical hypothesis, or to some claim of a historian, the arguments from phenomena to God are cumulative. Each phenomenon gives some degree of probability to the hypothesis; taken together with arguments from phenomena *against* the existence of God, they give an overall probability to the existence of God. I have argued at length elsewhere,[6] that overall these arguments make the

6. See my *The Existence of God*, 2nd ed. (Oxford: Oxford University Press, 2004); for a

existence of God significantly more probable than not. In this paper I hope to show in brief outline the force of the positive arguments for the existence of God from the first four phenomena listed above—the existence of a physical universe, its conformity to simple natural laws, those laws being such as to lead to the existence of human bodies, and those bodies being the bodies of reasoning humans who choose between good and evil. For reasons of space I shall not be able to discuss the negative argument against the existence of God from the existence of pain and other suffering.

Criteria for a probably true causal explanation

Theism, the claim that there is a God, is an explanatory hypothesis, one which purports to explain why certain observed phenomena (that is, data or evidence) are as they are. There are two basic kinds of explanatory hypothesis: personal and inanimate (= scientific) hypotheses.

A personal hypothesis explains some phenomenon in terms of it being caused by a substance, a person, acting with certain powers (to bring about effects), certain beliefs (about how to do so), and a certain purpose (or intention, to bring about a particular effect, either for its own sake or as a step towards a further effect). I (a substance) cause the motion of my hand in

---

shorter and simpler account of my natural theology, see my *Is There a God?*, rev. ed. (Oxford: Oxford University Press, 2010). My conclusion in *The Existence of God* was that when we take into account not merely the public evidence discussed in this chapter, but the additional compelling evidence of the religious experiences of millions of people (in the sense of it seeming to them that they are in the presence of God), our total evidence makes it more probable than not that there is a God (in virtue of the principles of credulity and testimony, which I discussed at the beginning of this paper). This is so, I argued there, even when we take into account any counter-evidence from the evidence of great human suffering. However, I did not take into account there any detailed evidence about the historicity of the events concerned with the life of Jesus, as I did briefly in the revised edition of *Is There a God?* (For more detailed exposition of this evidence, see my books *The Resurrection of God Incarnate* [Oxford: Oxford University Press, 2003], and *Was Jesus God?* [Oxford: Oxford University Press, 2008].) In view of that additional evidence I concluded that the (now) total available evidence makes the existence of God *significantly* more probable than not. It is impossible to give an exact value to how probable the evidence adduced in these arguments makes the existence of God, but that is not to the discredit of those arguments, since one cannot give exact values to the probability of any scientific or historical hypothesis. All one can conclude about any such hypothesis is something like "it is fairly probable" or "it is as probable as not," or "it is more probable than not," "it is significantly more probable than not," or "it is very probable."

virtue of my powers (to move my limbs), my belief (that moving my hand will attract attention) and my purpose (to attract attention).

An inanimate explanation is usually represented as explaining some phenomenon in terms of it being caused by some initial state of affairs and the operation on that state of laws of nature. The present positions of the planets are explained by their earlier positions and that of the sun, and the operation on them of Newton's laws. But I think that this is a misleading way of analyzing inanimate explanation—because "laws" are not things; to say that Newton's law of gravity is a law is simply to say that each material body in the universe has the power to attract every other material body with a force proportional to mm'/r^2 and the liability to exercise that power on every such body. So construed, like personal explanation, inanimate explanation of some phenomenon (e.g., the present positions of the planets) explains it in terms of its being caused by substances (e.g., the sun and the planets) acting with certain powers (to cause material bodies to move in the way codified in Newton's laws) and the propensity always to exercise those powers. So both kinds of explanation explain phenomena in terms of the earlier actions of substances having certain powers to produce effects. But while personal explanation explains how substances exercise their powers because of their purposes and their beliefs, inanimate explanation explains how substances exercise their powers because of their propensities to do so.

I suggest that we judge a postulated hypothesis (of either kind) as probably true insofar as it satisfies four criteria. First, we must have observed many phenomena which it is quite probable would occur, and no phenomena which it is quite probable would not occur, if the hypothesis is true. Secondly, it must be much less probable that the phenomena would occur in the normal course of things if the hypothesis is false. Thirdly, the hypothesis must be simple. That is, it must postulate the existence and operation of few substances, few kinds of substance, with few easily describable properties behaving in mathematically simple ways. We can always postulate many new substances with complicated properties to explain anything which we find. But our hypothesis will only be supported by the evidence if it is a simple hypothesis which leads us to expect the various phenomena that form the evidence. And fourthly, the hypothesis must "fit in" with our knowledge of other hypotheses, which provide probable explanations of phenomena other than those that our hypothesis purports to explain—what I shall call our "background evidence." Our hypothesis will "fit in" with these other hypotheses, if they in turn do not give some probability to a wider theory inconsistent with our hypothesis.

I now illustrate these criteria at work in assessing postulated explanations. I begin with a postulated personal explanation. Suppose that there has been a burglary; money has been stolen from a safe. A detective has discovered these pieces of evidence: John's fingerprints are on the safe; someone reports having seen John near the scene of the burglary at the time it was committed; and there is in John's house an amount of money equivalent to the amount stolen. The detective puts forward as the explanation of the burglary the hypothesis that John robbed the safe. If John did rob the safe, it would be to some modest degree probable that his fingerprints would be found on the safe, that someone would report having seen him near the scene of the crime at the time it was committed, and that money of the amount stolen would be found in his house. But it would be much less probable that these phenomena would occur if John did not rob the safe; they therefore constitute positive evidence, evidence favoring the hypothesis. On the other hand, if John robbed the safe, it would be most unexpected (it would be most improbable) that many people would report seeing him in a foreign country at the time of the burglary. Such reports would constitute negative evidence, evidence counting strongly against the hypothesis. Let us suppose that there is no such negative evidence. The more probable it is that we would find the positive evidence if the hypothesis is true, and the more improbable it is that we would find the negative evidence if the hypothesis is false, the more probable the evidence makes the hypothesis.

But a hypothesis is only rendered probable by evidence insofar as it is simple. Consider the following hypothesis as an explanation of the detective's positive evidence: David stole the money; quite unknown to David, George dressed up to look like John at the scene of the crime, Tony planted John's fingerprints on the safe just for fun; and, unknown to the others, Stephen hid money stolen from another robbery (coincidentally of exactly the same amount) in John's house. If this complicated hypothesis were true, we would expect to find all the positive evidence which I described, while it remains not nearly as probable otherwise that we would find this evidence. But this evidence does not make the complicated hypothesis probable, although it does make the hypothesis that John robbed the safe probable; and that is because the latter hypothesis is simple. The detective's original hypothesis postulates only one substance (John) doing one thing (robbing the safe) which leads us to expect the various pieces of evidence; while the rival hypothesis which I have just set out postulates many substances (many persons) doing different unconnected things.

But as well as the evidence of the kind which I have illustrated, there may be "background evidence," that is, evidence about matters other than those which the hypothesis purports to explain, but which itself gives some probability to a wider theory that fits well or badly with the hypothesis which we are considering. We may have evidence about what John has done on other occasions, for example evidence making probable a hypothesis H* that he has often robbed safes in the past. This latter evidence would make the hypothesis that John robbed the safe on this occasion much more probable than it would be without that evidence. This is because in its turn H* makes probable a theory of wider scope (e.g., that John is a regular safe-robber) which in turn makes the hypothesis in question more probable than it would otherwise be. Conversely, for similar reasons, evidence that John has lived a crime-free life in the past would make it much less probable that he robbed the safe on this occasion.

The same four criteria are at work in assessing postulated inanimate hypotheses. Consider again the hypothesis that the present positions of the planets are to be explained by their positions and that of the sun five hundred years ago (which we learn from reports of observers) and the operation of Newton's laws—which I'll rephrase in due course in my preferred way. Newton's theory of gravitation consisted of his three laws of motion and his inverse square law of gravitational attraction. The evidence available at the end of the seventeenth century favoring this theory consisted of evidence about the paths taken (given certain initial positions) by our moon, the planets, and the moons of planets; the velocities with which bodies fall to the earth; the motions of pendula; the occurrence of tides; and so on. Newton's theory made it very probable that these phenomena would occur as observed. It would be very unlikely that they would occur if Newton's theory were not true. There was no significant negative evidence. The theory was very simple, consisting of just four laws which postulated very simple mathematical relations ($F=Gmm'/r^2$ being the most complicated one). Yet innumerable other laws would have satisfied the first two criteria equally well. Within the limits of accuracy then detectable any law in which you substitute a slightly different value for the "2" (e.g., "2.0000974") would have satisfied the first two criteria as well as did the inverse square law. So too would a theory which postulated that the inverse square law held only until AD 2969 after which a quite different law, a cube law of attraction, would operate, or a theory containing a law claiming that quite different forces operate outside the solar system. But Newton's theory, unlike such theories, was rendered probable by the evidence because it was a very simple theory. There was no relevant background evidence, because there was no evidence available in the seventeenth century outside the scope of Newton's theory giving any degree of probability to any wider explanatory theory of the forces which physical bodies exert on each other (e.g., a theory of electromagnetism) with which Newton's theory needed to fit. Hence Newton's theory was very probable on the evidence available in the seventeenth century because it satisfied our four criteria; and so therefore is the hypothesis that it, together with the initial positions of the sun and planets, explains the present positions of the planets. Rephrased in a more satisfactory way, that hypothesis is the hypothesis that the sun and each of the planets have simple powers and propensities (as codified by Newton's laws) and initial positions which explain the present positions of the planets.

I stress the importance of the criterion of simplicity, as the crucial criterion for distinguishing among hypotheses which all make the occurrence of the phenomena fairly probable when their occurrence would not otherwise be very probable. There are, I suggest, several different facets of simplicity. One hypothesis is simpler than another hypothesis if it postulates fewer entities, fewer properties, fewer kinds of entity, or fewer kinds of property. Astronomers postulate the existence of as few planets as are needed to explain their observations. Particle physicists postulate that particles have properties of as few kinds as are needed to explain their observations—they only postulate color charge, as well as mass, electric charge, and spin, because they need to do so in order for their hypothesis to make it more probable that they would observe what they do. Further, entities and properties are simple insofar as they are readily observable (or experienceable) or definable in terms of things readily observable (or experienceable). Also, one hypothesis is simpler than another insofar as it has fewer laws postulating mathematically simpler relations between the properties of objects. Mathematical entities (that is, primarily numbers) and mathematical operations (such as addition or multiplication) are simpler than other ones if it is necessary to understand the former in order to understand the latter, but not conversely. Thus the number 3 is simpler than the number 4, because 4 is defined as 3+1, and so you couldn't understand 4 without understanding 3, but you could understand 3 without understanding 4. And you can't understand multiplication without understanding addition, but you can understand addition without understanding multiplication; hence addition is a simpler operation than multiplication. It is because you couldn't understand 2.0000974 without understanding 2, but you could understand 2 without understanding 2.0000974, that the hypothesis that the force of gravity is $F=Gmm'/r^2$ is simpler than the hypothesis that it is $F=Gmm'/r^{2.0000974}$. So if both hypotheses make the observations equally probable, the observations make the former hypothesis more probable than the latter one. A crucial consequence of this account of mathematical simplicity for our concern is that 0 (zero) is a simpler number than any large finite number, because one can understand what it is for there to be 0 objects of a certain kind without understanding what it is for there to be 2,786,895 (or any other large finite number) objects of that kind. Hence the hypothesis that there are zero limits to some quantity is simpler than the hypothesis that that quantity has some very large finite value. So the hypothesis that some object has existed for 0 limits to the number of years, that is, for an unlimited number of years, is simpler than the hypothesis that it has existed for 2,786,895 (or any other large finite number of) years.

These (and other) facets of simplicity have to be weighed against each other. Some hypothesis may be simple in respect of one facet, but complex in respect of a different facet, and so not infrequently it is not possible to say whether overall a certain hypothesis is simpler than a certain other hypothesis. But very frequently it is possible to compare hypotheses in respect of overall simplicity, especially when they differ from each other only in respect of one of the various facets of simplicity. There are always an infinite number of mutually incompatible theories which could be constructed which predict all the observed data when the occurrence of these was not otherwise probable, yet make different predictions from each other about what will happen tomorrow. Without the criterion of simplicity it would be impossible to predict anything beyond what we immediately observe.

If the hypothesis is concerned only with a narrow field, it has to fit with any background evidence. But for many hypotheses there may be no relevant background evidence, and the wider the scope of a hypothesis (that is, the more it purports to explain about the world), the less background evidence there will be. For a very large-scale theory of physics (such as quantum theory) there will be few physical phenomena (which alone would support a theory inconsistent with quantum theory) apart from those within its scope (ones which it purports to explain), and so little—if any—background evidence.

Theism as a simple hypothesis

Such are the criteria for the probable truth of some postulated explanatory hypothesis. I now spell out the hypothesis of theism. Theism is clearly a personal hypothesis. God is supposed to be one person who is essentially omnipotent, omniscient, perfectly free, and eternal. (If you emphasize that God is a Trinity, "three persons of one substance" as Christianity claims, regard these arguments as arguments to the existence of God the Father who is the cause of everything else, including the other persons of the Trinity who are essentially dependent on him.) It is simpler to suppose that there is one person rather than many independent persons (many independent gods) who are the cause of the universe.

God is supposed to be omnipotent. A person is a being who has powers to perform intentional actions (that is, actions which he or she means to do), beliefs, and purposes (choosing among alternative actions). It is simpler to suppose that the cause of the universe has zero limits to his power (that is, is omnipotent), rather than that he can only make a universe of a certain size and duration. This is because zero is a simpler number than some very large finite number; we can understand the number zero simply by understanding a few small numbers, but we can only understand the very large finite number if we can define it in terms of other numbers and these in terms of yet other numbers until we reach a few small numbers. An omnipotent person can do any logically possible action, that is, any action which can be described without contradiction; and so he cannot make me both exist and not exist at the same time. But since it makes no sense to suppose that I could both exist and not exist at the same time, a logically impossible action is not really an action at all—any more than an imaginary person is really a person.

A truly omnipotent person would not be subject to irrational forces in forming his purposes, as so often are the choices of humans; he would be influenced by reason alone and so by what he believes good to do. In that sense of "perfectly free," an omnipotent person is necessarily perfectly free. A truly omnipotent person would know all the possible actions open to him, and so know whether they are good or bad, and so being perfectly free would do actions only insofar as they are good. So he would be perfectly good. A truly omnipotent person would be *essentially* omnipotent, for otherwise his omnipotence would be precarious. It is simpler to suppose that God is unlimited in time as well as in power, and so essentially eternal. In my view that should be interpreted as God being everlasting (existing at every moment of past and future time), since I regard the Boethian view of God as outside time, yet simultaneously present at all moments of human time, as a view to which it is very difficult to give any sense, and a totally unnecessary burden on theism.

So often there must be before God, as there is before us, a choice between equally good incompatible actions, which are better than any alternative actions, and which I call "equal best" actions. And, since God is omnipotent, the range of incompatible equal best actions available to him would be so much greater than the range available to us. Further, God must often be in a situation where we cannot be, of having a choice between an infinite number of possible actions, each of which is less good than some other action he could do. For example, angels and bears and elephants are good things; they can be happy and loving. So, the more of them the better (given that in the case of bears and elephants they are spread out among an infinite number of planets, so that they do not crowd each other out). So however many of these creatures God creates, God would believe it better if he had created more. (And he could still have created more, even if he created an infinite number of them.) It may be, however, that when there is no best or equal best action available to God, there may be a best kind of action available to God, such that it would be better to do some action of that kind than to do any number of actions of any other incompatible kind. For example, God can create creatures of many different types, including angels, humans, and animals. If it were the case that it would be better to create at least some humans (even if he creates no angels or animals), than to create any number of angels and animals and no humans or to do an action of any other incompatible kind, then it would be a best kind of action for God to create some humans, although there would be no best number for him to create. In that case, I suggest, God, being influenced by reason alone, would inevitably create some humans. And if there are two or more equal best kinds of action (that is, equally good kinds of action better than any other kinds) available to him he will inevitably do some action of one of these kinds. So God will inevitably always do the best or an equal best action, or if there is no such action, some action of the best or equal best kind, and otherwise some good action; but he would never do a bad action.

Given the logical impossibility of backward causation, God will not be able to cause past events, but he will be able to cause any future event. The simplest supposition about God's knowledge is that there will be zero limits to it, compatibly with his omnipotence. Hence his knowledge will be confined to knowledge of the past and of any necessary truths, but the future will be entirely subject to his choice. Just as omnipotence is to be understood as the power to do anything logically possible, so omniscience should be understood as knowledge of everything logically possible to know. (Of course on the Boethian account of God's eternity, then God's omniscience would include knowledge of the whole (to us) future as well as of the whole past.)

Insofar as moral principles (e.g., that one ought to keep one's just promises) are necessary truths, and so independent of the will of God,[7] God will have true beliefs about what they are; and so not merely do what he believes to be the best (or whatever), but what is in fact the best or equal best (or one of the best or equal best kinds of action) or otherwise any good action. In that case he will be as good as it is logically possible to be, which is to say that he will be perfectly good.

I conclude that theism is a very simple hypothesis indeed. It postulates just one substance, God, having essentially the simplest degree of power, and lasting for the simplest length of time; all the other essential divine properties follow from that. God being what he is in virtue of these essential properties makes God a "person" in a sense somewhat analogical to the sense in which we are persons. Theism is such a wide-ranging hypothesis (it purports to explain all the most general features of the universe) that there is no background evidence; all the evidence (whether positive or negative) is within its scope. So the hypothesis of theism satisfies the third criterion superbly well; and does not need to satisfy the fourth criterion. Hence whether the hypothesis of theism, that God exists, is probable on the evidence of the phenomena which I outlined earlier, turns on how well that evidence satisfies the first two criteria.

It is quite probable that God will bring about the observed phenomena

First, are the phenomena such as, if there is a God, it is probable that he would bring them about? If there is a God, he will seek to bring about good things. It is good that there should be a beautiful universe. Beauty arises from order of some kind—the orderly interactions and movements of stars

7. For argument that the fundamental moral truths are necessary truths independent of the will of God, see for example my paper, "What Difference Does God Make to Morality?" in R. K Garcia and N. L King, eds., *Is Goodness without God Good Enough?* (New York: Rowman and Littlefield, 2009), 151–63. I argue there that one of the necessary moral truths, which atheists as well as theists may come to recognize, is that it is obligatory to thank and please benefactors. Hence, in virtue of God being our supreme benefactor who has given us our life and everything we possess, we have an obligation to obey his commands: and so his commands (both with respect to our duties to God and to our duties to our fellow humans) form much of the morality which we are obliged to follow. See also for further development of these points chapter 11 of my *The Coherence of Theism,* 2nd ed. (Oxford: Oxford University Press, 2016).

and planets in accord with natural laws is beautiful indeed; and even more beautiful are the plants and animals which evolved on Earth. Animals have sensations, beliefs, and desires, and that is clearly a great good. Humans have the power to reason and understand the universe, and that is an even greater good. But all these kinds of goodness are kinds of goodness which God himself possesses. God is beautiful and has beliefs and desires (and in my view, also sensations), and the power to reason and understand. But there is one kind of great goodness which God himself does not possess—the power to bring about good or evil. God can only bring about good. Yet it would be very good indeed that there should be persons who have the free will to make this all-important difference to the world, the power to benefit or harm themselves, each other, and other creatures. So, if there is a God, we have very good reason to suppose that there will be persons who have, as I believe humans have, that freedom.[8] But clearly there is a bad aspect to the existence of such persons; they may cause much evil. So it cannot be a unique best action to create such persons, but in view of the unique kind of goodness which they would possess, surely it must be an equal best action to create such persons; and, if so, it is as probable as not that if there is a God, there will be such persons, that is persons like us humans. But if God is to create us, he must provide a universe in which we can exercise our choices to benefit or harm ourselves and each other. We can only do that if we have bodies, through which we can learn about the world and make a difference to it, and which are places where we can get hold of each other, and escape from each other. But only if there are comprehensible regularities which we can discover will there be ways in which my doing this or that will make a predictable difference to me or you, and so we can have a choice of how to treat each other. Only if humans know that by sowing certain seeds and weeding and watering them, they will get corn, can they develop an agriculture. And only if they know that by rubbing sticks together they can make fire, will they be able to burn the food supplies of others. But comprehensible observable regularities are only possible if the fundamental laws of nature are simple ones. Further, if God is to create embodied humans, the laws must be such as to allow the existence of human bodies, either brought about by an evolutionary process or created directly by God. And finally, human bodies only have a point if they are controlled by conscious persons.

8. For the argument that probably humans do have free will, see my *Mind, Brain, and Free Will* (Oxford: Oxford University Press, 2013), especially chapter 7.

So the four phenomena to which I have referred are to be expected (that is, it is quite probable that they will occur) if there is a God.

The phenomena would be immensely improbable if there were no God

But if there is no God, it is immensely improbable that these phenomena will occur. It is enormously improbable that each of the innumerably many fundamental particles, or rather chunks of compressed energy, immediately after the Big Bang, should just happen to exist. And it is even more improbable that each such chunk should behave in exactly the same fairly simple way as each other chunk (the way codified in the laws of relativity and quantum theory and the four forces). So while there are fairly simple laws, their instantiation in each of innumerably many chunks of matter-energy would be an enormous coincidence unless caused by some external agent. And even if such an enormous coincidence occurred by chance, it is immensely improbable that those laws should be such as together with the boundary conditions of the universe (which are its initial conditions if the universe had a beginning) should have given rise to human bodies. And even if this too occurred by chance, as far as any plausible system of scientific laws of the kind just described are concerned, the laws might just as easily have given rise to robots. There would need to be innumerable independent scientific laws connecting physical events such as brain events with different conscious events if science is to explain consciousness; and it is *a priori* most improbable that there should be a system of innumerable such laws of a kind such that our brain events cause our human kind of rational consciousness, which is sensitive to evidence from the outside world. Consciousness, and especially consciousness of the kind that humans have, is totally improbable, unless there is a creator who gave it first to the higher animals and then to us.

Some contemporary physicists will tell you that we live in a multiverse such that many different possible universes (with different laws of nature, and different initial conditions) will eventually occur, and so it is not surprising that there is one like ours. But we could only have reason to believe what they tell us, if the most probable explanation of phenomena observable in our universe was that the most general laws of nature are such as to bring about these many universes; and to postulate that is to postulate that all the particles, not merely of our universe, but of the vastly bigger multiverse behave in accord with the same very general laws, which throw up particular variants thereof in different universes—which is to postulate an even bigger coincidence. And the laws of that multiverse would have to be such as to produce at some stage a universe like ours which in turn produces us, when almost all logically possible multiverses would not have this characteristic. So even if our universe does belong to a multiverse, it is immensely improbable (if there is no more ultimate explanation thereof—e.g., God) that that would be a multiverse of the kind to bring about the existence of humans. So the possible existence of a multiverse makes little difference to the force of the arguments which I have discussed.

So these four general phenomena are such as it is moderately probable will occur if there is a God, and almost certainly will not occur if there is not a personal being or personal beings who created the universe. And the simplest possible such personal being is God, as I have described him. So theism is a very simple hypothesis indeed, and simpler—I suggest—than any inanimate hypothesis which could be constructed. I conclude that arguments from the phenomena which I have discussed are strong cogent arguments to the existence of God, which give a significant degree of probability to that conclusion.[9]

My argument and that of Athanasius have a similar structure

Furthermore, I suggest, the pattern of argument which my own natural theology exemplifies and which I believe to be the pattern of argument used by scientists and historians to establish their lower-level theories, is exemplified in some of the natural theology of the Fathers. And I now proceed to exhibit the structure of one detailed teleological argument developed by Athanasius, to which Alexey Fokin's chapter refers. Athanasius argued that it follows from the nature of God that he would make a beautiful and orderly universe, for the purpose of showing that the creator of the universe is a rational and benevolent being:

9. The evidence considered in this paper is only the main public evidence of a very general kind in favor of the existence of God. See note 6 above, for the final conclusion (for which I have argued elsewhere) about the degree of the probability of the existence of God, when the widespread evidence of religious experience, as well as historical evidence about the life of Jesus, and also any evidence against the existence of God, are also taken into account.

> For God, being good and loving to mankind, and caring for the souls made by him . . . by his own Word gave the universe the order it has, in order that . . . men might be enabled to know him at any rate by his works.[10]

And he describes at considerable length the various patterns of order which we find in the universe:

> Who that sees the sun rising by day and the moon shining by night, and when waning and waxing without variation exactly according to the same number of days . . . can fail to perceive that they certainly have a creator to guide them? . . . By reason of him the water is suspended in the clouds, the rain showers upon the earth, and the sea is kept within bounds, while the earth bears grasses and is clothed with all manner of plants.[11]

Athanasius took for granted the teaching of Greek science that physical matter is of four kinds—earth, air, fire, and water—and then points out that, despite their contrary natures (earth and water move downwards, air and fire upwards), they are put together in such a way as to produce an environment in which humans can flourish. Thus:

> Who that sees the clouds supported in air, and the weight of the waters bound up in the clouds, can but perceive Him that binds them up and has ordered these things so? Or who that sees the earth, heaviest of all things by nature fixed upon the waters, and remaining unmoved upon what is by nature mobile, will fail to understand that there is One that has made and ordered it, even God? Who that sees the earth bringing forth fruits in due season, and the rains from heaven, and the flow of rivers, and springing up of wells, and the birth of animals from unlike parents, and that these things take place not at all times but at determinate seasons,—and in general, among things mutually unlike and contrary, the balanced and uniform order to which they conform,—can resist the inference that there is one Power which orders and administers them ordaining things well as it thinks fit? For left to themselves

10. Athanasius, *Against the Heathen* 35.1; NPNF 2/4:22.
11. Athanasius, *Against the Heathen* 35.4, 40.5; NPNF 2/4:22, 25–26.

> they could not subsist or ever be able to appear, on account of their mutual contrariety of nature.[12]

He is claiming that matter has been put together in a way not to be expected unless a creator had so ordered it, and the universality of the order shows that there is a single orderer: "If the universe had been made by a plurality of gods, its movements would be diverse and inconsistent."[13] So, Athanasius is claiming in effect, the universe is such as we would expect if God (understood as one omnipotent creator and sustainer) caused it to exist and keeps it in being—that is, satisfies my first criterion for a probably true hypothesis; it is not such as we would expect if it had been ordered by chance or created by many less powerful gods—that is, satisfies my second criterion. And he rules out the hypothesis that it was made by many very powerful gods on the grounds that "if each one was sufficient for the creation of the whole, what need of more than one, one being self-sufficient for the universe?"[14] So in effect he is employing my third criterion (simplicity). As I argued above, the fourth criterion is irrelevant to a theory of such wide scope as theism. So Athanasius is giving an argument with a similar structure to my own.

Shorter versions of the same argument were put forward by Gregory of Nyssa,[15] the *Clementine Recognitions*,[16] John of Damascus,[17] and (very briefly) by Gregory Palamas. In a passage (discussed by David Bradshaw in this volume) which would be almost impossible to understand without any familiarity with simpler accounts of it, Gregory wrote:

> Who that possesses reason and beholds such manifest differences among beings—both the oppositions of hidden forces and the compensating kinetic impulses, and again stability that compensates in another way; the ceaseless resolutions arising out of contrary affections and the unconfused harmony arising out of irreconcilable strife; the cohesion of things that are distinct and the continuing distinction of those that are united, whether they be minds, souls, or bodies; the harmony among so many, their established positions and relations; the conformity of their states and ranks to their essence, the indissolubility

12. Athanasius, *Against the Heathen* 36.2–4; NPNF 2/4:23.
13. Athanasius, *Against the Heathen* 39.5; NPNF 2/4:25.
14. Athanasius, *Against the Heathen* 36.4; NPNF 2/4:25.
15. Gregory of Nyssa, *On the Soul and the Resurrection* 1.
16. *Clementine Recognitions*, book 8, especially ch. 17.
17. John of Damascus, *On the Orthodox Faith* 1.3.

> of their connection—who that attends to all these points would not form a conception of the One who has so well established each thing in itself and wondrously harmonized each with the others, so as to come to know God from his image and that which he has caused?[18]

It was, I presume, an argument of this kind which Gregory Palamas called in his first letter to Akyndinos a method by which thinkers ascend from creation to the Creator:

> Those who have not attained to this contemplation are able to apprehend from the forethought about all things the common Forethought; from those who are made good, Goodness itself; from those who are made wise, Wisdom itself; and, in general, from all things the One who transcends all and is established above all, the many-named and unnameable Being beyond being. Are not all these immaterially contemplated around that One, whatever it may be? And is it not through them as evidence that there is a demonstration free from deceit (ἀψευδὴς ἀπόδειξις) that there is One who leads forth all, who before the ages has forethought for all, who is all-mighty, overseeing all, all-good, and the cause of all, transcending nature?[19]

Robert Sinkewicz comments that "there emerges from this letter a notion of demonstration quite distinct from that advocated by Barlaam and ultimately by Aristotle. It is a notion that seeks its justification not in the Greek philosophers but in the tradition of the Fathers."[20]

Although Gregory Palamas hints that arguments to God may be *sui generis*, he and his predecessors are in fact giving an argument of just the same kind as those of my own natural theology. Although neither Aristotle nor the medievals, East or West, had the slightest conception of the nature of inductive inference, and of the criteria which a cogent inductive inference needs to satisfy, I claim that nevertheless in effect some of them, and in particular

18. Gregory Palamas, *Triads* 2.3.44; Greek text in *Défense des saints hésychastes*, ed. John Meyendorff, 2nd ed. (Louvain: Specilegium Sacrum Lovaniense, 1973), 477–79; trans. David Bradshaw in this volume.

19. Palamas, *First Letter to Akindynos* 12, in P. Chrestou, ed., *Gregoriou tou Palama: Syngrammata*, 6 vols. (Thessalonica, 1962–2015), vol. 1, 216; trans. by David Bradshaw in this volume.

20. Robert Sinkewicz, "The Doctrine of the Knowledge of God in the Early Writings of Barlaam the Calabrian," *Mediaeval Studies* 44 (1982): 181–242, at 201.

Athanasius and those who reproduced his arguments, were implicitly using just the same criteria for a probably true hypothesis as I have claimed are at work in assessing the probable truth of hypotheses of science and history, and as I am claiming can be used to show the existence of God. Of course, all the Fathers from Athanasius to Gregory Palamas took for granted a totally erroneous physics, in assuming that all mundane substances are made of earth, air, fire, and water. But their main point was that the chemistry of substances is such that different elements fit together in such a way as to produce an orderly world (of day and night, winter and summer, rain and sun, plants and animals) fitted for humans—which would be very improbable unless a divine person had made it. And I too am arguing from the powers and propensities of the elements, now known to be quarks, electrons, and so on, and their initial arrangements being such as to produce an orderly world, fitted for humans, which would be very improbable unless a divine person had made it. My basic point is the same as that of the Fathers, expressed in terms of modern physics, and articulated in a much more sophisticated and rigorous way than theirs. Clearly in order to appeal to modern humans, it needs to be expressed in terms of modern physics; and in order to appeal to modern humans who see science as the paradigm of knowledge, it needs to be shown that the pattern of argument is just the same as that of science, of the kind that modern philosophers of science have been elucidating.

Of course we cannot come to know the essence of the God to whom the argument leads; but we can know that that God is a God who has the "energies" (that is, "properties" or "attributes" as Western philosophers and theologians call them) traditionally ascribed to him of (in some sense) eternity, omnipotence, omniscience, and perfect goodness. In patristic and medieval times there was far less need of natural theology than there is today, because in those earlier times there were relatively few atheists (in the sense of persons who believed that there was no kind of god at all). But in our day in the Western world there are hundreds of millions of atheists; and in consequence of this even many believers are doubtful about whether there is a God. They can be helped to have a stronger belief in God by reflecting on natural theology. As Gregory of Nyssa put it:

> It is necessary, therefore, to regard the opinions the persons have taken up and to frame your argument in accordance with the error into which each has fallen, by advancing in each discussion certain principles and reasonable propositions, that thus, through what is agreed upon on both sides, the truth may conclusively be brought to light. . . . Should

[someone] say there is no God, then, from the consideration of the skilful and wise economy of the Universe he will be brought to acknowledge that there is a certain overmastering power manifested through these channels.[21]

21. Gregory of Nyssa, *The Great Catechism*, prologue; trans. William Moore and Henry Austin Wilson, NPNF 2/5:474 (slightly modified).

Index

Made in the USA
Columbia, SC
16 July 2021